AUSTRALIAN WINE
from the vine to the glass

ENJOY WINE

with food

with others

and in moderation.

D1316040

This book aims to enhance the knowledge, appreciation and enjoyment of Australian wine. It is dedicated to the grapegrowers and winemakers of Australia, without whom none of this would be possible.

First published in Australia in 1997 by
Patrick Iland Wine Promotions
PO Box 131, Campbelltown
Adelaide, South Australia 5074
Telephone (08) 8337 1484
Facsimile (08) 8337 0592

Acknowledgements
Many sectors of the Australian wine industry have helped in various ways. We particularly acknowledge their support.

Some of the graphics in the Viticulture and Winemaking Sections were originally prepared by Graeme Lavis and Melanie Horsman for our previous book 'An Introduction to Wine' and 'Discovering Australian Wine - a taster's guide'. These have been redesigned for this book by Marcella St Claire, who has also designed and created all the new diagrams.

We thank Margaret Cargill for doing a splendid job of editing the text.

National Library of Australia
Cataloguing-in-Publication data:
Iland, Patrick
Gago, Peter
Australian Wine - from the vine to the glass
Includes index

ISBN 0646 31855 1

1. Australian Wine 2. Wine and Winemaking 3. Title

Project co-ordinator: Judith Iland
Design: Marcella St Claire and Patrick Iland
Computer layout and illustrations: Marcella St Claire
Graphic Reproductions: Skanz, Graphic Communications, Adelaide, South Australia
Printer: Newstyle Printing, Adelaide
Research assistants: Judith Iland and Julie Iland

Cover photography:
Jacob's Creek Vineyard provided by Orlando Wyndham;
Chardonnay vine by Patrick Iland;
Wine glasses by Prima Photographics
Inside front:
Henschke's Lenswood Vineyard by Patrick Iland;
Pumping over a red wine fermentation at Magill Estate by Prima Photographics;
People enjoying wine with food supplied by South Australian Tourism Association
Inside back: Wine and food by Prima Photographics

The Australian Wine Industry is undergoing dramatic change. The information given in this publication is as accurate as possible at the time of printing. We acknowledge that the Geographic Indications of Australia Wine Regions will evolve and that some of the names in this book may change or even be deleted in the future. Production statistics and names of wineries will or may also change. The characters of wine and food are perceived in different ways by different people and the sensory descriptors and the examples given in this book are a general guide to describing and choosing wines.

Publisher: Patrick Iland Wine Promotions
Adelaide, South Australia

Patrick Iland is a senior lecturer in viticulture in the Department of Horticulture, Viticulture and Oenology at The University of Adelaide, South Australia. Prior to 1991, he was a lecturer at Roseworthy Agricultural College (the first college of viticulture and oenology in Australia), which has amalgamated with The University of Adelaide. Patrick teaches and conducts research in viticulture, winemaking and sensory evaluation.

He is a past winner of The Vin de Champagne Award and one of the two inaugural winners of the Stephen Hickinbotham Memorial Trust Award, the latter for his research work on Pinot Noir grapes and the viticultural factors influencing their composition. In 1993 he was one of the three recipients of the Stephen Cole the Elder Award for Excellence in Teaching awarded by The University of Adelaide.

He has experienced vintages in Australia and France, and enjoys tasting wines from different regions. He believes it is important to appreciate the diversity of wine styles. Patrick has a strong interest in and commitment to wine education and the promotion of a greater understanding of the culture of wine.

Drawn to the wine industry after eight years of secondary school teaching (mathematics and chemistry) in Victoria, **Peter Gago** completed a degree in Applied Science (Oenology) at Roseworthy Agricultural College in 1989, graduating Dux of the Course.

After four years as a maker of sparkling wines for the Penfolds Wine Group (now Southcorp), he joined its red winemaking department. He now functions in an extended winemaking role across the Southcorp wineries.

An avid wine collector and taster, Peter is passionate about Australian and overseas wine. He believes it is essential for a winemaker to gain an intimate appreciation of wine style differences and an understanding of a wine's development with time. Above all else, he advocates that wine is to be shared and enjoyed.

Peter's breadth of winemaking and tasting experience provide him with excellent credentials for co-authoring this authoritative text on Australian wine.

CONTENTS

AN INTRODUCTION TO AUSTRALIAN WINE

THE WINE IN THE GLASS

THE VINEYARD

THE WINERY

SPARKLING WINES

DRY WHITE TABLE WINES

SEMI-SWEET AND SWEET WHITE WINES

Wood ducks in flight over Mountadam vineyard, Eden Valley, South Australia

AN INTRODUCTION TO AUSTRALIAN WINE

Built on the pioneering spirit of Australia's early vignerons, the Australian wine industry, with its 200 year heritage, is now spread across all states and territories of our vast nation.

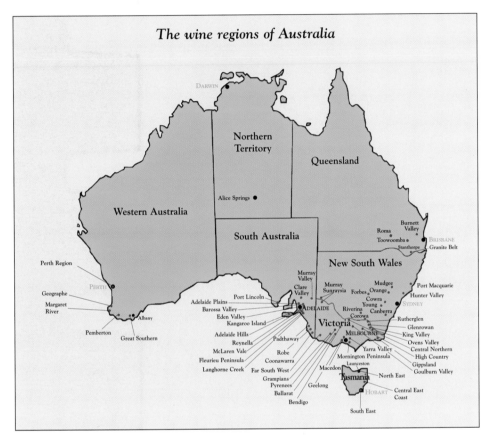

The last 40 years have seen enormous change. The adoption of modern and innovative practices in both the vineyard and winery, coupled with a sensitivity to and appreciation of tradition, has led to a modern, expanding and exciting industry where wine is part of the lifestyle enjoyed by many Australians and international visitors.

Australia's winemakers now produce wine of a wide diversity of styles, wines recognised worldwide for their quality and character.

WHAT IS WINE?

The alcoholic drink produced by the fermentation of grapes is called wine, but wine is more than an alcoholic drink.

Wine contains many components which
- give interesting and enjoyable taste sensations,
- contribute to what we call the character of the wine, and
- are appreciated most when wine is accompanied by food and shared with others.

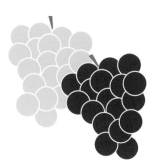

Crushing or pressing the berries releases the juice and mixes the components of the grape.

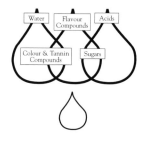

Yeasts convert the sugar to alcohol.

The other components are carried over into the wine. The amount of each component will vary depending on the type of wine: red, white, dry, sweet, sparkling or fortified. It is the sugar, acid, alcohol and colour, phenolic and flavour compounds, present in different amounts in different wines, that give a wine its style and character.

Some components of wine:
approximate percentage composition
(by weight)

Flavour Compounds
0.1%

Colour and Tannins
0.3%
(in red wines)

Acids
1%

Sugar
0.1% - 8%
(dry wines)   (sweet wines)

Water 80-90%

Alcohol
10% - 20%
(table wines)   (fortified wines)

Note: Alcohol content is normally expressed as % by volume, not weight. However, the values are similar to those given in this illustration.

1

White wines are made from white wine grape varieties (which are coloured various shades of green or yellow), and red wines from red wine grape varieties (which are coloured red, purple or black).

Some white wine grape varieties:
Chardonnay
Riesling
Sauvignon Blanc
Semillon

Some red wine grape varieties:
Shiraz
Cabernet Sauvignon
Pinot Noir
Grenache

2

Crushing the bunches breaks each berry into its parts and releases the juice. The mixture of juice, pulp, skins and seeds is called *must*.

To make white wine the *must* is pressed to separate the juice from the solids. Sometimes, the crushing operation is avoided and whole bunches are gently pressed to release the juice.

Red wine is made from the mixture of berry parts (the *must*) obtained after crushing bunches of black grapes. The colour of black grapes is contained in the skin of the berry, and thus the skins need to be kept in contact with the juice to provide colour in the wine.

The winemaker has to make decisions about how he/she will ferment and handle a particular batch of grapes.
What temperature?
Which yeast?
How long to leave the skins in contact with the fermenting liquid?
Whether to store the wine in oak barrels?
When to bottle?

3

The sugars present in the liquid are then converted to alcohol by the action of yeasts. The yeasts are either naturally present on the skin of the berries or are added to the juice or must by the winemaker. This process, whereby the juice or must is converted to wine, is called fermentation. Other components of the grape (eg acids and flavour and colour compounds) are also carried over into the wine. Some remain unchanged, while others are modified through winemaking techniques or by the passage of time.

4

The alcoholic drink produced by the fermentation process is called wine. Wine comes in different types and styles. Throughout this book we take you on a journey to discover what happens from the vine to the glass. We hope it will help you to appreciate the fascinating diversity of Australian wine styles and enhance your enjoyment of drinking Australian wine.

A dry white table wine, semi-sweet white table wine, dry red table wine, sparkling wine and fortified wine

AN INTRODUCTION TO AUSTRALIAN WINE — types and styles

Wine type

Variations in grape composition and winemaking technique lead to sensory differences in wines. We use the word *type* to distinguish between wines with large differences in their chemical make up: whether they are red or white, taste dry or sweet, contain bubbles of carbon dioxide, or have low or high alcohol content.

Australian wines can be classified into a number of wine types according to their chemical composition.

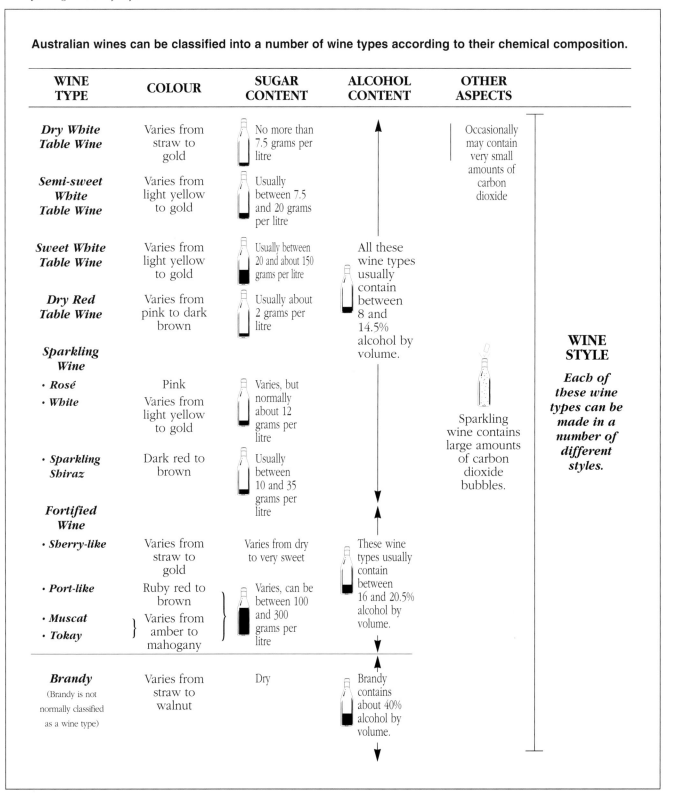

WINE TYPE	COLOUR	SUGAR CONTENT	ALCOHOL CONTENT	OTHER ASPECTS	WINE STYLE
Dry White Table Wine	Varies from straw to gold	No more than 7.5 grams per litre		Occasionally may contain very small amounts of carbon dioxide	
Semi-sweet White Table Wine	Varies from light yellow to gold	Usually between 7.5 and 20 grams per litre			
Sweet White Table Wine	Varies from light yellow to gold	Usually between 20 and about 150 grams per litre	All these wine types usually contain between 8 and 14.5% alcohol by volume.		
Dry Red Table Wine	Varies from pink to dark brown	Usually about 2 grams per litre			
Sparkling Wine					**WINE STYLE**
• **Rosé**	Pink	Varies, but normally about 12 grams per litre			*Each of these wine types can be made in a number of different styles.*
• **White**	Varies from light yellow to gold				
• **Sparkling Shiraz**	Dark red to brown	Usually between 10 and 35 grams per litre		Sparkling wine contains large amounts of carbon dioxide bubbles.	
Fortified Wine					
• **Sherry-like**	Varies from straw to gold	Varies from dry to very sweet	These wine types usually contain between 16 and 20.5% alcohol by volume.		
• **Port-like**	Ruby red to brown	Varies, can be between 100 and 300 grams per litre			
• **Muscat**	Varies from amber to mahogany				
• **Tokay**					
Brandy (Brandy is not normally classified as a wine type)	Varies from straw to walnut	Dry	Brandy contains about 40% alcohol by volume.		

Wine style

Each type of wine can be made in a number of different styles. Wines grouped into particular types do not all taste the same; some will smell and taste distinctively of the grapes from which they were made, while others will be more influenced by the winemaking technique or by age. These (often more subtle) differences between wines of the same type are described as *style variation*. The words that describe style indicate whether the wine is light-, medium- or full-bodied and what specific aromas, flavours, tastes and mouthfeel sensations are evident at the time of tasting.

Wines made from Riesling, Chardonnay, Semillon and other white wine grape varieties can be the same type (dry white table wine) but of different styles. The style will be different because they are made from different grape varieties. Similarly the different red wine grape varieties can be made into different styles; for example dry red wines can be made from Pinot Noir, Cabernet Sauvignon and Shiraz or from other red wine grape varieties and/or blends. You have to taste the wine to assess what style it is; the label may give some clues.

A selection of different styles of dry white table wine

A selection of different styles of dry red table wine

Even wines from the same variety may vary in style, depending on where the grapes were grown and how the wine was made.

A selection of different Chardonnay wines

A selection of different Shiraz wines

Australian wines come in a diversity of styles. They reflect the characters that come from the various climates and soils of our viticultural regions and the skills of our grapegrowers and winemakers.

Australian wine — a diversity of styles

The Wine in the Glass

Sensory evaluation of wine is an appraisal of wine by the action of observing, smelling and tasting. The terms 'tasting wine' and 'to taste wine' as we use them in this chapter and throughout the book are used in a broad sense to describe the actions of sensory evaluation, and take in an appraisal of the colour and clarity, the aromas and flavours, the basic tastes and the mouthfeel of the wine being tasted. We refer to these sensory sensations as the character of the wine.

The prime components of character, the sugars, acids, aromas, flavours and phenolic compounds, are present in the grape at harvest. These provide the foundation of character, which then evolves with time. The sensory characters that come from winemaking complement the inherent qualities of the grape to create the total sensory experience.

The sensory experience is sensed through the eyes, nose and mouth. The sensory signals are registered and interpreted in the brain and we form an overall impression of the characters of the wine and whether or not we enjoy it. In the following chapters we provide guides to describing the character of the different styles of wine.

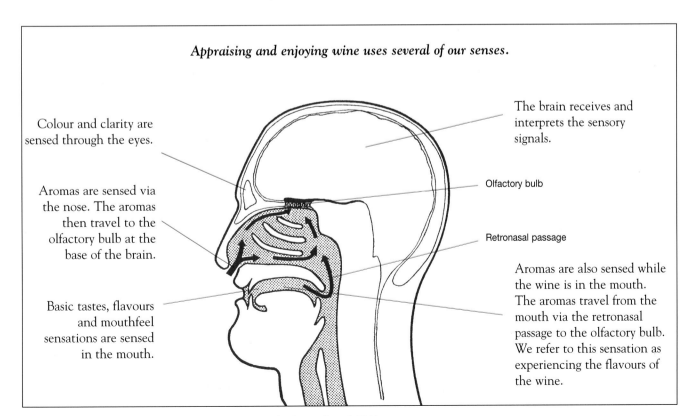

Appraising and enjoying wine uses several of our senses.

Colour and clarity are sensed through the eyes.

Aromas are sensed via the nose. The aromas then travel to the olfactory bulb at the base of the brain.

Basic tastes, flavours and mouthfeel sensations are sensed in the mouth.

The brain receives and interprets the sensory signals.

Olfactory bulb

Retronasal passage

Aromas are also sensed while the wine is in the mouth. The aromas travel from the mouth via the retronasal passage to the olfactory bulb. We refer to this sensation as experiencing the flavours of the wine.

Diagram adapted from Tasting and Enjoying Wine, page 57, by Rankine (1990).

TASTING WINE — step by step

Pour about 30 ml of wine into a glass.

1. Observing

- Tilt the glass slightly.
- Check that the wine is clear (not hazy).
- Observe its colour against a white background and determine the depth (intensity) and shade (hue) of colour. Look at the rim and the body of the wine: the colours may be different. Are the colours brilliant or dull?
- Look for viscosity: if a wine is high in alcohol, droplets of the wine may adhere to the side of the glass after the wine is swirled.
- Record the words that describe the wine's appearance.

2. Smelling

Sniff the wine. The volatile compounds are detected by the olfactory bulb in the brain. Swirl the glass and then sniff the wine again.

A couple of sniffs are sufficient as our sense of smell is easily fatigued, and when this happens it becomes more difficult to detect and discern the aromas.

- Check if the wine is clean, ie does not have any mouldy, acetic (vinegar-like) or dirty (smelly) characters.
- Attempt to recognise and describe the various aromas. These fall into three possible categories: primary fruit characters, developed fruit characters and characters derived during the winemaking process.

The words that we use to describe aromas (as well as flavours) are referred to as descriptors, eg fruity, floral, raspberry, toasty, smoky.

- Estimate the intensity of these smell sensations: are they light, medium or intense?
- Assess the harmony of the various sensations: no one smell, with the possible exception of fruit characters, should dominate.
- Record your impressions.

Some exercises to familiarise yourself with these basic tastes: Take a small portion of each of the solutions below into your mouth separately, move it over your tongue and experience the taste.

sweet
mix a teaspoon of sugar into a cup of water.
sour (acid)
squeeze a lemon into a cup of water, mix.
bitter
mix 2 teaspoons of instant coffee into a cup of warm water, or taste some tonic water which contains quinine.

3. Tasting

Take a small volume of wine (about 10 ml) into your mouth. Move the wine around in the mouth for about 10-15 seconds. While the wine is in the mouth, think about the flavours, tastes and mouthfeel sensations that you are experiencing. Then swallow or spit out the wine. Have you ever wondered why wine tasters make those peculiar noises when tasting wine?

It actually helps to get the most out of the wine. The warm environment of the mouth releases the volatile compounds from the wine, which then pass through the retronasal passage to the olfactory bulb in the brain. Opening the mouth slightly and drawing air in help to aspirate the volatile compounds out of the wine. This action, although a bit noisy, does enhance the perception of the wine's flavour.

There are four basic tastes: sweet, sour, bitter and salty. We normally encounter only the first three when tasting wine. Detection of these tastes does not take place exclusively in any particular region of the tongue, and it is important to move the wine around your mouth and over all parts of the tongue to appreciate them fully. Bitterness is the most localised of the taste sensations and its perception is concentrated towards the back of the tongue. The presence of bitterness can lessen the enjoyment of the wine.

The compounds that give wine its aroma also contribute to flavour sensations experienced in the mouth. Similar descriptors are used to describe flavours as are used for aromas. Flavour sensations are also described as being light, medium or intense. Some sensations are more obvious immediately the wine enters the mouth, while others intensify as the wine warms up. The ever-changing nature of these flavour experiences is often referred to as the development or evolution of the wine in the mouth.

Another commonly used term is complexity. It describes the diversity of the aroma and flavour sensations. We also use the terms length and aftertaste when referring to the flavour attributes of a wine; these relate to the intensity of flavour over the palate and how long the flavour sensations last in the mouth after the wine is tasted. Acidity also contributes to the length and finish.

Astringent sensations (puckering of the mouth) are often experienced when tasting red wines, especially those high in tannins. The tannins interact with the saliva in the mouth, nullifying its lubricating action, and thus the mouth feels dry (as with a lack of saliva). Tannins can also contribute textures; some of the words that are used to describe the feel of the tannins are soft, silky, supple, grainy, furry and puckering.

Textural features are not exclusive to red wines. White wines, particularly those that have been stored on yeast lees, can have a creamy feeling in the mouth. Another tactile sensation is that due to high or unbalanced alcohol levels present in some wines. These wines (either red or white) will give a warm or hot feeling at the back of the mouth, particularly after the wine has been swallowed.

Experience the wine on the palate and look for
- the type, intensity and harmony of the sensory characters
- the weight of the wine in the mouth
- the balance between the acid and sweet tastes
- the balance between fruit characters and those of, for example, acid, sugar, alcohol, tannins, wood
- richness and fullness on the palate
- pleasant mouthfeel (tactile sensations)
- overall structure
- contribution of negative characters (eg bitterness, coarseness, hotness, dirty or unpleasant odours, tastes or taints). These normally should not be present, but if they are, they should be minimal. Quality wines do not have to be squeaky-clean. It is the overall impression of the wine's positive features that portrays its quality, providing negative characters are not dominant.
- the length
- the finish
- the aftertaste.

Although the nose of the wine may build our expectations, it is only when the wine is in the mouth that the full coming together of all the sensations is experienced — tastes, aromas and flavours — their intensity, development and balance — the richness, feel and structure of the wine.

Aromas and flavours
We use the word flavours to describe the sensory sensation of the aromas of the wine while it is in the mouth, ie the detection of the volatile components that pass via the retronasal passage connecting the mouth to the olfactory bulb in the brain. *You are actually smelling the wine while it is in the mouth.* Other components which also give sensory sensations in the mouth may either enhance or subdue the impression of flavour.

All these tasting terms are described in the following pages.

If you are tasting a wine during a meal, or over a period of time, the characters of the wine may change as some air is absorbed into the wine in the glass. It is interesting to see how the wine develops and how it matches the food.

9

Check the colour of the rim

and the body of the wine.

The term bouquet
Often this term is used to describe the overall smell which originates from the winemaking process and the maturation and ageing stages in the development of a wine, ie the smell of a more mature wine. We use the terms aromas and flavours irrespective of the age of the wine, and refer to them as primary fruit characters, developed fruit characters and the characters derived from winemaking, either separately or combined. Hence we do not generally use the term bouquet throughout the book.

Descriptive terms/words
People associate certain images with particular experiences. A raspberry smells and tastes like a raspberry, a pineapple like a pineapple, etc. Similarly, Chardonnay grapes smell and taste like Chardonnay grapes. However, we often have less experience with the smell and taste of grape varieties and how they change from year to year and from vineyard to vineyard. Grapes develop characters recognised in other fruits, vegetables, etc, and it is often useful to describe grape varieties and wines with familiar terms such as raspberry, plums, citrus or licorice. These terms help us to communicate when tasting wines, to describe the aromas and flavours.

These terms should be used in conjunction with words like 'is', 'smells like' or 'tastes like', as appropriate.

Some of the terms used may need to be imagined and others may not be grammatically correct, but they are nevertheless the commonly used terms and provide a basis for communication.

Some terms used when observing wine

Terms used to describe the colour of white wines include — *various depths (pale, mid or deep) of straw, yellow, gold or amber*.
Those for red wines include — *light red, mid red, dark red, purple, brick-red, brownish-red, tawny* and *brown*.

These colours can further be described as being bright or dull. As well as the colour of the body of the wine, some wines will have a particular hue at the rim. In young white wines this can be a greenish hue, in young red wines there may be purple tones, while in older red wines brownish tinges may be apparent.

Some terms used when smelling wine

The nose: the overall smell sensations of a wine.

Aromas: volatile compounds that evaporate from the surface of the wine and are detected when the wine is smelt. These include the smells of the wine that are derived from compounds present in the grape at harvest (termed primary fruit characters) and the smells that evolve in the wine via the winemaking process and with time. Each variety of grape imparts its own distinctive character to the wine, eg citrus, floral, minty, herbaceous, blackcurrant. Characters that are not distinctive but give wine-like impressions are described as vinous. As the wine matures, the primary fruit characters are modified and now convey new sensations, termed developed fruit characters, eg the chocolate, gamey or earthy aromas that are obvious in some aged red wines. These developed characters are associated with the grape variety/varieties from which the wine was made. As well as changing with time, they integrate with any other characters that are derived from the winemaking process. This mixing and modification of characters starts during fermentation and continues while the wine is stored in the cellar and then in the bottle, this last stage being referred to as bottle age. Throughout this maturation the intensity of developed characters increases, and the wine grows in complexity.

Some terms used when tasting wines

The palate: the overall impressions of flavour, basic tastes and tactile sensations on the tongue and mouth.

Sweetness: a sweet taste sensation due mainly to the sugar content of the wine. Sweet impressions unrelated to the sugar content can also be perceived; flavour compounds derived from ripe fruit and associated levels of alcohol and glycerol present in the wine can give an apparent sweetness on the palate. Sweet sensations are experienced all over the tongue.

Acidity: a crisp, refreshing taste sensation from the natural acids present in the wine. High levels of acid can have a drying effect in the mouth. (The concept of acidity is discussed further in the vineyard and winemaking sections.)

Freshness: a sensation. A wine that portrays freshness will not only be crisp, but will also have associated stimulating and fresh (not dulled with time) fruit aromas and flavours. Freshness is a quality that is derived from the grapes and needs to be preserved throughout the winemaking process.

Astringency: a puckering (drying out) sensation over the mouth due to the reaction of tannins with the saliva in the mouth. Tannins are derived from the grape and from the wood of oak casks. Astringency is more common in red wines.

Hotness: a warming, heated, sometimes almost burning sensation in the back of the mouth due to a high or unbalanced level of alcohol.

Tactile sensations: a 'tangible' or 'feel' effect on the mouth, tongue and lips when wine is tasted. For example, tannin may have an astringent, drying (or 'chewy'!) effect. Oak may have a powdery, sometimes gritty effect. Alcohol may provide a hot or burning sensation.

Flavours: aroma sensations experienced while the wine is in the mouth. Like aromas, flavours associated with the grape variety are referred to as either primary or developed fruit characters.

Other flavours come from winemaking practices, eg from the oak during storage in oak barrels. Wine flavours, like aromas, change with time. At the stage of drinking, individual flavours should be distinct yet in harmony with each other. No one flavour, with the possible exception of fruit characters, should dominate.

Synergy: the combination of separate aromas/flavours to produce new aroma and flavour sensations, quite different from the individual components. It also applies to the combination of structural features. Although present in all wines, the effects of synergy are most obvious when winemakers blend wines.

Balance: the combined effects of the different flavour and structural components of the wine. When the wine is ready for drinking, all the wine components should blend to convey harmonious flavours, tastes and mouthfeel sensations, without any particular character dominating. The examples below attempt to explain these interactions. It is important to realise that it is the sum total of many diverse effects that conveys the impression of a well-balanced wine. Balance changes with time, as the wine ages.

Acid-sweetness balance
A wine too high in acidity tastes sour and harsh and often displays unripe characters, whereas a wine high in sugar may taste sickly sweet or cloying. These sensations become apparent when the wine is out of balance. Attaining balance requires adjustment of either the acid or sugar level to nullify the excessive expression of the other. A well-made sweet wine, although very high in sugar content, can still taste refreshing and finish with apparent dryness if it is balanced by good acidity and/or phenolics from ageing in wood. Acidity is also balanced by the sweetish impression of the alcohol and/or glycerol present in the wine.

Other balances
Primary and/or developed fruit character must also be in balance with each of the acid, sugar, alcohol, tannin and wood components. Wine must be flavoursome. The quality and quantity of the fruit sensations (primary and/or developed) must be easily recognisable, while integrating with the array of other components. These fruit profiles or images bring flavour, richness and interest to the palate. They should not be masked by excessive levels of other wine components, especially those derived from the winemaking process.

The aromas and flavours of wine come from:

the vineyard

the winery

and time.

Faults

Sometimes during the winemaking process smells and flavours will evolve (eg due to oxidation or spoilage) that give the wine an unpleasant character. When these characters are present in excessive amounts the wine is said to be faulty.

Bitterness: a bitter (unpleasant) sensation on the back of the tongue and mouth, due to certain types of compounds such as phenolics in the wine.

Volatility: the smell of vinegar (acetic acid) and/or nail polish remover (ethyl acetate) in a wine. In small amounts it can contribute to complexity, but when present in large amounts it is regarded as a fault. Certain yeasts can produce these compounds or they can be present as a result of oxidation, a concept we discuss in the section on winemaking.

Aldehyde: the smell that you find in sherry style wines. In these wines it is a positive feature, but in table wines it is generally considered a fault, as it detracts from the fruit characters of the wine. It appears as a result of oxidation.

Hydrogen sulphide: the smell of rotten eggs, not a very pleasant odour to find in wines. It is produced by yeast, but does not persist very often in modern winemaking practices. Other related unpleasant odours that are sometimes present in wines can be described as garlic, onion and cabbage.

Corked: a mouldy and/or wet hessian bag type of smell, which can come from a contaminated cork. Cork is a natural product and sometimes it can contain moulds. These moulds react with some of the chemicals used during the production of corks to produce a compound which remains in the cork. When the cork is inserted in the bottle and then comes in contact with the wine, the contaminating compound diffuses into the wine and gives it a mouldy smell and flavour. The wine is then said to be 'corked'. Apart from this mouldiness, the aroma and flavour of the wine is masked. The contamination of the wine by this corked character can spoil an otherwise good wine.

Body: one of the more difficult concepts. Wines are described as being light-bodied, medium-bodied or full-bodied; these terms help to express the weight of the wine (how 'heavy' the wine feels) in the mouth. Body results from the combined effect of many of the wine's components but especially the amount of flavour, phenolics (tannins), sugar, glycerol and alcohol present in the wine. Essentially a dry, lower alcohol wine (eg about 10% v/v) with medium flavour intensity will fall into the light- to medium-bodied category, whereas a wine with plenty of flavour and tannins and higher alcohol (eg about 13% v/v) will be classified as full-bodied. There are no definitive rules since wines will differ in their make up and different components may be responsible for the expression of body in any one wine. Wines lacking in body can tend to taste watery (thin). Alcohol is one of the more important contributors to the impression of body, and generally wines higher in alcohol content are more full-bodied. However, wines very high in alcohol and low in flavour will be unbalanced, in that the alcohol sensation will dominate the other features of the wine. Wine has many facets and 'getting the balance right' is part of the art of winemaking.

Weight: a measure of a wine's mouthfeel that incorporates not only flavour intensity, but also other compounded effects derived from residual sugar, alcohol and oak.

Attack: the effect of the wine on the palate immediately it enters the mouth: whether it is smooth, soft, acidic, hard, aggressive. Notice, for example, the effect of the flavour impact, acids, tannins, oak and alcohol.

Length: the degree to which the sensations stretch across the palate.

Finish: the final experience of the wine immediately it is swallowed. Some words used to describe the finish of a wine include: rich, alcoholic, hot, bitter, watery, abrupt, short, sharp, long, crisp, acidic, dull, flat, cloying, sour, clean, dirty, tannic, phenolic and oaky.

Aftertaste: desirable sensations which linger in the mouth after the wine is swallowed. Aftertaste follows the finish. A wine is described as having a long, persistent or lingering aftertaste when the flavour sensations linger for about 20 seconds or longer.

Richness: an enhanced intensity of sumptuous aroma and flavour tones, coupled with enjoyable fullness on the palate. Rich wines do not have to be sweet wines, or full-bodied wines. Richness is associated with grapes that really get ripe, ie both sugar and flavour ripe: grapes from good vineyards and good years. It is associated with both primary and developed fruit characters.

Smoothness/Softness: a pleasing all-over mouthfeel sensation, displaying no unbalanced, harsh or aggressive impressions. It also relates to the finish on the back palate. Glycerol contributes to the smoothness of a wine, increasing the viscosity (the thickness of the texture).

Roundness: a sensation that appears to fill the mouth all over, apparent in wines with good flavour and structure.

Tightness: a highly defined balance of structure, weight and flavour (often intense) on the palate.

Finesse and elegance: terms used to describe well-structured wines exhibiting delicate characters with all the desired features of the style present in perfect balance.

Complexity: a wine is described as complex when it provides a diversity of desirable sensory sensations in harmony with each other. Complexity is derived from the various combinations of:
- primary fruit characters
- developed fruit characters
- winemaking contributed characters.

Sometimes terms like layers of flavours and layered complexity are used to describe a complex wine.

Structure: a difficult concept to explain. A wine is said to be well structured or to have good structure when the flavour properties (type, intensity, persistency) fit well with the taste and tactile qualities of the wine. All the parts of the wine are integrated and complement each other. The overall taste just feels right. Good structure indicates a propensity to age (longevity). It incorporates the interrelationship between many of the terms (flavour, balance, freshness, etc).

Many sensations combine to produce 'the character' of any wine. Although we often tend to describe a wine by its parts, it is the coming together of these parts that makes the wine. The types and intensity of aromas and flavours, the complexity, balance, finesse, structure and mouthfeel, and their interrelationships, are what really indicate the quality of the wine — just like the pieces of a jigsaw fusing together to reveal the finished picture.

Tasting wine — putting it all together

A check list:

Observe the colour, its depth and hue.

Are there any off smells?

Are the aromas and flavours distinct, intense and complex?

How would you describe them?

What about the balance: is the wine too acidic? too sweet?

Is there good balance between the fruit characters and those of, for example, acid, sugar, alcohol, tannin and oak?

Is the wine showing freshness and/or richness and/or roundness on the palate?

Does it have good mouthfeel?

For red wines, what is the 'feel' of the tannins?

Is it well-structured?

Are any negative characters dominating the palate?

How does the wine finish?

Is the aftertaste short or long?

Is the wine interesting and enjoyable?

Although it is not necessary to describe or record your impressions of the wine to fully enjoy its sensory experience, a few words about its flavour, balance, weight, mouthfeel, structure and interest can readily convey your impressions of the wine. The occasion and the wine will often dictate how little or how much you need to say. Simply expressing your appreciation of the quality and interest of the wine may be all that is necessary, especially when it is accompanied by food and shared with friends, and when it adds to the overall enjoyment of the occasion.

The enjoyment of drinking the wine is, after all, what it is all about.

Wine is made up of many components;

all components should blend together

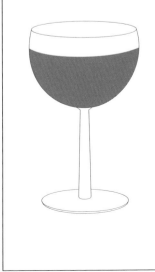

to structure a particular type and style of wine.

Leeuwin Estate Vineyards in the Margaret River Region

THE VINEYARD

The culture of the vine is spread over many parts of Australia. Some areas are already famous for their wines: Coonawarra, the Barossa Valley, the Hunter Valley, the Yarra Valley, to name a few. However the expansion of the wine industry into new vinegrowing regions is bringing other sites to prominence, names such as Pipers Brook in Tasmania, Margaret River in Western Australia, Cowra in New South Wales, Mornington Peninsula in Victoria and the Adelaide Hills in South Australia. These and many other regions are emerging as quality wine producing areas.

At any site the complex interactions between variety, climate, soil and vineyard practices control the growth of the vine, its performance and the composition of its grapes. Grapes will develop and ripen differently in different vineyards, and it follows that the wines from each vineyard will also be different since many of the wine's sensory characters come from the grapes. Australian vineyards span a wide range of climatic environments, are planted on an assortment of soils and are managed in different ways. You should not be surprised then to discover that there is a range of wine types produced in Australia and that these come in many styles, the diversity of our vineyards being portrayed in the diversity of our wines.

It is not easy to describe why grapes from one vineyard are different to those of another, as there are so many contributing factors; grape variety, the climate and its variability, soil type and management practices associated with each site are some of the things we need to consider. They all form part of the big picture where the work of the grapegrower complements the influence of the natural environment in producing grapes for the many styles of Australian wine. Sugar, acid, colour, aroma and flavour compounds (and varying levels of these that are specific to the site) are formed in the grapes, and these largely determine the wine style coming from that vineyard.

Typically, Australian wines are full of flavour. They are made from grapes that come from well managed vineyards in sunny, non-polluted environments; such conditions ensure clean, flavoursome grapes from which our winemakers can begin to craft their wines.

Grapevine varieties

Wine grape varieties

Grapevines come in many shapes and forms. The vines that you see in Australian vineyards belong to the species referred to as *Vitis vinifera*. This species, which has its origins in the Middle East and Europe, has about 5000 different types, called varieties. There are about 60 varieties in Australia, although most wine drinkers will be familiar with only twenty or so, names such as Riesling, Chardonnay, Semillon, Sauvignon Blanc, Pinot Noir, Cabernet Sauvignon and Shiraz. But we also grow many varieties that you do not often see on wine labels, such as Palomino and Pedro Ximenes, which are used for making sherry, and Pinot Meunier, a variety used in sparkling wine production. Each variety has specific aroma and flavour sensations, which we call varietal characters. Some varieties have more distinctive characters than others, and it is these varieties that we commonly see on labels of varietal wines (wines made predominantly from a single variety). Often wines from different grape varieties will be blended to produce a wine of more complexity, structure and interest.

Some white wine grape varieties
(grapes are coloured various shades of yellow or green)
Chardonnay
Riesling
Muscat Gordo Blanco
Semillon
Chenin Blanc
Crouchen
Sauvignon Blanc
Traminer (Gewürztraminer)
Frontignac
Marsanne
Sultana

Some red wine grape varieties
(grapes are coloured various shades of red and purple and are often referred to as black grapes)
Cabernet Sauvignon
Grenache
Shiraz
Malbec
Merlot
Pinot Noir
Cabernet Franc
Ruby Cabernet
Touriga

Clones

Clones are sub-types within varieties. These sub-types differ in their genetic make up or, as scientists put it, in the DNA structure of their cells. DNA is the component of living cells that gives each cell its genetic fingerprint and which governs every process and structure associated with that cell.

If over time some mutation occurs in the cell of a bud on a shoot on a particular vine and this shoot is taken as a cutting for planting in a new vineyard, the vine that arises from that cutting will be slightly different from all the other vines that have come from cuttings of unchanged vines. If there were many vines in the original vineyard that have undergone mutation, the new vineyard will now be a mixture of vines of the two clones (the original one and the mutated one). When this process occurs over many years, some vineyards may be made up of a number of different clones of the same variety. Therefore, differences may exist in the shape of the vines, in berry size, in berry colour and/or other features between vines in the same vineyard.

Varieties that have been used in winemaking for many years, such as Pinot Noir, have many clones, because there has been plenty of opportunity for mutation to occur in the vineyards. Other varieties, such as Ruby Cabernet, show less clonal variation since they are more recent and have had less opportunity to undergo changes.

Some clones seem to perform better than others under different environmental conditions. However, while there may be obvious differences between some clones, most mutations result in very slight differences and so-called clones will differ little in their performance in the vineyard.

Some winemakers prefer a specific clone for a certain style of wine and will select this clone when planting their vineyards, while others will choose to plant a selection of desirable clones, aiming for greater variability in the characters of the grapes coming from the vineyard and thus increasing the complexity of the resultant wine.

Recently, Australian grapegrowers have had greater access to the clones used in the vineyards of Europe. The future will be exciting as the search continues for the clones that are most suitable for our different grapegrowing regions. These improvements in planting material can only mean better quality grapes and wines.

Grapevine rootstocks

Vitis vinifera vines often do not perform well when planted on their own roots in soils with high lime or salt content and where pests such as phylloxera are present. In these circumstances it is best to plant grafted vines, where the root system is from a species other than *Vitis vinifera*, and which thus allows the vines to grow in these unfavourable soil conditions.

Diagram of a grafted vine

This part of the vine (upper wood, shoots, leaves and fruit) is from the *Vitis vinifera* variety. It could be Chardonnay, Shiraz or any of the many *Vitis vinifera* varieties.

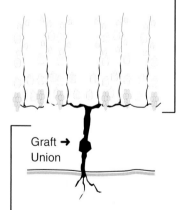

Graft ➜
Union

This part of the vine (the rootstock), which provides the roots, comes from another species (normally a native American species or a hybrid), which is resistant to attack by soil pests or grows well in certain soils.

Effects of phylloxera on a vineyard
The vines in the foreground are on own roots and have been attacked by phylloxera, while those in the background have been planted on resistant rootstocks and have survived.

Grape phylloxera is a small aphid that lives on the roots (and sometimes leaves) of grapevines. This pest attacks the roots, which eventually decay, and the vine dies. In areas where phylloxera is present in the soil, *Vitis vinifera* vines must be grafted onto resistant rootstocks before they are planted. These grafted vines, now with a resistant and efficient root system, produce grapes of the selected *Vitis vinifera* varieties.

Phylloxera is present in most countries. It destroyed the vineyards of Europe in the late 1800s and in more recent times it has ravaged vineyards in California. Phylloxera was found in Australia in the 1880s and destroyed many of the vineyards of Victoria during the late 1800s and early 1900s.

The spread of phylloxera in Australia has been controlled by quarantine regulations that restrict the movement of grapevines between regions, and thus many Australian vinegrowing regions are not troubled by this pest.

Rootstocks are also used to combat nematodes, which are small worm-like organisms that live in some soils and disrupt root function, affecting the growth of the vine. But rootstocks are used for other reasons than controlling soil pests; there are rootstocks that work better in salty soils and others that work better in soils of high lime content. Researchers are now looking for rootstocks that will decrease the vigorous growth that often occurs in vines growing in rich deep soils.

Over the years, grapevine breeders have conducted extensive research to find varieties suitable for the many different soil and environmental conditions in which the vine grows. The task of these researchers is not only to combat such pests as phylloxera, but also to breed varieties that are resistant to diseases that attack the grapevine. The aim is that the vineyards of the future will be planted with the best planting material, ie the best clones and the best rootstocks which are the most resistant to diseases and pests and which produce the highest quality of the desired style of wine.

How grapes grow

Once the vineyard is established, each vine grows according to an annual growth cycle. Temperature regulates the timing of each stage, and since temperature conditions vary from site to site the stages of vine growth occur at different times of the year in different vineyards. Each stage of growth occurs earlier in hotter regions than it does in cooler regions.

Temperature conditions also change from year to year. Hence, at any one site, the stages of vine growth will either be early or late depending on the conditions of that year. Therefore grapes, either from different vineyards in any one year or from the same vineyard in different years, will ripen under different temperature and other climatic conditions.

These climatic differences, which influence how the grapes ripen, contribute to differences in wines produced from different vineyards (*the regional variation*) and from the same vineyard from year to year (*the vintage variation*). However, many other factors also contribute to the sensory characters that develop in grapes, including variety, vineyard site, management practices and time of harvest.

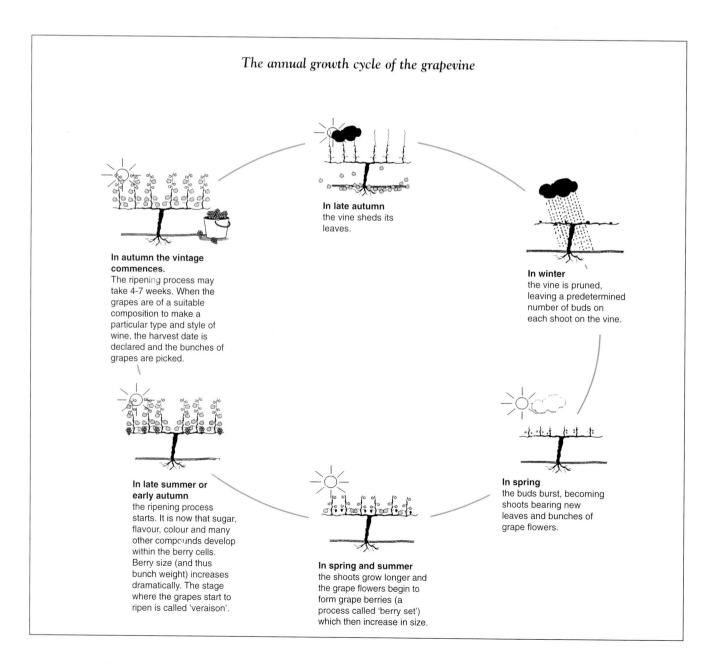

The annual growth cycle of the grapevine

In late autumn
the vine sheds its leaves.

In winter
the vine is pruned, leaving a predetermined number of buds on each shoot on the vine.

In autumn the vintage commences.
The ripening process may take 4-7 weeks. When the grapes are of a suitable composition to make a particular type and style of wine, the harvest date is declared and the bunches of grapes are picked.

In spring
the buds burst, becoming shoots bearing new leaves and bunches of grape flowers.

In late summer or early autumn
the ripening process starts. It is now that sugar, flavour, colour and many other compounds develop within the berry cells. Berry size (and thus bunch weight) increases dramatically. The stage where the grapes start to ripen is called 'veraison'.

In spring and summer
the shoots grow longer and the grape flowers begin to form grape berries (a process called 'berry set') which then increase in size.

GRAPES — the ripening process

The sugar story

The leaves of the vine act like miniature chemical factories and produce sugar (a process called photosynthesis). The sugar is then moved through the shoot to other parts of the vine, including the developing berries. When the berries are small, hard and green (during the stage from berry set to veraison) this sugar is mainly used for berry growth and chemical reactions within berry cells. However, veraison signals the onset of ripening and now sugar begins to be stored in special compartments within the berry cells. From veraison to harvest the sugar content of the berries increases dramatically and berries become obviously sweet to taste. Prior to harvest samples of berries are collected regularly from each vineyard and crushed to release the juice. The sugar content of the juice is measured and usually expressed in units of either °Baumé (degrees Baumé) or °Brix (degrees Brix). One °Baumé is equivalent to 1.8° Brix. °Baumé is more commonly used since it gives a convenient indication of the potential alcohol content of the wine produced from those grapes, eg:
• a grape juice with 10° Baumé (18° Brix) will, if fermented completely, produce a wine of about 10% alcohol by volume; and
• a grape juice with 13° Baumé (about 23° Brix) will, if fermented completely, produce a wine of about 13% alcohol by volume.

Hence a measure of °Baumé taken prior to harvest gives the winemaker a guide as to the type of wine he/she could make from that batch of grapes, eg:
• sparkling wines are normally produced from grapes with sugar levels in the order of 9 to 11° Baumé;
• a full-bodied red wine requires grapes with a higher sugar level, about 13° Baumé; and
• to make a muscat the grapes should be very high in sugar, sometimes up to 22° Baumé.

Apart from the increase in sugar in the berries during the ripening process, many other changes also occur. It is a period of great chemical activity within the berry. The berries soften, take up water, increase in size, decrease in acidity, change colour and develop distinctive aromas and flavours. While the sugar level at harvest essentially dictates wine type, it is the types, amounts and balance of these other components which are largely responsible for the style of any particular wine type.

Photosynthetic reactions occur in the leaves

(where carbon dioxide and water react to form sugar. The main sugars in grapes are glucose and fructose.)

The energy for this reaction comes from sunlight.

The sugar produced in the leaves is moved through the shoot to the grape berries on each bunch.

The water comes from the soil via the roots.

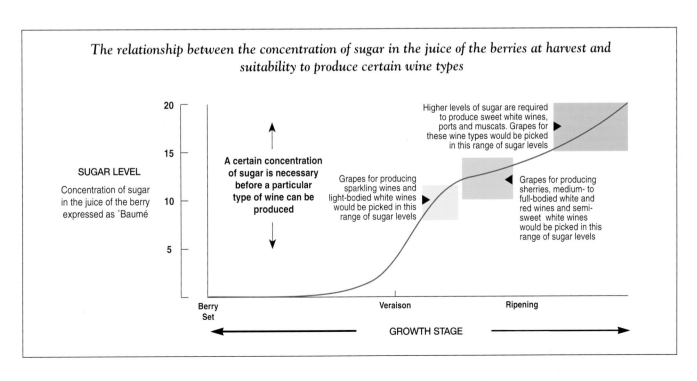

The relationship between the concentration of sugar in the juice of the berries at harvest and suitability to produce certain wine types

SUGAR LEVEL

Concentration of sugar in the juice of the berry expressed as °Baumé

A certain concentration of sugar is necessary before a particular type of wine can be produced

Grapes for producing sparkling wines and light-bodied white wines would be picked in this range of sugar levels

Higher levels of sugar are required to produce sweet white wines, ports and muscats. Grapes for these wine types would be picked in this range of sugar levels

Grapes for producing sherries, medium- to full-bodied white and red wines and semi-sweet white wines would be picked in this range of sugar levels

Berry Set   Veraison   Ripening

GROWTH STAGE

The acid story

Acids are the components that give wine its fresh, crisp taste sensation. The main acids in the grape are tartaric acid and malic acid. They originate in the grape but some may also be added during winemaking. Just as the sugar level is expressed by the term °Baumé, there are special terms that relate to the concept of acidity. The overall concentration of acid present in the juice of grape berries is expressed as titratable acidity, while the chemical effectiveness of the acids (how they influence chemical reactions in the juice) is referred to as pH. These terms are also used to describe acidity levels in wine and are often seen on wine labels. A more detailed coverage of acidity concepts is given in the section on winemaking. Both tartaric and malic acids, which are produced in the berry during the early stages of berry growth, reach their maximum levels about veraison and then decrease in concentration during the ripening period. These changes are reflected in the measures of acidity; with berry ripening, titratable acidity decreases and pH increases. Measurements of pH and titratable acidity are taken on the juice of sample berries collected from each vineyard. The winemaker takes into consideration the values of these measurements and their balance with the sugar level in deciding when to pick the grapes.

The colour and tannin story

Colour and tannin compounds form part of the phenolic make up of wines. Phenolics are a group of chemical compounds that give wine its colour, influence its texture and palate weight and can contribute bitter and astringent (drying) taste sensations. Most of the phenolics are in the skins and seeds of the grape, and the compounds that give red wine its colour (the anthocyanins) are found only in the skins of black grapes. Peel a black grape and you will observe that the flesh is clear and only the skin is coloured black.

The onset of colouring in grapes is the most obvious change occurring at veraison. Berries of red wine grape varieties change from green to red; this colour is modified during ripening as the anthocyanin content in the skin increases, and the berries take on a purple-black appearance. Colour changes in white wine grape varieties, although less obvious, are also triggered at veraison, the dark green berries taking on either a lighter green or yellow appearance as ripening progresses. The amount of colour in black grapes at harvest determines in part the colour of the wine made from them; lightly coloured grapes produce lightly coloured red wines while more intensely coloured grapes produce darker coloured wines.

The drying (puckering) sensation in the mouth, often experienced when tasting red wines, is associated with compounds called tannins. These have their beginnings in the skin and seeds of black grapes. As the berry ripens the tannin level in the skin generally increases, but as well as this the tannins that are formed are continually changing their structure. Both the amount and types of tannins in the grapes at harvest influence the mouthfeel of the resultant wine.

A black grape with and without its skin

Veraison — the beginning of ripening and the time when the grapes start to change colour

The aroma and flavour story

The aroma and flavour compounds which are present in the juice and skin of the berries are responsible for the distinctive aroma and flavour sensations of wines made from those grapes. These aroma and flavour sensations are often referred to as varietal character. As the berry ripens, there are changes in the types of characters expressed and an increase in the overall level of aroma and flavour compounds, albeit only in minute amounts. For example, with Pinot Noir grapes from some vineyards the juice from the berries may exhibit aroma and flavour character similar at first to strawberries, then raspberries and then plums during the ripening process. Each variety of grape has its own set of varietal characters and its own pattern in which these change during ripening; we refer to this as the primary fruit spectrum. The descriptors used in the spectrum are guides only; other terms which express particular varietal characters can also be used.

Examples of the primary fruit spectrum for some varieties

These are examples of words that can be used to describe the aromas and flavours of grapes and wines of the particular variety. Generally there will be a mixture of words that best describes any particular wine. For example for Pinot Noir, one wine may express strawberry, violets and raspberry characters while another wine may express raspberry and plum characters. The two wines would be described as being different in style because the aromas and flavours are different. Also the other characters of the wine, for example the acid structure and phenolic makeup, are likely to be different. For any one vineyard there is a general association between the progression of aroma and flavour development in the berry and sugar accumulation. Descriptive characters at the early ripening stage are usually associated with lower sugar levels, and those at the later stage appear as sugar ripening continues. But the combination of characters present in the berries at harvest depends very much on the climatic conditions during ripening and the management practices employed in the vineyard.

RIESLING
floral | perfumed | apple | pear | citrus | lime | passionfruit | tropical fruit

SAUVIGNON BLANC
asparagus | capsicum | herbaceous | grassy | gooseberry | tropical fruit

SEMILLON
herbaceous | straw | gooseberry | apple | lemon | lime | passionfruit
grassy | quince | citrus | tropical fruit

CHARDONNAY
cucumber | grapefruit | apple | lime | rockmelon | fruit salad | tropical fruit
tobacco | gooseberry | melon | peach | fig

PINOT NOIR
cherry | strawberry | violets | raspberry | plum | stewed plum

GRENACHE
floral | boiled lolly | spice | raspberry | pepper | plum | stewed plum | prunes | licorice

MERLOT
herbaceous | leafy | perfumed | sappy | cherry | plum | fruit cake | blackcurrant
fruity | violets | raspberry | beetroot

CABERNET SAUVIGNON
herbaceous | capsicum | tomato bush | leafy | minty | dusty | black olive | blackcurrant

SHIRAZ
herbs | spice | raspberry | plum | pepper | blackberry | mulberry | licorice | black olive | jammy

EARLIER RIPENING STAGE → LATER RIPENING STAGE

However aroma and flavour ripening does not necessarily progress through the whole spectrum in every situation. Some grapes will ripen to a stage where the characters are described more by those terms earlier in the spectrum, while others will ripen to a stage described by characters more in the middle or later in the spectrum. Variety, climate and grapegrowing practices all influence the types of aroma and flavour compounds (and their intensity) in the grapes at harvest.

Grapes of the same variety but from different vineyards can ripen to the same sugar level, but with different expressions of aroma and flavour.

SITE 1		SITE 2
RIPENING PATTERN ONE		**RIPENING PATTERN TWO**
	13°	
peach/tropical fruit/fig	12°	melon/peach
melon/peach/tropical fruit	11°	melon
melon/peach	10°	tobacco/melon
tobacco/melon	9°	cucumber/tobacco/grapefruit
cucumber/tobacco/grapefruit	8°	cucumber
cucumber	7°	unripe characters
unripe characters	Sugar Level °Baumé	unripe characters

Possible changes in aroma and flavour sensations of Chardonnay grapes during ripening under two ripening patterns

Defining ripeness now takes on new dimensions. Viticulturists and winemakers refer to grapes not only as being sugar ripe (at the right sugar level), but also as being flavour ripe (having the right aroma and flavour compounds present in the grapes for the style of wine that they intend to make from those grapes). Flavour ripeness may occur at different sugar levels for different vineyards.

The varietal characters present in the grapes at harvest are carried over into the wine during winemaking and form a critical part of the style of the wine produced. The aromas and flavours of wines, particularly young wines, resemble those of the grape variety from which they were made.

Whether
a Sauvignon Blanc wine will have grassy, capsicum, tropical fruit, or other characters;
or a Chardonnay wine will have tobacco, melony, peachy or other characters;
or a Pinot Noir wine will have strawberry, raspberry, plum or other characters;
or a Cabernet Sauvignon wine will have minty, herbaceous, blackcurrant or other characters;
or a Shiraz wine will have peppery, spicy, plum, mulberry or other characters
depends on whether these characters were present in the grapes at harvest.

As well as measuring the concentration of sugar and acid in the juice of the berries sampled from the vineyard, winemakers also appraise the types and intensity of varietal characters in those berries (normally by tasting the berries or by smelling the juice samples). They may be looking for the presence or absence of specific characters. This assessment, and the measurements of sugar and acid, are all taken into account in deciding when to harvest the vineyard.

Matching sugar and flavour ripeness requires not only an understanding of the principles of grape ripening, but also many years' experience of assessing fruit and making wine from that vineyard. Traditional practices in certain vinegrowing regions reflect this knowledge that comes with time. Winemakers are always mindful of the type and style of wine they plan to produce. Often wines from different vineyards and/or varieties will be blended to give a range of desirable characters, enhancing the interest and enjoyment of that wine.

Some of the fruits that can be used to describe the aromas and flavours of Chardonnay wines

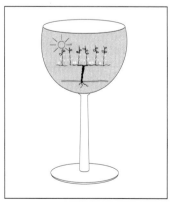

Wine style commences in the vineyard, as this is where many characters of the wine originate.

Vintage (*the period during which the grapes are harvested*) normally occurs in Australian vineyards during the months of February, March and April. It occurs at different times in different regions and for different varieties. Generally the warmer the region, the earlier the commencement of vintage. For any one region the varieties Pinot Noir and Chardonnay are, as a rule, the first to reach a stage of ripeness suitable for harvest, while Cabernet Sauvignon is one of the last varieties to be harvested. The Hunter Valley region in New South Wales is often the first to finish vintage activities, while the cooler areas of Victoria and Tasmania can still be harvesting grapes into late April and early May.

At the stage of harvest the berries contain varying amounts of sugar, acid, colour and aroma and flavour compounds, as well as minerals and other nutrients — all the ingredients for making wine. The exact time of harvest will depend on many factors, including not only the amounts and balance of these compounds but also the physical condition of the grapes and the prevailing weather conditions.

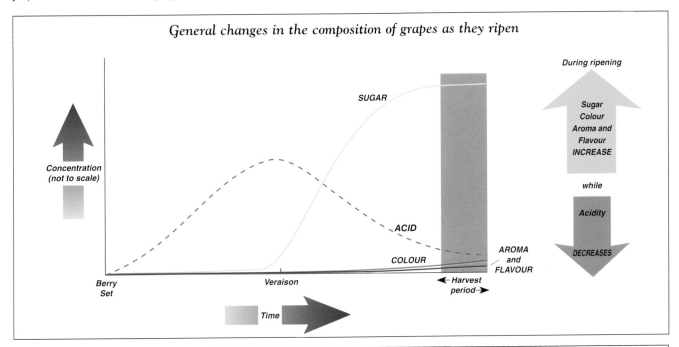

General changes in the composition of grapes as they ripen

A general guide to the composition of grapes used to make the various types of wine

Composition of the juice
(shown as typical ranges of values)

Wine type/style	Sugar (°Baumé)		Acidity (grams per litre)	
Table wines				
Sparkling wine	9 - 11	LOW	8 - 12	HIGH
Light-bodied dry white	10 - 12		7 - 9	
Full-bodied dry white	12 - 14		6 - 8	
Light-bodied dry red	10 - 12		7 - 9	
Full-bodied dry red	12 - 14		5 - 9	
Semi-sweet white wine	13 - 16		7 - 9	
Sweet white wine (eg botrytis styles)	17 - 22		6 - 9	
Fortified wines		HIGH		LOW
Sherry-like	10 - 11		6 - 9	
Port-like	14 - 16		4 - 6	
Muscat, Tokay	17 - 22		4 - 6	

There will be a large range of grape colours and flavours that accompany the above values, which create different styles of wine within each wine type.

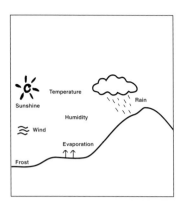

The elements of climate

CLIMATE, GRAPES AND WINE
Describing the climate of vinegrowing regions
All the climatic elements are important in grape production; however if emphasis were to be given to one it would be temperature. Temperature affects vine growth and berry composition, in some cases quite dramatically. Temperature also forms the basis for the various classification systems for describing vinegrowing regions. It is often the most obvious difference between sites.

Temperature
One approach to classifying vineyards according to their temperature characteristics is to categorise them in relation to the mean January temperature at that site. This classification was developed by two Australian viticulturists, Dr Richard Smart and Mr Peter Dry. Although January does not correspond to the ripening period for most vineyard sites, the measure of the mean temperature for this month does broadly reflect the general climatic conditions during the ripening period in the different sites, and based on this index vineyards can be classified into very hot, hot, warm, cool or cold climatic sites, as described below.

Climatic description of site	Mean January temperature of site °C	
very hot	>23	There are no definite cut off points between classifications, but some arbitrary figures need to be set so that general groupings into the various climatic descriptions can be made.
hot	21 - 22.9	
warm	19 - 20.9	
cool	17 - 18.9	
cold	<16.9	

Leasingham's Provis Vineyard near Clare, South Australia

A combination of terms

A combination of the climatic terms gives the best description of a particular vinegrowing region. For example the Rutherglen region in Victoria could be described as having a hot, very sunny, continental type of climate, while the climate of the Launceston region in Tasmania could be described as cool, moderately sunny, humid and moderately maritime. If a region is described as having a continental climate, it means that there is generally a large difference between summer and winter temperatures. Maritime climates on the other hand show smaller fluctuations between summer and winter temperatures. Regions with continental climates are normally further inland, while regions categorised as maritime are near the coast or in close proximity to large bodies of water.

Heat summation index

Another climatic index that is frequently used in describing vineyard sites is *Heat Degree Days*. It is a heat summation index, ie how much heat a particular vineyard site receives over the growing season, and is an alternative expression of the temperature conditions at that site. It is a more quantitative way of describing the temperature conditions of different vineyards. Various modifications of this index have been advanced by viticulturists over the years.

In this book we have chosen to use a modification of the heat degree day system termed *biologically effective day degrees*. This was developed by an Australian agricultural scientist, Dr John Gladstones, who was also involved in identifying many of the new vinegrowing areas in Western Australia. This index links temperature conditions of the site more closely with the biological activity of the vine and, as John Gladstones argues, it gives a better relationship with actual observations of vine growth and performance seen in the vineyard. A general association exists between the words we use to describe the temperature conditions of a vineyard site and the biologically effective day degrees of that site. Vineyard sites classified descriptively as hot normally have higher values for biologically effective day degrees, and so on. Because the terms evolve from different concepts it is not appropriate to define sharp cut-off points between the various gradations of the two systems; however the diagram on the following page does give a guide to the relationship between the two expressions.

Delatite's vineyards in the foothills of the alps near Mansfield in the High Country region of Victoria

Taltarni's Clover Hill vineyard in Tasmania

Yalumba's Oxford Landing Vineyard in the Riverland region of South Australia

Some climatic data for Australian grapegrowing regions

A general guide to the heat summation index and climatic classification (vertical axis), average % relative humidity (horizontal axis) and an estimate of the average daily mean temperature during the ripening period (numbers in brackets) for some of Australia's vinegrowing regions.

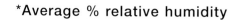

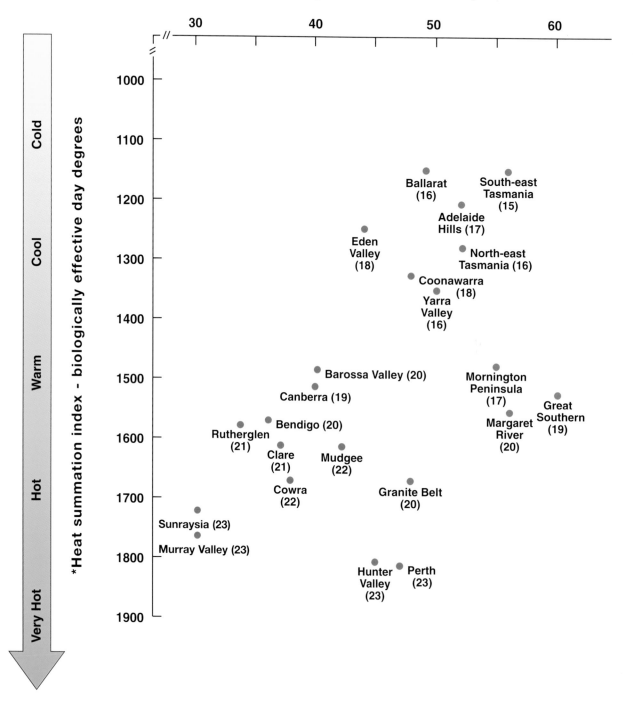

* This data should be used in conjunction with other climatic indices for an accurate comparison of regions. The book 'Viticulture and Environment' by Dr John Gladstones gives an excellent coverage of these issues.

Some words of caution on interpreting the climatic classification

Variation within a region due to location

Temperature conditions may change over a very short distance within a region. Individual vineyards within each region may not match the classification of the overall region, since they may be at a higher elevation and thus cooler than the climatic station where the temperature is recorded. For example, many sites within the general classification of Clare, in South Australia, are cooler than suggested by the data from the recording station, due to quite large differences among the vineyards in their altitudes, latitudes and individual topographics. These differences justify the description of the vineyards in the Clare region as ranging from cool through to cool to warm and warm. Similar arguments apply to specific vineyards in other sites.

Other climatic factors can modify the effects of temperature

The temperature conditions during the ripening period are important in setting the balance between the sugar, acid, flavour and phenolic compounds of the berries.

However, other aspects such as wind, humidity, whether the vineyard is on a slope, in a valley or near a large body of water may also modify the temperature conditions of individual vineyards.

Because of the influence of other climatic factors, temperature conditions cannot always be taken as a direct indication of ripening conditions and potential wine style. For example, in the Hunter Valley the conditions are more suitable for ripening grapes for table wine styles than would initially be expected from observation of temperature conditions. It is likely that the higher humidity and sea breezes that occur in this region have an effect in relieving vine stress during ripening, providing more efficient ripening conditions.

Therefore, within each region it is important to know the particular conditions of any site in relation to the region as a whole.

The vintage variation

Because the climate of any region may vary from year to year, some vineyards will fluctuate from their normal classification each year. For example, a cool vineyard site may experience cold, cool or warm conditions during the period of grape development and ripening, depending on the climate of that year.

Similarly, sites classified as warm fluctuate from cool to hot depending on the year. The wines will reflect the prevalent climatic conditions experienced up to and during the ripening period.

In hotter vinegrowing regions, although temperature does vary from year to year, the temperature conditions generally remain hot. The climatic conditions during ripening are more consistent from year to year, and thus there is usually less vintage variation in the wines produced from these regions. However, the cooler years in these regions are generally associated with better wines.

Vineyard management practices can modify the effects of climate

Sound vineyard management practices are required to bring out the best in grapes from any climate. Practices that provide conditions which lead to vines with open canopies and which are adequately supplied with water and nutrients generally enhance grape composition. The vineyard management practices must be matched to the soil and climatic conditions of the site.

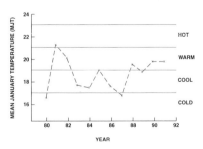

This illustration shows how the Mean January Temperature has changed over recent years for a vineyard sited in a cool region.

All grape varieties do not ripen at the same time

The cycle of vine growth occurs at different times of the year for different vineyard sites. Budburst and shoot growth commence in spring, normally when the mean daily temperature reaches about 10°C, and thus these stages of vine growth occur first in hotter regions. As a rule these differences in growth pattern are carried through to harvest. For example, budburst and shoot growth occur in the Barossa Valley (a warm region) about mid-September and harvest takes place during March, while in a cool vineyard area, such as sites in Tasmania, budburst occurs about the beginning of October and harvest not until early to mid April or later.

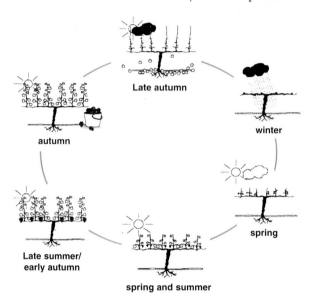

The annual cycle of vine growth occurs at different times for different vinegrowing regions.

However within each climatic region all grape varieties do not grow and ripen over the same time period. Grape varieties can be grouped into early, mid or late ripening varieties; at any one site the early ripening varieties are normally harvested earlier than varieties in the other groups.

Early ripening varieties include Pinot Noir and Chardonnay, while Shiraz and Riesling are classified as mid ripening varieties and Cabernet Sauvignon is a mid to late ripening variety. Tarrango, a new red wine grape variety bred by researchers at the CSIRO laboratories at Merbein (Victoria), is a late ripening variety.

A comparison of the times of ripening for some of the more well known grape varieties

In any one area these varieties are likely to be harvested first, signalling the start of vintage.

Early ripening	Mid-season ripening	Late ripening
Pinot Noir	Cabernet Sauvignon	Grenache
Chardonnay	Malbec	Tarrango
Sultana	Shiraz	Muscat Gordo Blanco
Traminer	Cabernet Franc	
Verdelho	Ruby Cabernet	*These varieties will be*
	Chenin Blanc	*amongst the last to be*
	Colombard	*harvested. The vintage*
	Crouchen	*for that year is almost*
	Marsanne	*over.*
	Riesling	
	Sauvignon Blanc	
	Semillon	

Matching the variety and the climate

Another difference between grape varieties is their ability to reach an adequate grape sugar level for the production of particular types of wine. This feature is linked with the concept of heat summation, some varieties having a lower heat summation requirement to attain the grape sugar level appropriate for making certain wine types. Dr John Gladstones categorises varieties into groups according to their biologically effective day degrees requirement to reach a certain level of sugar in the grapes. The example given below relates to a variety's heat summation requirement to attain a sugar level of about 12° Baumé (ie a level suitable for the production of dry red or dry white table wine).

The heat summation requirement for different varieties	
Variety	**Heat summation requirement** (biologically effective day degrees)
Pinot Noir	1150
Chardonnay	1150
Traminer	1150
Riesling	1200
Shiraz	1250
Cabernet Sauvignon	1300
Tarrango	1400

Varieties which require a larger heat summation to ripen fully are not suitable for cold and cold to cool sites. Grown in these cooler conditions, these varieties will be ripening during a period (eg April and May) when mean daily temperatures are falling as winter approaches. Varieties such as Cabernet Sauvignon may have difficulty in achieving good grape sugar levels for production of medium- to full-bodied dry red wine and, if adequate sugar is attained, the accompanying varietal aroma and flavour may often be dominated by capsicum-type characters, a feature frequently associated with Cabernet Sauvignon grown in cooler climates. A variety such as Tarrango would have little chance of ripening fully in cool conditions as there would simply not be sufficient heat for its particular growth and ripening pattern. It was in fact developed specifically to match the ripening conditions occurring in hot areas and under these circumstances produces a light-bodied, well flavoured red wine with good natural acidity.

Varieties which require less heat to ripen, such as Chardonnay, Traminer, Riesling and Pinot Noir, will ripen adequately in cool, warm or hot regions but they produce a different style of wine in each climatic region.

In cold, cool and cool to warm climatic regions the vineyards are planted predominately with the varieties Pinot Noir, Chardonnay, Traminer and Riesling. Often, and particularly in the cooler regions, Pinot Noir and Chardonnay will be used to make sparkling wine. In warm, warm to hot and hot regions we are more likely to find plantings of Cabernet Sauvignon, Shiraz, Grenache, Muscat Gordo Blanco and Frontignac, as well as Chardonnay. Chardonnay appears to be a very adaptable grape variety and produces well flavoured wines (but of different styles) right across the climatic spectrum. Chardonnay is grown in many Australian regions and consequently we see many styles of Chardonnay wines.

Temperature: how it influences wine type

Temperature affects the photosynthetic process in the leaves since the function of the enzymes involved in sugar production is temperature sensitive. Enzymes are chemical substances that cause reactions in living cells to go faster. These sugar enzymes work best at between about 18 and 33°C. If the leaf temperature is either cold or extremely hot, production of sugar in the leaves is slowed, and subsequent accumulation in the berries may be low and inappropriate for the production of certain wine types. Overall, most sites classified as very hot, hot, warm or cool have sufficient periods (photosynthetic hours) during each day of the ripening period to satisfy this temperature requirement and almost always produce grapes with sugar levels appropriate for the production of most wine types.

However, in cold and cold to cool sites where daily temperatures are lower, particularly towards the end of ripening, there may be insufficient hours of this necessary temperature range to produce adequate amounts of sugar in the leaves and thus in the berries. In Australia these regions would include some of the more southerly and/or higher altitude vineyard sites (areas with low values for biologically effective day degrees). Delicate, light-bodied dry whites and sparkling wines are often produced from grapes grown in these regions, since these wine styles are made from grapes with lower sugar levels. Grapes grown in cool to warm, warm and warm to hot regions normally reach adequate sugar levels for the production of medium- to full-bodied white and red table wines. Warm to hot and hot regions are often suited to growing grapes for the production of full-bodied white and red table wines as well as fortified wines. Under these conditions there is a greater chance of attaining the higher sugar levels (between 16 and 20° Baumé) required for the production of fortified wines.

Temperature: creating characters of wine style

As well as influencing sugar accumulation in grapes, temperature also regulates the amounts and types of acid, colour, tannins and aroma and flavour compounds that develop in grapes during ripening. It thus has a controlling role in determining the style of wine produced from those grapes: how crisp the wine is on the palate (the acidity component), how the wine smells (the aroma and flavour component) and for red wines, how red coloured the wine will be (the colour component) and how the wine feels in the mouth (the tannin component).

Acidity

During berry ripening, the overall decrease in juice acidity level is partly due to the breakdown of malic acid, a process also controlled by enzymes. As a rule the higher the temperature, the greater the loss (breakdown) of malic acid. Grapes from vineyards in warm to hot climates will on average have lower natural levels of acid than grapes from cooler conditions and may require acid adjustment prior to winemaking. Cool climates normally produce grapes which contain higher amounts of acid and the resultant wines will be more naturally acidic and fresher.

Colour

Production of colour (compounds called *anthocyanins*) occurs in the skin of black grapes, again modified by specific enzyme activity. These colour enzymes work best between 17 and 26°C. This range is somewhat lower than that for photosynthetic reactions and thus, while most grapegrowing regions have temperature profiles that fulfil the temperature requirement for sugar production, some very hot regions will not be optimal for grape colour production. The temperature during a large part of the day in these sites will be too high for colour production, although adequate amounts of sugar may be obtained. In cold regions both sugar and colour production may be limited by the low temperature conditions. Thus, black grapes from vineyards in different climatic regions may ripen to similar sugar levels, but the accompanying colour in the grapes may vary widely. The wines produced from those grapes will also be different; although of similar type (eg dry red table wine) they could range in sensory characters from lightly coloured and light-bodied to highly coloured and full-bodied wines, ie they will be of different styles.

Aroma and flavour

Temperature also regulates the production of aroma and flavour compounds in grapes. As yet we do not know the optimum temperature range for the enzymes involved in varietal aroma and flavour production, although it is likely to be similar to or slightly lower than that for colour production.

Experience does give us some clues as to the type of primary fruit characters to expect from grapes and wines from diverse temperature conditions. Each variety responds uniquely. Shiraz wines from cooler climates often display distinctive primary fruit characters described as peppery, while those from warmer regions may express more plum and mulberry-like aromas and flavours. Cooler growing conditions highlight the floral, fragrant aromas and flavours of Riesling grapes (and wines) while cool to warm and warm sites bring out more lime-like characters. The primary fruit characters of Chardonnay wines generally range through apple, lime, gooseberry, melon, rockmelon, peach, fig and fruit salad to tropical fruit-like sensations as we progress from cool to hot vineyard sites.

Wine style

Wine style is not just influenced by the temperature conditions in which the grapes grow; many other factors of climate, vine management and winemaking technique also play a role in influencing the make up of grapes and the character of the wine. However, the effects of temperature produce a range of combinations of sugar, acid, colour and aroma and flavour compounds in grapes, which when carried over into the wine create different wine styles for each variety, ie wines of varying alcoholic strength, acidity and aroma and flavour sensations.

The following comments on the effects of temperature on wine style are given as a general guide to the types and styles of wine to expect from different climatic regions.
These comments assume that the vines are grown according to sound management practices.

The most suitable grapes for premium sparkling wine production come from Chardonnay and Pinot Noir vines grown in cold to cool climatic sites. Under these conditions they produce a high intensity of the right aromas and flavours at the lower sugar levels required for the production of these wines.

Medium-bodied white table wines (for example, Rieslings, Traminers, Chardonnays and Sauvignon Blancs) are normally produced from grapes grown in cool and cool to warm conditions. Their sensory characters will be described by terms more towards the earlier to mid stages of the primary fruit spectrum. Their natural acidity is frequently high, reflected by a crispness on the palate.

Cool to warm, warm and warm to hot climatic conditions appear to be most suited to the production of medium- to full-bodied white and red table wines, such as Chardonnay, Pinot Noir, Cabernet Sauvignon and Shiraz. A range of rich but distinct aroma and flavour profiles may be evident, those in the middle and towards the later stage of the primary fruit spectrum. These wines can often not only have rich primary and developed fruit characters, but will also show complexity and a pleasing mouthfeel sensation. Red wines generally show good tannin structure. Alcohol levels of these wines are often around 12-14% v/v.

Grapes grown in hotter climates often, but not always, produce medium- to full-bodied wines with medium intensity of colour and overall aroma and flavour. Palate structure of the wine produced in such conditions may not be as good as that of wines from warm conditions. Acidity adjustment is normally required prior to winemaking.

Warm to hot and hot conditions are also suited to the production of fortified wine styles, in this case higher sugar levels, as well as intensity of flavours, being an important requirement.

The changes do not occur in distinct steps and for any situation there is an overlap of sensations. Most often it is groups of characters that are associated with specific climatic sites.

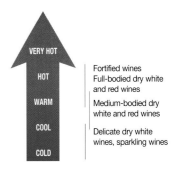

VERY HOT
HOT — Fortified wines / Full-bodied dry white and red wines
WARM — Medium-bodied dry white and red wines
COOL — Delicate dry white wines, sparkling wines
COLD

A general relationship between temperature conditions of the vineyard site and the likely types/styles of wine that will be produced.

Examples of primary fruit descriptors for the different grape varieties are described on page 21 and in the relevant sections on wine styles.

Sunshine within the vine canopy

Temperature: only part of the climate story

Although a critical aspect in setting wine style, temperature is only part of the complex array of events that influence grape composition and wine style. The effects of other climatic elements such as sunshine hours, humidity, rainfall, evaporation and wind on vine growth and grape ripening also need to be considered before deciding on any particular site for growing grapes.

Sunshine

Sunshine provides the energy for photosynthesis. Most Australian vinegrowing regions have sufficient sunshine hours during the growing season to provide adequate ripening conditions. Many of our vineyard sites are aptly described as sunny and warm, conditions that are conducive to producing not only well flavoured grapes with adequate sugar levels, but also grapes that are free of disease and in sound condition at harvest.

However, it is not only leaves that benefit from sun exposure; grape berries also require light to initiate reactions that lead to colour, aroma and flavour development. For vineyards in cool and warm climatic sites the more the bunches are exposed to sunlight, generally the greater the production of colour and aroma and flavour compounds in the berries. However exposure, as well as increasing light interception, may also raise the temperature of the berry; in hotter environments this may be detrimental to the reactions causing colour, aroma and flavour development. Thus in hot climates some but not total bunch exposure may be the best option. Viticulturists need to set their management practices to complement the effects of the environment.

Humidity and evaporation

Sites that have high evaporation and low humidity are associated with higher transpiration rates (ie water loss through the leaves). Irrigation may be necessary to maintain efficient leaf function in order to prevent the vines becoming stressed during critical growth periods. Water is essential to the functioning of the vine and many Australian vineyards benefit from regulated irrigation, improving grape and wine quality.

Environments with lower evaporation and higher humidity are more favourable for avoiding vine moisture stress; however such environments are often associated with higher rainfall during the growing season, which can lead to a higher incidence of fungal diseases. In these sites good vine management practices are required to provide sound grapes for winemaking.

Wind

Some wind may be beneficial to vines; it can dry out the leaves after rain and help prevent the onset of disease. On the other hand, very windy sites can impair vine growth, and vineyards in such environments are often protected by wind breaks.

Site selection

The effects of all these climatic elements guide the viticulturist in selecting an appropriate vineyard site. The first decision, though, must be: 'What type/style of wine is to be produced?' Selecting a site with the appropriate temperature conditions for that type/style of wine is the next step. Within the selected site the best position is then chosen in relation to soil type and other climatic considerations such as protection from wind and frost.

The methods employed in selecting new vineyard sites now involve extensive surveys of climate, soil and water resources and consideration of the most appropriate varieties to match the climatic conditions.

Modern technology and management practices are employed in the construction and maintenance of these new vineyards.

The development of the modern Australian vineyard

Many companies, aiming to meet the future needs of consumers of Australian wine, are undertaking vineyard expansion programmes in both traditional and new viticultural areas. The establishment of these vineyards involves the application of sophisticated technology to select and develop the site. Climatic locations are chosen for their suitability to produce specific wine styles. Detailed soil surveys are conducted, which provide information on soil structure, depth and readily available water. Varieties are allocated to specific soil types, eg often red wine grape varieties are matched with soils having the lowest available water with the aim of controlling growth through regulated irrigation, thus leading to more open canopies and improved berry development and ripening. Vine rows are set up using laser technology. Modern trellis and canopy management techniques are also utilised. Irrigation, where necessary, is applied through computer controlled drip irrigation systems, where water requirements are determined by soil moisture measuring devices. Generally, pruning and harvesting operations are partially or fully mechanised. All the above practices are designed to ensure the production of flavoursome grapes.

An example

Orlando Wyndham's vineyard development at Langhorne Creek in South Australia — Here the climate is ideally suited for the production of grapes for red wine, and most of the plantings are Cabernet Sauvignon, Shiraz and Merlot. A thirteen kilometre pipeline has been built from Lake Alexandrina to supply water to the site. The pipeline, one of the largest privately owned lines in South Australia, can carry twenty million litres of water a day to feed an eighty million litre dam. The vineyard is now a patchwork of different varieties planted on specific soil types with matching irrigation schedules.

Orlando Wyndham's new vineyards at Langhorne Creek. Lake Alexandrina is seen in the background.

The dam that supplies the water for irrigating the vines

MANAGING THE VINE

Microclimate

Climate and other environmental influences are only part of the wine style equation. How the vine is managed also plays a part in the development and ripening of the grapes.

Leaves and fruit require sunlight, and the arrangement of the shoots should enable as much sunlight as possible to penetrate the canopy. Small vines with spacious canopies achieve this naturally, while for other situations human intervention is needed to order the vine's shape through trellising. A great variety of trellis systems has been developed, particularly in the last few decades, and this area has developed its own jargon: G.D.C. (Geneva Double Curtain), V.S.P. (Vertical Shoot Positioned), Scott-Henry and Lyre to give a few examples.

Essentially these trellis systems all serve the same purpose: to arrange the shoots of the vine in such a way that the leaves and fruit receive optimal sunlight in that particular site. Vines that are grown on shallow or poor soils normally require simple trellis systems, while those grown on rich, deep soils usually require more elaborate trellis systems. Viticulturists refer to this as *getting the microclimate right*. The right microclimate enhances the biological activity of leaves and fruit and adds to, rather than detracts from, the desired grape composition. Grapes from open canopies, as a rule, have improved sugar accumulation and sugar/acid balance, increased grape colour and more desirable primary fruit characters.

Viticulturists have found that they can modify wine style through canopy management. For example, some wines made from the variety Cabernet Sauvignon can have dominant capsicum-like aromas and flavours, a feature originating in the grapes and very often associated with grapes coming from cooler growing conditions and/or from shaded canopies. The intensity of this character in the grapes can be decreased by changing the trellis system so that leaves and bunches are more exposed to light. The changes in the primary fruit spectrum of the grapes lead to a refinement of the style of the wine coming from those grapes.

Some definitions of climate:
• *Regional climate* - the climatic conditions that apply to a particular region.
• *Site climate (also called mesoclimate)* - the climatic conditions that apply to a particular site within a region.
• *Microclimate* - the climatic conditions around and within the canopy, in the immediate vicinity of the leaves and bunches.

In addition to selecting the right trellis, other cultural practices may be required to enhance fruit quality. Leaves may be removed in the vicinity of the bunches to ensure maximum sunlight interception, a practice that can increase grape colour as well as modifying fruit flavours. Special machines have been developed to carry out this operation, although in many vineyards it is still done manually.

A vine before and after leaf removal; an example of 'getting the microclimate right'

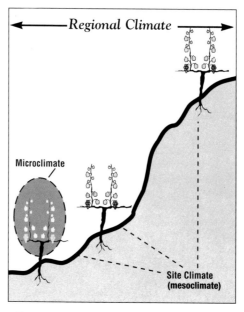

Climate can be defined in different ways.

Some options in canopy management ...

Not all vines require a trellis system. These bush vines in the Barossa Valley are small enough to support themselves.

Some vines will only need a simple trellis system where a single wire is erected along the row to hold the arms of the vine and its foliage off the ground. The spiky nature of the canopy allows sunlight to penetrate into the interior of the canopy.

Vertical shoot positioning
This is a system where all the shoots are trained upwards through foliage wires.

The Scott-Henry system
In some sites positioning all the shoots upwards may cause crowding and shading within the canopy. A Scott-Henry trellis system can be used, where half the number of shoots for any section of the row are positioned upwards and the other half downwards.

The Lyre system
Canopies can also be divided horizontally to form two sections which are positioned upwards.

Geneva Double Curtain (GDC) system
Canopies can also be divided and positioned downwards.

Yield

This is commonly referred to as the weight of grapes per area of vineyard and is expressed as tonnes per hectare or tonnes per acre. One tonne per acre is equivalent to 2.5 tonnes per hectare. Yields of Australian vineyards range from about 3 to about 40 tonnes/hectare, depending on the variety, site and associated vineyard practices. There is no magical figure for the optimum yield at any one site. It depends on the style of wine that the winemaker wishes to produce and relates to establishing conditions which provide adequate active leaf area to ripen the amount of grapes on each vine for that style of wine (both sugar ripe and flavour ripe). These conditions will vary with variety, site and desired wine style.

In the main, wines that are highly regarded as benchmarks for their style of wine are produced from lower rather than higher yielding vineyards. Wines showing great structure and intensity of flavours are, as a rule, produced from well managed vineyards yielding less than 10 tonnes per hectare and frequently lower than 5 tonnes per hectare. However any specific relationship must be judged with caution, as assessment on yield alone ignores the other aspect of vine management. With sound vine management, vineyards yielding in excess of 10 tonnes per hectare can produce excellent wines. Each particular situation must be judged on its merits, and the judgement ultimately rests with the quality of the finished wine in the glass.

There may be one, two or three bunches of grapes and anywhere from ten to thirty leaves on a shoot, and many combinations of numbers of leaves and bunches can occur in different situations. However, it is the overall ratio of active leaf area to the weight of grapes that appears to be crucial. Within limits, quality grapes may be produced from vines which have short shoots and small bunches or from vines with longer shoots and larger bunches.

If the ratio is very low (too few active leaves or too high a weight of grapes), accumulation of sugar in the berries may be slowed and the fruit may not be sugar ripe at harvest for particular wine types, a circumstance referred to as overcropping. Accompanying levels of grape colour, aroma and flavour will also be low. Overcropping may occur in very cool sites where low temperatures may limit leaf activity, in situations where leaf function is hindered by water stress or shaded canopy conditions, and/or where yield is excessively high. Simply put, there is not enough sugar to be shared among the berries on the vine.

active leaf area per vine:
the number and size of properly functioning leaves on a vine

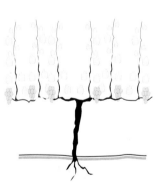

yield per vine:
the weight of grapes on a vine

In well-managed vineyards, overcropping is normally not a problem, and most vine-yards will produce fruit that is of the required sugar level for the desired wine type. However, this ratio of active leaves to the weight of the grapes also influences the amount of colour and the intensity and types of aroma and flavour compounds in the berries, since the reactions forming these require a supply of sugar. For any one variety, changing this ratio may also modify the style of the wine coming from those vines. Up to a point, the higher the ratio, the more sugar is available, and in these conditions grapes with similar sugar levels will have higher berry colour as well as a greater intensity of primary fruit characters. Again, simply put, there is more sugar to go around and so there are more aroma and flavour compounds produced in the berries. The ratio can be improved by manipulating the vine either to increase the leaf area or to decrease the weight of grapes.

Many vineyards are now fitted with trellis extensions so that another trellis wire can be fitted to hold the shoots upright, allowing them to grow longer and bear more leaves before they need to be trimmed during summer. But it is not just a matter of having more leaves; these leaves must be functioning efficiently, and for this to happen they must be well exposed to light, free of disease and supplied with adequate nutrients and water.

Some growers will cut bunches off (bunch thinning) at about veraison. This reduces the overall weight of grapes on the vine and in certain situations can improve not only sugar accumulation but also the development of colour and flavour of the grapes on the remaining bunches.

Irrigation

Many Australian vineyards are sited in environments with winter dominant rainfall and high evaporation during the summer months, conditions which can lead to depletion of soil moisture during the growth of the vine and the ripening of the grapes. Under such conditions it is critical that additional water be supplied to the vine by irrigation, relieving vine stress and improving vine performance overall. On the other hand, too much irrigation or rain during berry development can swell the berries and dilute the concentration of sugar and other berry components.

Controlled irrigation is the best approach, and modern vineyards are now irrigated so that different sections of the vineyard receive different amounts of water, depending on the soil type in that section.

Irrigation scheduling should be such that soil water content is maintained so that the vine is neither stressed nor overwatered. In many Australian vineyards this is now achieved by applying water through drip irrigation systems where the amount and timing of water is regulated by computer controlled technology.

Water is a valuable resource and the Australian wine industry is sensitive to its use and the impact on the environment. An example of this approach is the management of BRL Hardy's Banrock Station vineyard on the banks of the River Murray in South Australia's Murray Valley. This new 1700 hectare property is set up with modern trellising and drip irrigation systems. The practices in managing the vineyard are sensitive to the environment. About 300 hectares will be used for vineyards while the remaining land is being restored to native vegetation status. The management also has a wetlands preservation strategy where, with the environment group Landcare, BRL Hardy are maintaining and restoring natural water flow in the neighbouring wetlands to allow native fauna to breed. Establishments such as this indicate that development and environmental concerns can be balanced.

BRL Hardy's Banrock Station vineyard: new development (foreground), established vineyard (middle) and the wetlands (background)

Hand pruning vines at Mitchelton Winery, Victoria

Mechanically pruning vines

Pruning

Pruning is an annual activity normally carried out in winter, in which parts of the dormant shoots are cut off the vine. Traditionally it has been done by hand, but now it is more common to prune with the aid of various forms of machines. Machine pruning (also called mechanical pruning) reduces the time and high cost involved in hand pruning.

In some cases vines are essentially not pruned at all. This concept of minimal pruning, in which only shoots hanging close to the ground are trimmed (either in winter or summer), was developed in Australia and has proved to be successful in many vinegrowing regions. Minimally pruned vines have many more shoots and smaller bunches per vine and generally are higher yielding than conventionally pruned vines. The shoots are short and grow on the outside of the canopy, providing good leaf and bunch exposure. Berries are small, a feature which results in a concentration of sugar and other berry components. It has been convincingly demonstrated that well-managed mechanically and minimally pruned vines, as well as having cost advantages in grape production, can produce consistently good wines. Many highly regarded red and white table wines have their origins in vineyards using these techniques or modifications of them.

You will find that in any one vinegrowing region some growers will manually cane prune or spur prune their vines, while others will machine prune. Through experience, each chooses to use a system that gives the best grapes for the desired style of wine. Wines that command high prices can justify extra work in the vineyard, such as hand pruning and other costly vineyard practices, while wines that are sold at lower price points require application of cultural practices in the vineyard that are highly mechanised. Mechanical pruning and machine harvesting are now widely accepted practices in Australian viticulture. Adoption of these practices has been significant in producing well flavoured wines at reasonable prices.

Spur pruned vines. The vines in the background are still to be pruned.

A cane pruned vine

Vines after mechanical pruning

Minimally pruned vines

Disease control

Most Australian vineyards are located in climates that are sunny and dry during the period of vine growth and grape ripening, conditions that are ideal for growing healthy, disease free grapes. In sites where rainfall or humidity during the growing season is higher, there will be a greater incidence of fungal diseases. The incidence and intensity of these diseases are much lower in open canopies where air movement can dry out the leaves and bunches. Integrating pruning and trellis systems to achieve open canopies can minimise the need for chemical sprays in preventing these diseases. Viticulturists, not only in Australia but world wide, are mindful of the environment and are moving towards management systems that will allow them to produce grapes with low, or in some cases no, chemical input. Luckily, in Australia the climate of many of our vineyards is favourable to such an approach.

Pests

In Australia there are no major pests that cause problems across the vineyards generally. But from time to time pests such as light-brown apple moth, mites, snails, termites and birds can cause damage by feeding on parts of the vine. Birds damage the bunches by eating whole berries or by pecking at the berries, causing them to split. Two bird species that cause damage in Australian vineyards are the silvereye and the starling. Methods to prevent birds from entering the vineyard include netting of vines, scare devices (which make noises) and scarecrows. Another pest is phylloxera. We discuss damage that phylloxera can inflict on vines on page 17.

Scarecrows in a Barossa Valley vineyard

The soil

The soil provides anchorage for the vine and acts as a source of nutrients and water, which are taken up by the vine roots. Grapevines will grow in a wide range of soil types; often the most limiting factor is availability of soil water, although this can normally be provided through irrigation. In general, suitable soils are those that have sufficient depth, are well-aerated and well-drained and have good water holding capacity. A range of soil types from sandy loams through to loam clays provide these conditions. Nutrient deficiencies, if any, can be supplied through the application of fertilisers.

It is debatable whether some soils have a magical chemical make-up that enhances grape composition. The amount and ratio of minerals such as nitrogen, phosphorus and potassium are important in the function of leaves and the development of berries. Therefore it may be argued that there is some optimal balance of minerals that provides special conditions relating to vine performance. Some soils do seem to have special properties, eg red earth over limestone, commonly called Terra Rossa. This soil is found in a number of Australia's grapegrowing regions. In the Coonawarra district, it is generally considered that wines made from vines grown in the Terra Rossa soil have more intense flavours and better structure that those from vines grown on neighbouring, deeper black soils. Whether these red soils have some special chemical properties remains debatable. It is more likely that it is the combination of soil properties (composition, structure and depth) that is important in influencing vine growth and berry ripening. The structure and depth of the red soils is such that they are very well drained, while maintaining adequate soil moisture to provide balanced vine growth and open canopies. These conditions are more favourable to berry development and ripening than the more vigorous, shaded conditions that can occur in vines grown on the black soil where the water holding capacity is higher.

The black soil

The red soil

Profile of the 'Terra Rossa' soil in Katnook's vineyard at Coonawarra

Getting it right in the vineyard

Variation in the style of wines produced from grapes grown in different regions can be partially explained by differences in regional climate, ie whether the region is regarded as being cool, warm or hot. For example, Shiraz vines grown in warm to hot climates can potentially produce full-bodied wines with plum and chocolate flavours and with soft, silky tannins, while Shiraz vines grown in cooler climates can potentially produce medium- to full-bodied wines with berry fruit and distinctive pepper characters, coupled with higher natural acidity and finer tannin structure. These differences in regional styles highlight the dominant influence of climate, and in particular temperature, on grape composition and wine style. Normally, but not always, the effects of large differences in climate override variations due to differences in soil characteristics and management practices between regions.

Wine style can also differ between wines produced from any one region, where wine style varies according to variations in mesoclimate, soil characteristics and management practices. For example, in Australia, in regions where vineyards are planted on slopes, sites with a northerly aspect intercept more sunlight and thus provide more favourable ripening conditions. This applies particularly to vineyards that are located further south. In regions that are generally flat the mesoclimatic effects are minimal.

Within a region, soil depth and structure may change, sometimes within small distances. These variations can dramatically affect the growth of the vine and how it ripens its grapes. Vineyard management practices, eg pruning, trellising and irrigation, may need to be modified to match the changing soil conditions.

The supply of water to the vine is one of the most critical factors in maintaining vine performance. If the vine becomes stressed due to lack of water, photosynthesis is slowed and overall there is less energy for the growth of the vine. Even though these vines may have open canopies, they may not fully ripen their fruit because the leaves are not working efficiently. Generally, the growth and ripening patterns could be improved if these vines were to receive some water through irrigation.

On the other hand, over-supply of water stimulates shoot and leaf growth and produces larger berries. In some cases vigorous growth can cause shading of leaves and bunches. Shaded leaves do not photosynthesise effectively; sugar supply to the berries may be limited and they may not fully ripen. Production of flavour (and colour in black grapes) in the berries is restricted in shaded bunches. This situation may be improved by opening up the canopy through pruning and trellising techniques. It may also be possible to control vigorous canopy growth by planting cover crops between the rows to utilise some of the excess water.

Superimpose the effects of soil and vine management onto those of climate, and you can well imagine the many possible combinations of sugar, acid, colour and aroma and flavour compounds that can develop in grapes in different regions and within regions. These variations in grape composition result in differences in wine style.

The concept of 'terroir'

The French term 'terroir' refers to the interaction of the vine with its soil and its climate. However it is important to realise that over time vineyard management practices have evolved to achieve the best result in any one site. Thus, the term 'terroir' really encompasses the interrelated and integrated effects of soil, climate and management practices on the function of the vine and the way that it ripens its fruit.

Accepting that between regions there is an over-riding influence of climate on wine style, the concept of terroir is more appropriately used to explain differences in wine styles within regions, ie how the mesoclimate, soil characteristics and management practices interact with each other at a particular site.

Sites where the combination of these separate but interrelated influences come together perfectly are regarded as having the best terroir. Here the pattern of ripening is such that the grapes have at harvest the potential to produce wines with strength and depth of flavour, complexity, structure and other apparent, but difficult to define, quality features. In some cases the major factor is the variation in soil characteristics; in others it is the combination of a number of factors that create different terroirs. In sites where the topography is generally flat, the terroir is determined mainly by differences in soil characteristics and management practices. In areas that are mountainous, elevation, aspect, soil characteristics and management practices all play a role in creating the terroir of any particular site. The terroir of any site is important in determining the accumulation of sugar and the accompanying amounts and types of acid, aroma and flavour and phenolics in the berries. These various combinations can result in wines of different styles being produced from different vineyards and even from different sections of one vineyard.

Some examples

Jasper Hill's Emily's Paddock and Georgia's Paddock — two Shiraz wines from different vineyards: Jasper Hill's vineyards and winery are located near Heathcote in Victoria. Emily's Paddock and Georgia's Paddock vineyards (both with plantings of Shiraz vines) are approximately 1 km apart, both planted on deep, friable, red brown gravelly loam, on well drained slopes with good water retention. The annual rainfall of 575 mm, in combination with the deep soil, is sufficient to enable healthy vine growth without the need for irrigation. Emily's Paddock has a north-east aspect while Georgia's Paddock has a north-west aspect. Emily's Paddock thus captures the morning sun earlier and is warmer and sunnier for a longer period during the day. It is also a little steeper and hence drier, and yields are lower. Grapes from both vineyards reach similar levels of maturity and are made into wine in a similar way. The wine from Emily's Paddock is stored in French oak barrels while that from Georgia's Paddock is stored in a combination of American and French oak barrels. Both wines are richly flavoured and well structured but with subtle differences in their flavour and tannin structure; differences which evolve from the terroir of each vineyard.

Emily's Paddock — generally slightly deeper coloured than the wine from Georgia's Paddock. A full flavoured and complex wine showing strong berry, plum and chocolate flavours that develop into meaty, earthy tones with age. Powerful well structured tannins complement these rich, fruit characters.
Georgia's Paddock — intense aromas and flavours in the red berry and plum spectrum with some spiciness, intermingled with fresh acidity and assertive yet supple tannins.

Grant Burge's Meshach and Filsell — two Shiraz wines from different sections of the same vineyard: The Filsell vineyard is located on the rich soils of the flats between Williamstown and Lyndoch in the Barossa Valley. The vineyard is planted with Shiraz vines of varying ages but over 8 hectares (20 acres) are over 80 years old. Experience gained over many years provides the base for managing these 'dry grown', low yielding vines. The vines are cane pruned to levels that produce between 3 and 6 tonnes per hectare of intensely flavoured berries. Soil characteristics vary across the vineyard, ranging from deep alluvial to light loam over light to medium clay. The grapes for Meshach are sourced from the best sections of the old vines grown on the light loam over light to medium clays. The grapes for the Filsell are the balance of the old vines and the younger vines situated across the vineyard. These variations in vine age and soil type and the effect of their interactions provide a difference in the characters of each of the wines produced from the vineyard. Careful selection of the blocks within the vineyard starts before the vines are picked. Sections of the vineyard are fermented separately and the final choice of the wines to make up the blend of the Meshach or Filsell is determined on the tasting bench. It is an interesting insight into the concept of terroir, when in tasting the wines the winemaker is checking if that section of the vineyard expresses the desired characters in that year, ie if it was true to its anticipated terroir. Only the very best wines will go towards the crafting of Meshach.

Meshach — a big, powerful complex wine, with plenty of tannins, intensity and depth of berry fruit, plum and chocolate characters, and the structure to improve for many years in the bottle.
Filsell — a wine with intense fruit and complexity of violets, berry, plum and vanillin oak flavours. The tannins provide a firm finish to the flavoursome palate.

Every vineyard has its terroir; it is just that some vineyards have special terroirs. The best terroirs, ones that consistently produce great wines, appear to be those sites that require least manipulation and where the vine is in harmony with its environment.

Often good terroirs are characterised by their ability to provide conditions in which the vine ripens its fruit faster than neighbouring sites. Not only does the sugar accumulate faster but there is greater intensity of aroma and flavour compounds coupled with higher acidity; a composition that reflects efficient vine functioning and continuous berry development and ripening. Such grape composition often leads to wines with depth of flavour and good structure.

As yet scientists cannot fully explain the mechanisms of the interaction between the vine and its soil, its climate and its grower, and the word terroir remains a term that captures the special nature of some sites and the individuality of the wine produced from vines grown and managed in that site.

Managing vineyards to achieve the desired grape composition for particular wine styles requires an integrated approach for each vineyard. The pruning method, the irrigation level, the trellis system and other viticultural practices all need to be matched to achieve the best from any one site. Sometimes this will be carried out through traditional and well established practices; in other cases it will be achieved through innovative technology. It is all about nurturing the vine in such a way that it readily captures the available sunlight and utilises it to the fullest.

Ripeness has many definitions, each closely linked to a particular wine style. Simply put, it is when the grapes have the right amount of sugar, acid and colour and the right types of aromas and flavours for a particular wine style. Ultimate ripeness occurs when the combined effects of climate, soil and management practices are fine-tuned in such a way that the grapes ripen completely and perfectly for the production and development of wines that epitomise that style. This is a ripeness that, with time, provides a wine that gives ultimate tasting enjoyment, this being the prime purpose of wine.

In summary
Wines made from the same grape variety, but grown in vineyards in different regions, differ due to the variations in regional climate, mesoclimate, soil characteristics and management practices of each vineyard.

Wines made from the same variety, but grown in vineyards in the same region, differ due to the variations in mesoclimates, soil characteristics and management practices of each vineyard, ie the terroir of any particular site within the region.

Add to the above the differences that come from various winemaking approaches and it can be fully appreciated that a diversity of wine styles can be produced from vineyards around Australia.

Terroir: the interrelated effects of the micro-environment in which the vine grows and the care given to it by its grower

Climate, soil and vine management affect vine growth, vine performance and grape composition.

Grape variety and vine management must be matched to the climatic and soil conditions of the vineyard.

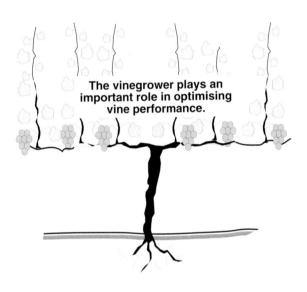

The vinegrower plays an important role in optimising vine performance.

Grape composition is the foundation of wine style.

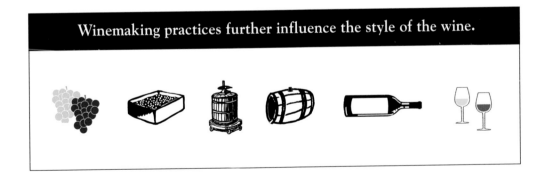

Winemaking practices further influence the style of the wine.

The winemaker crafts the wine to the desired style

Ultimately the combined effects of grape composition and winemaking practices influence the style of wine coming from any particular winery.

It is now widely acknowledged that the varied natural conditions present throughout Australia are highly favourable for the growing of vines of a range of grape varieties. These vines produce the grapes which in due course our winemakers craft into the many styles of Australian wine.

Images of winemaking — Seppelt Winery

THE WINERY

Winemaking is a dynamic process; many decisions need to be made during the life of every wine. In the following pages we discuss the steps in making white and red table wines, and particularly how the character of the wine is influenced by the different processing techniques. We focus on the options available to winemakers in crafting their wines.

The production of sparkling and fortified wines involves variations of the processes discussed below and is covered in more detail later in the book.

Harvesting the grapes

Vintage is the period when the grapes are harvested and the wine is made.

The decision to remove the grapes from the vine is based on several factors, including:
• an assessment of the sugar/acid balance and the aroma and flavour profile of the grapes in relation to the style of wine to be produced;
• the prevailing weather conditions;
• the availability of labour and machinery; and
• the condition of the grapes (whether the berries are shrivelling, or any disease is present).

Harvest commences when the winemaker considers that the grapes have ripened to the right stage for a particular style of wine.

Traditionally grapes have been hand-picked into baskets, buckets or crates, stacked and then transported from the vineyard to the winery by various means. Hand-picking removes whole bunches, leaving the berries attached to their stalks. While this practice still continues today, many of the larger vineyards are now picked by machines. We say that the grapes have been mechanically or machine harvested.

Mechanical harvesters operate by moving along the row and shaking the vines. The movement of the shoots causes the berries to be shaken off their stalks. The berries fall onto a conveyor belt contained in the machine and are carried by the moving belt to a bin for transport to the winery.

Compared to hand-pickers, these machines are able to pick grapes at a fraction of the cost and at greater speed, an advantage because the berries can be removed quickly when the fruit has reached the desired ripeness. Another advantage is that these machines can pick through the night; under these cooler conditions there is less oxidation (a term we discuss later) of the juice in the bottom of the container. The fruit arrives at the winery both cool and in good condition.

Mechanical harvesters cannot be used in situations where the vineyard is sited on steep slopes, or where the winemaking technique requires whole bunches of grapes, for example:
• in the production of premium sparkling wine, where whole bunch pressing is used to extract the juice;
• when red wines are made by the carbonic maceration method;
or
• where there is a need to select only parts of the bunches because disease is present.

Hand harvesting - the vertically shoot positioned canopy makes it easier to pick the bunches of grapes.

A Gregoire harvester working in the Yarra Valley at 4 o'clock in the morning

The rods inside the machine that shake the vine and cause the berries to be shaken off their stalks

Black grapes in the receival bin on their way to the crusher

Crushing grapes at Heemskerk Winery, Tasmania

Crushing

The grape berry must be broken to release its juice. The bunches (if hand-picked) or berries (if mechanically harvested) are normally crushed by passing them through a series of rollers which squash the berries and squeeze out the juice. The stalks (if present) are usually removed, and thus crushing produces a mixture of juice, pulp, skins and seeds, which we call *must*.

When harvested, the grapes will contain various proportions of sugar, acid, colour and aroma and flavour compounds. The winemaker can adjust the amount of sugar and acid to make the juice or must more suitable for a particular wine style.

Addition of sugar

The addition of sugar to juice or must is not permitted in Australia — an historic decision that was made when our vineyards were sited in mainly warm and hot climates. More recently many vineyards have been established in cooler regions and it seems logical that this law should be reconsidered in light of these developments. Grapes grown in cool climatic conditions may often attain preferred flavours at sugar levels slightly lower than desired, and it is here that some addition of sugar prior to fermentation may improve the sensory qualities of the resultant wine. The addition of sugar raises the alcohol level of the wine, improving its mouthfeel.

In cool to warm, warm, warm to hot and hot climatic regions, there is usually no need to modify the sugar content of the grapes, particularly if sound management practices have been used in their production.

In Australia the addition of grape juice concentrate is permitted and this can be used to raise the sugar content of the juice or must prior to fermentation; however this is considered to be a less satisfactory method than the addition of sugar.

Addition of acid

When grapes ripen in warm and hot climatic conditions there is more likely to be a deficiency of acid in the grapes at harvest, and it is more common that winemakers will need to adjust the acidity level of the juice or must prior to fermentation and/or during the winemaking process. To do this, tartaric acid (one of the natural acids of the grape) is usually added.

The concept of acidity was raised previously, in the section on grape ripening. Titratable acidity and pH are terms used to describe the acid conditions of grape juice or wine. Tartaric acid and malic acid are present in the grapes at harvest and are carried over into the wine. As well as these acids being present in wine, other acids may be formed by yeast and bacteria during winemaking, including lactic acid, acetic acid and succinic acid. In solutions such as grape juice or wine these acids can exist in different forms, one form being free hydrogen ions. Titratable acidity is a measure of all forms of all of the acids and gives an estimate of their overall concentration: how much acid (expressed as tartaric acid) is present in one litre of grape juice or wine. Values for titratable acidity in wine may be in the order of 6 to 10 grams of acid per litre. The concentration of acid relates to the acid taste of the wine, and generally the higher the titratable acidity, the more acidic the wine will taste.

It is more difficult to grasp the concept of pH. It gives a measure of the concentration of only the free hydrogen ions, but these are important in that they influence chemical reactions in the juice or wine. However, the concentration of these in grape juice or wine is very low, in the order of 0.001 to 0.0001 grams of free hydrogen ions per litre. In order to express these very low values more conveniently, chemists invented the pH scale, not just for wine, but also for expressing the acid conditions of other solutions, such as other beverages and the water in your swimming pool.

This scale covers the range from 0 to 14; values from 0 to 7 represent acidic solutions, and from 7 to 14 basic solutions. The lower the number on the pH scale, the higher the concentration of free hydrogen ions (ie the more acidic the solution). The lower the pH value of a juice or a wine, the less chance there is of oxidation and spoilage reactions occurring. Also, if the pH of a red wine is adjusted to a lower value (by the addition of acid) the wine will appear more red-coloured.

The pH value of grape juice and wine is normally in the range of pH 3 to pH 4, and even though this variation looks small, the differences in the chemical reactions and wine colour that occur in this range can be quite dramatic. Juices or wines at the higher pH values can oxidise very quickly. For this reason winemakers will adjust the pH to a lower value by the addition of tartaric acid, which also increases the titratable acidity. However, they must do this carefully and taste the wine after each addition, because if they add too much acid the wine will taste too acidic and thus out of balance. During the winemaking process, because of changes in the acid makeup of the wine, the pH will increase, and thus winemakers need to check the pH value of the wine regularly and adjust if necessary. The aim is to achieve an acid level that is in balance with the sugar, alcohol and fruit sensations in any particular wine.

In summary
Titratable acidity measures the concentration of acid in the juice or wine and gives the winemaker some guide as to how acidic the wine will taste, while pH measures the chemical effectiveness of the acids present and gives the winemaker a guide as to how protected the wine is from oxidation and spoilage. Some chemists offer an analogy to a bank account, where titratable acidity gives a measure of the total amount of money in the account (capital + interest) whereas pH gives a measure of only the interest, and thus how effectively your account is operating.

Although winemakers can adjust the sugar/acid balance in the juice, must or wine, they cannot modify the main ingredients of style: the aromas and flavours and phenolic compounds of the grapes. This emphasises the importance of getting it right in the vineyard, ie having the right amount and types of sugar, acid, phenolics, aroma and flavour present in the grapes at harvest. The best wines are often those made from grapes that require little or no adjustment of the juice or must components prior to fermentation.

Oxidation
Oxidation is another word that is frequently used when discussing the winemaking process and wines. The term oxidation embraces the chemical, physical and sensory changes that occur in the juice or wine when it is exposed to air (oxygen), changes that include: a reduction of varietal aroma and flavour; the appearance of vinegar, nail polish remover and sherry-like smells; a browning of the colour; and the development of bitterness. The wine is permanently modified once these changes occur, since they are irreversible. This is why winemakers are so careful to avoid oxidation (in delicate dry white table wines) or to control it to a level where its influence is deemed as contributing to complexity (in some full-bodied white and red table wines). Controlled oxidation is in fact an integral part of the winemaking process for sherry style wines, which we discuss later, in the section covering fortified wines.

Oxidation occurs to a greater degree when air is readily absorbed, when the juice or wine is hot, when it has a high pH, and when the grapes are mouldy. Winemakers will minimise these conditions by using inert gas (nitrogen and/or carbon dioxide) in any pumping operations and to fill the head space in storage tanks, by keeping the juice or wine cool and by the addition of chemicals (sulphur dioxide and ascorbic acid) which inhibit the activity of micro-organisms and oxidising enzymes and/or react with any air present.

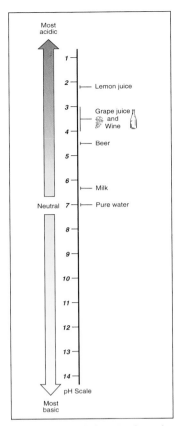

The pH scale and the pH values of some common beverages

Measuring the pH of a wine with a pH meter

Sulphur dioxide

Sulphur dioxide has been used in winemaking for many years; probably the Egyptians and Romans would have used it when making their wines. It is a unique compound in that it not only inhibits microbial activity, but also aids in preventing oxidation in wine. It is thus a very common and useful additive for maintaining the juice, must or wine in prime condition.

Sulphur dioxide can be added:
- to the bins in which the grapes are harvested and transported to the winery, preventing spoilage and oxidation of any juice in the bottom of the bin during transportation;
- to the juice or must prior to fermentation; and
- to the wine after fermentation and during storage.

Sulphur dioxide is only added in small amounts, and at these levels it is generally harmless to most wine consumers. A small proportion of consumers is sensitive to sulphur dioxide and may have adverse reactions when drinking wine. When sulphur dioxide has been added during winemaking, this will be indicated on the label by the code 220. The amount of sulphur dioxide added during white winemaking is normally higher than that required in processing red wines. Sweet white wines and cask wines will normally have higher levels of sulphur dioxide than bottled dry white wines, which will normally have higher levels than bottled dry red wines.

However, it is important to realize that sulphur dioxide is produced naturally by yeast during fermentation, and thus some sulphur dioxide will be present in wine even if it has not been added. People who are particularly sensitive are thus best advised to avoid drinking wine, unless they know that a particular wine has an extremely low level of sulphur dioxide and that they are not adversely affected by such wines.

Ascorbic acid

Ascorbic acid (a natural component of wine) may sometimes be added in white winemaking as it can react with any oxygen present in the juice or wine and thus prevent oxidation occurring. Again, the amounts added are very small. If ascorbic acid has been added to the wine during processing, the code 300 will appear on the label.

Pressing

In making white wines, the must is normally cooled immediately after crushing. It is then pumped to a draining vessel or to a press.

The juice that drains freely from either the draining vessel or the press is called the free-run juice. The remaining solids (pulp, skins and seeds) are pressed by some mechanical device to obtain more juice. Some of the juice obtained from the early stages of the pressing operation will be added to the free-run, while the juice obtained later in the cycle (when the pressing pressure is higher) may be discarded, because this fraction of the pressings may contain higher levels of compounds that impart bitter tastes in the final wine. After the pressing operation is completed the dry mass of skins and seeds is discarded.

Grapes intended for the production of delicate white wine styles and premium sparkling wine may not necessarily be crushed prior to pressing. Pressing directly, as whole bunches, minimises pick up of phenolic compounds from the skin and seeds, which may otherwise have produced slightly bitter tastes in the final wine.

Making red wines requires a different approach to that used for white winemaking. The skins need to be kept in contact with the fermenting liquid, since they provide the red colour. The alcohol produced during the fermentation aids in the extraction of colour and tannins from the skins. The mixture of juice, pulp, skins and seeds is kept together and is not pressed until some stage during or after the fermentation.

An air-bag press
After the press is filled and the lid closed, the bag in the centre is filled with air, and, as it expands, it presses the material and releases the juice (or wine) from the mass of solid material. The juice or wine drains through slats in the press and is pumped to a storage or fermentation vessel.

Transferring the mixture of pulp, skins and seeds to a press

Clarification of juice

Pressing only removes the larger particles from the juice or wine. Clarification is the removal of small solid particles (eg skin debris) that have not been removed by the pressing operation.

In white winemaking the white juice is allowed to stand while the small solid particles settle to the bottom of the tank. The clear juice (from above the solids) is then drawn off (racked) to the fermentation vessel. Additional clarification may be obtained by using centrifuges or filtration units. Sometimes winemakers will leave a small amount of solids in the juice during fermentation, and this may enhance the complexity of the resultant wine. This must be done with great care and after considerable experience, as too high an amount of solids will result in undesirable smells and coarse taste sensations in the finished wine. White wines are clarified again at the end of fermentation. In red winemaking the must is kept intact during fermentation and clarification occurs only at the end of this process.

Fermentation

Primary fermentation is the conversion by yeast of the sugar in the juice to alcohol and carbon dioxide.

Specially selected yeast is normally added by the winemaker to the juice or must. Yeasts are selected on their ability to conduct the fermentation efficiently and on the sensory features they add to the wine. For example, some yeasts produce compounds that add to the fruity and estery characters of the wine, while others are more neutral, allowing greater expression of the varietal characters. This is a critical part of the winemaking process, and the widespread use of specially selected pure yeast strains in Australian winemaking has contributed significantly to the quality of our wines.

Fermentation of white wines

White wines are usually fermented in temperature controlled stainless steel vessels or in wooden (oak) barrels stored in a cold room to regulate temperature. Fermentation temperatures are generally in the range of 8-18°C. These conditions help to retain the varietal aromas and flavours of the grapes in the finished wine. In the production of dry white table wines the fermentation is allowed to continue until all the sugar is fermented to alcohol, whereas for sweet white table wines the fermentation may be stopped part way through. This leaves some unfermented sugar present, which gives the wine its sweet taste. The fermentation is normally stopped by cooling the wine. Sweet white wines may also be produced by allowing the wine to ferment to dryness and then adding grape juice concentrate to sweeten the wine. On the completion of fermentation, wines are stored in either stainless steel tanks or oak barrels.

Some grape varieties, particularly those such as Riesling and Traminer which produce floral, fragrant wines, will be fermented and stored totally in stainless steel tanks.

Barrel fermentation and oak storage of white wines
Other varieties, such as Chardonnay, Semillon and Sauvignon Blanc, may be totally fermented in stainless steel tanks and then transferred to oak barrels, or they may be transferred to oak barrels part way through their fermentation, a process winemakers call barrel fermentation. Oak components are extracted into the wine, adding new aroma and flavour compounds.

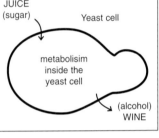

At the peak of fermentation there will be about 100 million of these cells in one ml of the fermenting liquid. It takes many yeast cells to make wine.

JUICE (sugar)   Yeast cell

metabolisim inside the yeast cell

(alcohol) WINE

Yeast settling to the bottom of the vessel at the end of fermentation.

Oak barrels for fermentation and storage of wine

The pictures below show how oak is prepared for processing into oak barrels

A view of an oak forest in the Troncais region of France

Logs ready for transport

Splitting the logs

Open air storage of staves

Time on lees

With barrel fermentation, the wine can be retained in the barrel on the completion of fermentation and kept in contact with the dead yeast cells, creating further dimensions of aromas, flavours and mouthfeel sensations. Winemakers refer to this practice as *time on lees*. The length of time the wine remains on lees is at the discretion of the winemaker, but generally this may be from 2-12 months. Often Chardonnay wines will be treated in this way, with various combinations of barrel fermentation, time on lees and storage time in oak barrels being used to provide a range of blending options.

Wines that have had time on lees will generally have improved mouthfeel, often described by saying that the wines have a creamy or cheesy texture on the palate. They also take on smells and tastes described as *creamy*, *yeasty*, *vegemite*, *bonox*, *marmite*, *cheesy*, *bready*, *toasty* and *leesy*.

Malo-lactic fermentation (MLF)

A second fermentation can also occur in wines, which does not involve sugar or yeast. In this so-called secondary fermentation, bacteria convert the malic acid in the wine to lactic acid. The bacteria are those naturally present in the wine environment or specially selected strains added by the winemaker. Grapes grown in cold and/or cool environments may contain high levels of malic acid which, when carried over into the wine, will make the wine taste too acidic. Winemakers can choose to put these wines through a malo-lactic fermentation. The lactic acid formed has a less acid taste than the malic acid, and the conversion thus results in a better acid balance in the wine; the wine tastes softer on the palate.

In addition, other chemical compounds are formed during the conversion which give the wine aroma and flavour sensations described by words such as *creamy*, *buttery*, *butterscotch*, *yogurt* and *caramel*.

Winemakers now use the technique of MLF for many of their wines, not just those produced from grapes that come from cool climates. It is used often for Chardonnay wines to give flavour enhancement and to improve complexity and mouthfeel.

The use of oak barrels in winemaking

During contact with oak barrels, whether it be during barrel fermentation or during storage, the wine takes on characters that are extracted from the oak wood. Some words frequently used to describe these oak characters include: *vanilla*, *toasty*, *sawdust*, *cedar*, *olives*, *spicy*, *bacon*, *coconut*, *pencil shavings*, *dusty*, *cashews*, *smoky*, *burnt*, *caramel*, *raisin* and *charred*. While the wine is in barrels slow oxidation also occurs, modifying the wine even further.

People talk about wines being 'woody', 'oaky', 'showing lots of wood' or 'lots of oak' or 'good wood' or 'oak complexity', terms that are all associated with storing wine in oak barrels. Wood is the general term that encompasses the use of oak; the terms are often used interchangeably. Oak barrels have been used as storage vessels for wine for over 2000 years and winemakers have a choice of barrels made from eg oak from French, German, American or other sources. The oaks are named after the forests where they grow. You will hear winemakers talk about, for example, Nevers, Limousin and Troncais, which are different types of French oak.

The use of oak barrels is an expensive winemaking procedure (some barrels cost about $800 each) and thus wines treated in this way are more costly. To overcome this cost, oak chips or pieces of oak wood can be added to the wine during either fermentation or storage. This imparts the oak aroma and flavour to the wine, but does not produce the same complexity as fermenting or storing in oak barrels.

The making of oak barrels

Oak forests are grown in parts of France, Germany, other European countries and the United States of America. Once a tree is cut, the log is taken to the mill where it is split by the millers into staves. The staves are then either kiln or air dried, a process called seasoning. If the staves are not seasoned to the appropriate moisture level they may dry out after they have been made into barrels; then the joints between the staves will separate and the barrel will leak. The seasoning process may take up to 3 years.

Staves ready for processing into barrels.

When the oak is deemed ready for processing into barrels, the staves are cut to length and then a sufficient number is selected for the type of barrel. The set of staves is then placed inside a hoop which holds the unbent staves at one end. This is called 'raising the barrel'. After raising, the barrel is ready to be bent. This is achieved by placing the set of unbent staves over a fire, which is normally fuelled by oak pieces. By constantly wetting the staves with water, steam is produced, which renders the staves pliable. Over a period of about 30 minutes, the barrel can then be shaped by placing a wire around the bottom end, which is winched into shape while being heated. When the bending is complete, the barrel is returned to the open fire for another 30 minutes to 1 hour. The inside of the barrel becomes toasted to various degrees, depending on how long it is left over the fire.

Assembling the cask

After the barrel is removed from the fire and cooled, the heads (ends) are fitted, and new hoops are then rivetted, fitted and driven into the barrel. It is now ready to be filled with wine.

Firing the cask

Oak barrels come in a variety of sizes:
Quarter casks — 160 litres
Barriques or — 225 litres
Hogsheads — 300 litres
Puncheons — 475 litres
and in some cases, much larger vats.

Bending the cask

The finished product

These pictures show the barrel making process at C. A. Schahinger Pty Ltd, Master Coopers in Adelaide, South Australia.

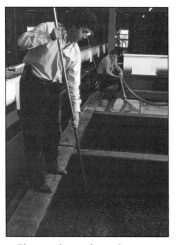

Fermentation of red wines

Fermentation temperature

Fermentation at a cool temperature (below 20°C) retains fruit characters and limits the extraction not only of colour and tannins from the skins, but also of bitter tannins from the seeds.

Higher fermentation temperatures (above 20°C) are required to extract more flavour, colour and tannins from the skins. More tannins may also be extracted from the seeds. Sometimes earthy and more complex characters are associated with hotter fermentations.

The fermentation process generates heat and therefore the fermenting liquid must be cooled to maintain the desired fermentation temperature range. Cooling and maceration operations are often combined.

Maceration techniques

As the fermentation progresses, carbon dioxide and alcohol are formed. The carbon dioxide gas pushes the mixture of skins and seeds to the top of the fermenting liquid. The alcohol produced in the fermenting liquid helps to extract the colour from the skins; therefore the cap of skins must be kept in contact with the liquid by frequent mixing. There are various methods for mixing the cap with the fermenting liquid, and we discuss some of the alternatives below.

Pumping over: pumping liquid from the bottom of the tank and splashing or jetting it over the top of the cap. As the liquid leaches through the cap it extracts the colour from the skins. The liquid can also be cooled as it is pumped, thus controlling the temperature of the fermentation.

Plunging down: pushing the cap down into the liquid with a plunger. This may be carried out a couple of times a day. An interesting variation is for people to stand on top of the cap and gently work a hole in it by moving their feet up and down, gradually pushing all the cap down into the liquid.

Heading down: placing boards across the tank (towards the top of the tank). The cap is trapped below the boards but the liquid can rise between the gaps (or through a central riser tube). The skins are then always in contact with the liquid. The liquid is also pumped over regularly during the fermentation.

Rotary Fermenters: vessels that look something like rotating cement mixers. After crushing, the mixture of juice, skins and seeds is pumped into the tank, the lid closed and the tank rotated regularly to keep the skins submerged in the liquid. This procedure enhances the extraction of flavour, colour and tannins in a short time.

A red wine fermentation in progress

Pumping over a red wine during fermentation

Plunging the cap during fermentation

Treading the cap during a red wine fermentation

Rotary fermenters at Leconfield Winery, Coonawarra

Time on skins

A short time on skins produces lighter coloured, more fruity styles, eg rosé or light-bodied reds. Longer skin contact increases flavour, colour and tannin extraction. At fermentation temperatures around 25°C, most of the flavour and colour is extracted from the skins by about midway through the fermentation, while tannin extraction continues for as long as the skins and seeds are kept in contact with the liquid. When the winemaker considers that the right balance between flavour, colour and tannins has been reached, the partly fermented wine will be drained off to another tank to finish fermentation. The wine obtained from this draining process is called the *free run*. The mass of skins and seeds is then pressed to recover more wine (called *the pressings*), which may or may not be added to the free run; it all depends on the quality of the pressings. A normal period of skin contact would be about 4-6 days.

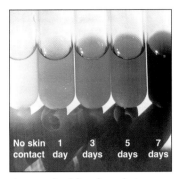

An example of the colour of wines made from the same fermentation but with different times of skin contact.

Extended Skin Contact

Some wines will be left in contact with the skins and seeds for much longer than this, even after the fermentation is complete, sometimes for up to 4 weeks, before they are drained and pressed. Winemakers refer to this as extended skin contact. This can produce a more complex wine, stabilise the colour and often soften the astringency of the tannins.

Barrel fermentation

Some free run wine may be transferred part way through fermentation to oak barrels to complete fermentation. Winemakers consider that this induces a more subtle integration of the oak and barrel fermentation characters into the wine.

Some red wines finish their fermentation in oak barrels.

Pressing of red wines

The pressings will normally be more highly coloured and tannic and, as the pressing continues, more bitter. The quality of the wine from the pressing stage is influenced largely by the maceration technique. Pressings from wines that have been fermented hot and/or heavily macerated are less suitable for adding to the free run. Often the wine from the last stages of the pressing operation, where higher pressures are used to extract the liquid, may be more bitter and will be kept separate. Gentle maceration combined with gentle pressing is an ideal approach to produce flavoursome, medium-bodied wines which still have good tannin sensation and a soft, pleasing mouthfeel.

Storage in oak barrels

Most red wines will be stored for some time in oak barrels. They take on new sensory characters that come from the oak barrels. During oak storage there is slow uptake of oxygen and developed (aged) characters may appear in the wine, which integrate with the oak and primary fruit characters. The wine is stored in the barrel until the winemaker considers that the balance is right; storage time may vary from a few months to two years or more.

Barrels at the twelve o'clock position

Twelve o'clock position — When the barrel is stored in this position it can be frequently topped to compensate for evaporation losses. Each time the barrel is topped with wine some oxygen may be dissolved in the wine, which modifies the maturation process and creates a more complex wine with altered tannins.
Two o'clock position — When the barrel is in this position it does not require frequent topping. There is less oxygen pick-up and thus maturation reactions are minimised. The wine retains more primary fruit characters.

Malo-lactic fermentation (MLF)

Most red wines (except rosé and light-bodied styles) will be put through a malo-lactic fermentation. The influence of the malo-lactic characters may not be as obvious as it is in white wines. There are changes in the sensory characters but they are difficult to describe. However, because of the decrease in acidity occurring during the malo-lactic conversion, the wines will feel softer on the palate and will be more pleasant to drink.

Barrels at the two o'clock position

The modifications that occur during maturation and ageing of wine are covered in the chapter on 'Choosing, cellaring and enjoying wine'.

Maturation

Wines that are meant to be consumed while they are young (eg most aromatic white wines and light-bodied red wines) will be bottled soon after they are made. Others, predominantly full-bodied white and red wines, may be matured in new or used oak barrels before they are bottled. Primary fruit flavours are gradually transformed to developed (aged) characters; white wines may take on *toasty*, *honey*, *nutty*, *cashew* and *kerosene* types of characters, and red wines may develop *gamey*, *meaty*, *earthy*, *leathery*, *mushroom*, *dusty*, *cowyard*, *barnyard*, *cigar box*, *licorice*, *chocolate* or *coffee-like* characters.

Wood characters (if present) harmonise with primary and developed fruit sensations. Red wines become browner and whites more golden. Astringency (in reds) decreases as tannins become larger and the wine appears softer on the palate and more pleasurable to drink. Apparent sweetness (from fruit and alcohol) may become more obvious.

All these balances change with time, both while the wine is stored in the tanks or barrels in the cellar and then while the wine is in the bottle.

Clarification, fining and stabilisation of wine

After primary fermentation the wine is left to settle, and then the clear wine is racked from the yeast lees at the bottom of the tank. Further clarification of the wine can occur through centrifuging or filtering.

Stabilisation is the removal of unstable compounds which may otherwise form a haze or deposit in the bottled wine. This ensures that the wine will be bright and free of deposits when enjoyed by the consumer.

Unstable proteins which can form a haze in the wine are removed by the addition of a natural clay compound called bentonite, which combines with the protein and settles to the bottom of the tank to give clear wine.

In some bottles of wine you may see a small deposit of crystals, particularly after the bottle has been stored in the refrigerator. These are tartrate crystals, a natural part of the wine; they precipitate out under cool conditions. They are not harmful and a small amount of these crystals is acceptable. However, most consumers prefer their white wine to be perfectly clear. To ensure this winemakers will, after fermentation and usually after any blending operations, chill the wine and hold it at about minus 3°C to precipitate out all or most of the unstable tartrate crystals before the wine is bottled. This process is called *cold stabilisation*.

Many red wines are not filtered and cold stabilised to the same extent as white wines. Thus, in some red wines, crystals of tartrate and sediments of coloured tannins may appear in the wine as it ages. These are natural products and are not harmful. They can easily be removed by decanting the wine prior to serving.

During the period from the end of fermentation to bottling, the winemaker may refine the taste of the wine by the addition of fining agents such as gelatine, casein and egg white, which react with and remove phenolic compounds in the wine which would otherwise give bitter and coarse tastes. In using these agents the winemaker is further fine-tuning the structure of the wine.

The use of small amounts of additives and of fining agents is generally necessary to ensure that the wine will be clear, stable and sound, have longevity and be enjoyable to taste.

Unstable tartrate crystals settled on the inside of the bottle

Blending

Some wines are made from one grape variety harvested from one vineyard, but many wines are the result of blending different wines: wines from different varieties, wines from different vineyards and even wines of different ages.

Winemakers mix the different wines in order to achieve a certain wine style, relying on their tasting abilities to indicate the mix which will give the most enjoyable taste.

Components of each wine in the blend contribute complexity, balance and structure, creating an improved wine overall.

The decision to bottle

The winemaker is continually making decisions throughout the winemaking process to ensure that the wine fits the desired style and that it is ready for bottling: how to ferment? whether and how long to store in oak barrels? will a malo-lactic be beneficial? cold stabilisation? fining? filtering? when to bottle?

The winemaker constantly tastes the wine and decides how a particular wine will be treated depending on an assessment of how the above operations will influence the sensory features of the wine. It is a continual process of crafting and fine-tuning the character of each wine, each step in the winemaking process linking the wine more closely with its maker.

Bottling

When the winemaker decides that the wine is ready for bottling, it will be checked for clarity and stability and then filtered into a bottle or cask. Most white wines, particularly sweet white wines, will be sterile filtered into their container, which ensures that the wine will be free of any yeast or bacteria that could grow in the wine after bottling. Red wines are usually filtered, but not to the same degree of sterility as white wines. Reds contain low amounts of sugar, have normally undergone a malo-lactic fermentation, and have been stored for longer periods of time. Thus the chance of any yeast or bacterial activity occurring after bottling is low. The aim of the bottling process is to maintain the quality of the wine. Very sophisticated bottling lines are used in the wine industry to sterile filter the wine and also to protect it from oxidation during bottling.

Sealing the bottle

The bottle is then sealed with either a cork or a screw cap. Cork is the more common seal.

A wine cork comes from the bark of cork-oak trees. These trees are mainly grown in Portugal and production of corks is based in this country. The bark is cut from the tree and then a cylinder of cork is cut from the bark. It takes about 12 years for the bark to regrow before it can be harvested for cork production. Recently there have been some problems with spoilage of wine by contaminated corks; about 3 to 5% of Australian wines have been reported to have a mouldy or hessian bag character referred to as 'corked' or 'showing cork taint'.

We discuss 'corked character' on page 12 under the heading 'Faults'. Currently the Portuguese cork industry is investigating ways to avoid the occurrence of cork taint. As well, other approaches such as screw caps and artificial corks are being explored by the wine industry as alternatives to natural corks. It will be some time before all these issues are resolved.

Removing the bark from a cork-oak tree

The finished product: a cylinder of cork cut from the bark

Collecting and storing the bark

Packaging

Once the wine is bottled and sealed, the next step is to label and package the product. This is all part of the image of the wine that the winemaker wishes to portray to the consumer.

A superb Coonawarra red from Penley Estate, one of the wineries based in Coonawarra, Australia's most famous red wine district

A collection of quality wines from Evans & Tate Winery, one of Western Australia's leading wine producers

Croser, one of Australia's premium sparkling wines - from the Petaluma Winery in the Adelaide Hills

The collection of fine wines that make up All Saints Estate Pioneers Selection

Maturation in the bottle

Some wines, mainly full-bodied whites and reds, will benefit from being allowed to mature in the bottle prior to drinking, more time being required for the integration of primary fruit, developed fruit and oak characters, and in red wines for the tannins to soften. Each wine will be perfected in its own time. Some wines will be ready to be enjoyed when young, sometimes within a year of their making, while others will require many years to reach perfection.

Explore the following pages and discover the character of the different styles of Australian wine.

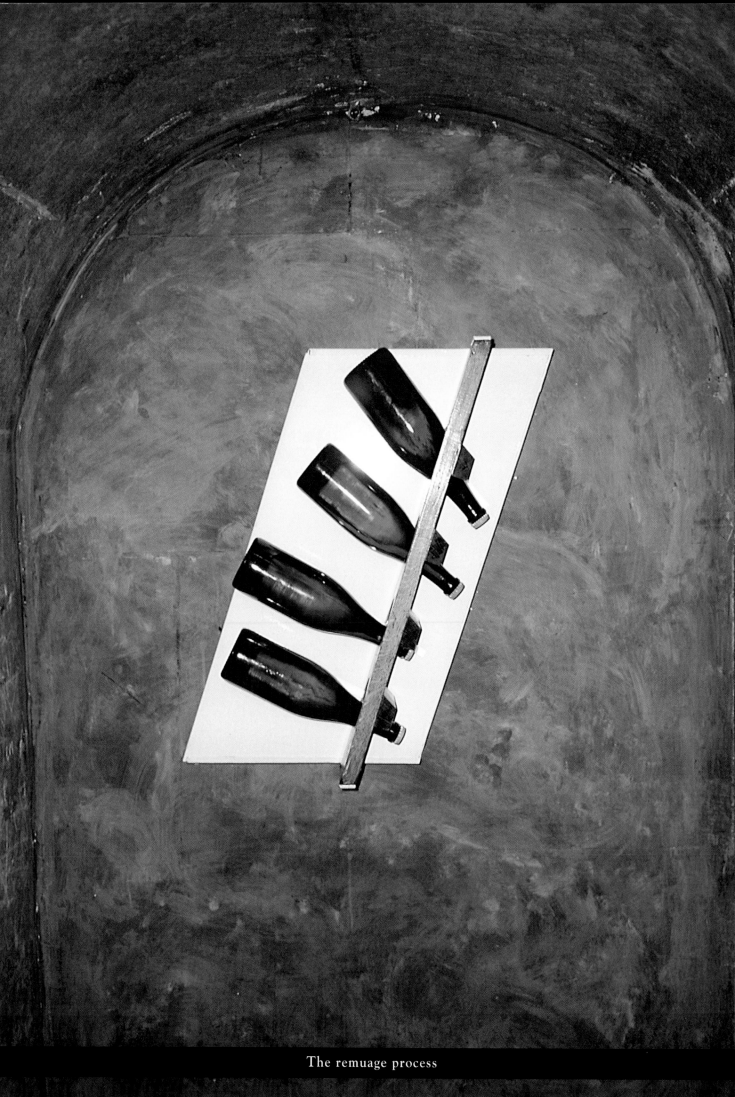

The remuage process

SPARKLING WINES

SPARKLING WHITE AND ROSÉ

The wines

Sparkling wines are made from both white and red wine grape varieties. Normally only the juice is used, although in the production of rosé wines some skin contact occurs. The first step is to make a still wine, a wine without bubbles, called the *base wine*. This wine then undergoes a secondary fermentation and the carbon dioxide gas produced in this step is trapped in the wine, changing it into a sparkling wine. When the wine is poured into the glass, the gas is released and a steady stream of bubbles (the bead) rises to the surface of the wine and forms the mousse. The bubbles are an exciting part of the appeal of sparkling wine, but it is the flavours and mouthfeel of these wines that are most rewarding. Traditionally they are wines of celebration but they can be enjoyed on many occasions, either as an apéritif or as a partner to food.

The grape varieties

Grape varieties used in the production of sparkling wine in Australia include:

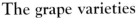

Chardonnay	Muscat Gordo Blanco	Riesling
Chenin blanc	Ondenc	Semillon
Colombard	Pinot Meunier	Trebbiano
Muscadelle	Pinot Noir	

Quality sparkling wines are made exclusively from Chardonnay, Pinot Noir and Pinot Meunier.

The wine styles

At the bottom end of the quality range are wines that are sweet and fruity, often having large bubbles. They are made from a large range of grape varieties and by the simplest method, where carbon dioxide gas is injected into the base wine. Then there are wines which are made most often from Muscat Gordo Blanco, Colombard, Chenin Blanc, Semillon and sometimes from the juice of black grape varieties, and which are usually fresh and fruity and vary in taste from slightly sweet to sweet. They are relatively inexpensive and most likely are made by a method called the Charmat process, with the secondary fermentation occurring in a pressurised tank.

Another style, slightly more expensive than the previous one, is made from similar varieties but with more Chardonnay and Pinot Noir included. These wines are more flavoursome, somewhat more complex and fuller and richer on the palate. They can be made dry or slightly sweet. They will probably be made by the Transfer method, which is a modification of the Méthode Champenoise process on which we elaborate in the following pages.

And then there are the styles made exclusively from the traditional varieties, Chardonnay, Pinot Noir and/or Pinot Meunier. They vary from the lighter bodied styles through to the more full-bodied styles. Both styles can show, as well as enticing aromas and flavours, a wonderful creaminess and complexity on the palate. They are made by either the Transfer or the Méthode Champenoise method. Ever increasing in number, these wines represent the highest quality of Australian sparkling wine.

What you may see on the label
Although you will see the word Champagne on labels of bottles of Australian sparkling wine, the wine is not Champagne, or even similar to it. Champagne is a region and a wine. The word Champagne rightly belongs to the famous wines produced in the Champagne region of France. With time the word Champagne will not be used on Australian wine labels, according to the agreement between the Australian Wine Industry and the EEC. Australian sparkling wine is developing its own image with names such as Croser, Yalumba D, Jansz, Salinger, Clover Hill and Domaine Chandon.

Sparkling red wines
Discover the characters of sparkling red wines, an unique Australian sparkling wine style, later in this section.

Where do the bubbles come from?

It all depends on how the wine is made.

Carbonated

The base wine blend is sweetened with sugar, filtered, chilled and infused with carbon dioxide gas in large refrigerated pressure tanks. It is then bottled under a counter-pressure filling system.

The wines are often sweet and fruity, with large bubbles which dissipate quickly.

Charmat process (fermentation in tanks)

The base wines, sugar and yeast are mixed in large refrigerated pressure tanks. The secondary fermentation occurs in these tanks and then, after a period of time on yeast lees, the wine is sweetened, filtered (under pressure) and bottled.

Transfer process

This is a modification of the Méthode Champenoise process. The secondary fermentation still occurs in the bottle, but at the end of the period on yeast lees, rather than each bottle being handled individually (as in the Méthode Champenoise), the contents of the bottles are transferred under counter pressure to a pressure tank. The wine is mixed and filtered (to remove the yeast lees), dosage is added and then the wine is filled into new bottles. The main advantage of this process is that it avoids the time and labour of the remuage operation and provides for greater uniformity in the finished wine. The wine can be labelled 'bottle fermented' but it cannot be labelled 'fermented in this bottle' as is the case for Méthode Champenoise wines.

Wines made in this manner cover a wide range of quality from large commercial brands to premium sparkling wine. The major difference in quality comes from the use of different grape varieties, and where and how the grapes were grown.

The higher quality wines are made from Chardonnay, Pinot Noir and Pinot Meunier and these wines can show similar characters and qualities to those made by the Méthode Champenoise process.

Méthode Champenoise

This is the traditional method used in France to produce Champagne. The method has been adopted by sparkling wine producers around the world. We describe this method in detail later in this chapter.

Bubbles — part of the appeal of sparkling wine

The different methods of making sparkling wine

CARBONATED	CHARMAT PROCESS	TRANSFER PROCESS	MÉTHODE CHAMPENOISE
Mix of classic and other varieties	Mix of classic and other varieties	Usually classic varieties	Usually classic varieties
Hand or machine picked grapes	Hand or machine picked grapes	Hand or machine picked grapes	Usually hand picked grapes
Primary fermentation	Primary fermentation	Primary fermentation	Primary fermentation
Blending process	Blending process	Blending process	Blending process
Filtering and transfer to pressure tanks	Transfer to pressure tanks	Transfer to bottles	Transfer to bottles
No secondary fermentation; carbon dioxide gas is bubbled into the wine in the pressure tank. The wine is sweetened and mixed	Secondary fermentation occurs in pressure tanks	Secondary fermentation occurs in individual bottles	Secondary fermentation occurs in individual bottles
	Clarified and transferred under pressure to a pressure tank where it is sweetened and mixed	Transfer (under pressure) of contents of each bottle to a pressure tank, where they are sweetened and mixed	Remuage Disgorgement and liqueuring
Filtration	Filtration	Filtration	
Bottling	Bottling	Bottling (in a different bottle to that in which secondary fermentation occurred)	Bottling (in the same bottle in which secondary fermentation occurred)
Packaging	Packaging	Packaging	Packaging

THE MÉTHODE CHAMPENOISE

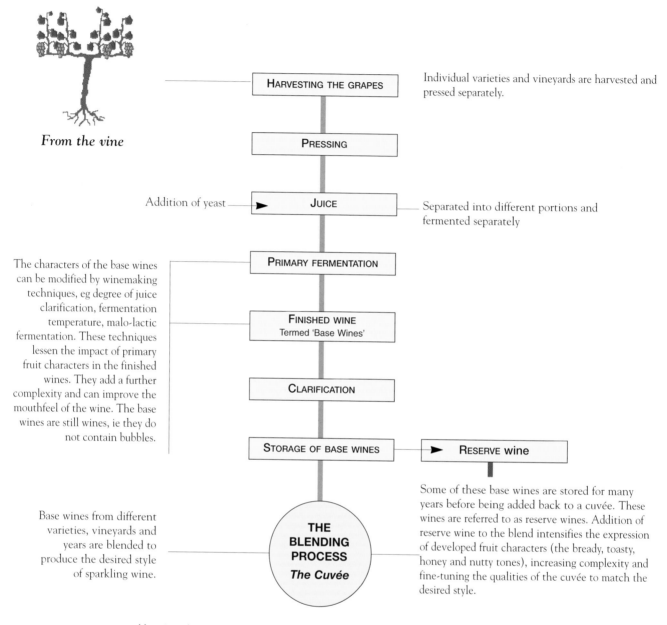

From the vine

HARVESTING THE GRAPES

Individual varieties and vineyards are harvested and pressed separately.

PRESSING

Addition of yeast — JUICE

Separated into different portions and fermented separately

PRIMARY FERMENTATION

The characters of the base wines can be modified by winemaking techniques, eg degree of juice clarification, fermentation temperature, malo-lactic fermentation. These techniques lessen the impact of primary fruit characters in the finished wines. They add a further complexity and can improve the mouthfeel of the wine. The base wines are still wines, ie they do not contain bubbles.

FINISHED WINE
Termed 'Base Wines'

CLARIFICATION

STORAGE OF BASE WINES ► RESERVE wine

Base wines from different varieties, vineyards and years are blended to produce the desired style of sparkling wine.

THE BLENDING PROCESS
The Cuvée

Some of these base wines are stored for many years before being added back to a cuvée. These wines are referred to as reserve wines. Addition of reserve wine to the blend intensifies the expression of developed fruit characters (the bready, toasty, honey and nutty tones), increasing complexity and fine-tuning the qualities of the cuvée to match the desired style.

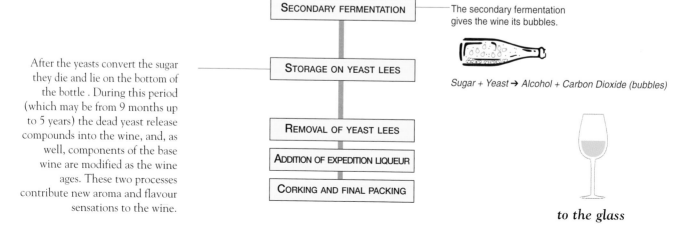

Yeast and sugar are added to the blended wine which is then divided into individual bottles where the secondary fermentation occurs.

SECONDARY FERMENTATION

The secondary fermentation gives the wine its bubbles.

After the yeasts convert the sugar they die and lie on the bottom of the bottle . During this period (which may be from 9 months up to 5 years) the dead yeast release compounds into the wine, and, as well, components of the base wine are modified as the wine ages. These two processes contribute new aroma and flavour sensations to the wine.

STORAGE ON YEAST LEES

Sugar + Yeast → Alcohol + Carbon Dioxide (bubbles)

REMOVAL OF YEAST LEES

ADDITION OF EXPEDITION LIQUEUR

CORKING AND FINAL PACKING

to the glass

THE INTRICACIES OF THE MÉTHODE CHAMPENOISE

The role of the vineyard

Premium sparkling wine is made from various combinations of the grape varieties Chardonnay, Pinot Noir and Pinot Meunier. Bunches of grapes are normally picked in the earlier stage of ripening, when sugar levels are about 10 to 11° Baumé, when acid levels are high (about 9 to 12 grams per litre) and when the grapes show desirable aroma and flavour characteristics.

Making sparkling wine from fruit grown in warmer climates requires careful selection, as grapes from these climates do not necessarily have the intensity of the right types of characters and/or the structure suitable for making wines intended for longer ageing on yeast lees. However, by picking the grapes in the earlier stages of ripening, juice with sufficient acid and some appealing characters can be obtained. Wines made from these grapes are released early and are often described as having more primary fruit characters and being less complex, but they can still be refreshing, flavoursome and enjoyable.

Cooler climates, on the other hand, bring out the best features of Chardonnay, Pinot Noir and Pinot Meunier for the making of premium quality sparkling wines. Grown under these cool conditions, the grapes have high natural acidity, a high intensity of desirable varietal characters, and good structure, features which after long ageing on yeast lees produce sparkling wines with rich but subtle and complex flavours and alluring creamy textures. It is difficult to describe the desirable varietal characters in the grapes at harvest. They are quite delicate and are associated with the early to mid stages of the ripening spectrum for each variety. Winemakers often use descriptors such as grapefruit, green apple, lemon, tobacco and melon to describe Chardonnay, but it is really the overall structure (high acid and intensity of delicate flavours) that is important. It is often easier to recognise desirable characters at the end of primary fermentation than in the fruit. It is at this stage that the different wines are selected for their suitability to contribute to blends for making particular sparkling wine styles.

Harvesting and pressing

Once the decision to pick the grapes is made, normally they are hand picked into crates and then often stored in a coldroom prior to pressing. Whole bunches of grapes are pressed as gently as possible so that there is minimal contact between the expressed juice and the grape skins and seeds. This avoids extraction of phenolic compounds which may cause bitterness, and with black grape varieties it also avoids any leakage of colour from the skins into the juice. The pressing operation can be carried out with traditional presses or with modern presses which often utilise computer controlled programmes to regulate the pressing cycle. This gentle pressing can produce clear juice even from the black grape varieties Pinot Noir and Pinot Meunier.

The juice released first contains the most sugar, acid and desirable flavour compounds and the least pickup of phenolic compounds. As the pressure is increased during the pressing cycle, the composition of the pressed juice changes. It becomes less acidic and more phenolic. With black grapes more colour is extracted from the skins. The juice obtained from the different stages of the pressing cycle is drawn off and stored in separate vessels; there may be three or more separate fractions. The juice from the first stage of pressing is more suitable for the production of high quality sparkling wine.

Chardonnay grapes, picked into small crates, ready to be transferred to the press

The pressing operation is carried out in stages.

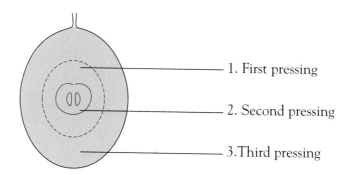

1. First pressing

2. Second pressing

3. Third pressing

1. The first pressing releases the juice from the mid-section of the berry.
It is:
• the most easily extracted,
• the richest in sugar,
• the richest in acid, and
• the lowest in phenolics.

2. The second pressing (or as the pressure is increased) releases juice from the sections closest to the seeds.
It is:
• harder to extract,
• lower in sugar,
• lower in acid, and
• higher in phenolics.

3. The third pressing (or as the pressure is increased further) releases the juice that is nearest to the skin.
It is:
• even harder to extract,
• even lower in sugar,
• even lower in acid,
• sometimes 'oily' in flavour, and
• even higher in phenolics.

A traditional Champagne press in the Woolshed Winery at Padthaway Estate

The press filled with grapes prior to pressing

Redistributing the load in between pressing cycles

Primary fermentation (creating the base wines)

Each batch of juice is clarified, yeast is added and the juice is then fermented in a similar way to a normal white wine fermentation. Sometimes with whole bunch pressing, the juice goes directly to the fermenter without, or with very minimal, clarification. The resultant wines are called *base wines*. The winemaker thus ends up with at least three base wines from each pressing operation. The different pressings from the different grape varieties and from each vineyard are usually stored and fermented separately. Makers of sparkling wine thus have many different wines in their cellars at the end of vintage, increasing their options in the blending process that follows.

Additionally, the base wines may be made in different ways, influencing their structure and suitability for blending for certain sparkling wine styles. Included in the options that winemakers have to mould the structure of their base wines are yeast selection, fermentation temperature, the degree of clarification of the juice prior to fermentation and the type of fermentation vessel (stainless steel or oak vats). Some winemakers also put varying portions of their base wines through a malo-lactic fermentation, the flavours of which may carry through to the final wine. Because base wines are quite acidic, the malo-lactic fermentation, as well as adding complexity, also softens the palate due to a decrease in perceived acidity.

Blending — the art of making sparkling wine

After vintage, all the base wines are assembled and assessed. Various combinations of the different base wines are made up so that the winemaker can decide which is the best blend for the style of sparkling wine to be produced.

The blend of the different wines is called the *cuvée*. The cuvée may not be made up of only the current year's wine, but may be modified by the use of reserve wine (wine kept from previous years). The task of blending requires a great deal of skill and experience, as it is the characters of the cuvée that dictate the structure and style of the finished sparkling wine. The blender must almost be able to look into the future and anticipate how the blend will develop and how it will then fit the desired style of sparkling wine. With many different base wines available, the winemaker strives to combine their individual flavours and structural components so that a cuvée is assembled that will produce a sparkling wine of the desired House Style(s) and brand names.

The cuvée must be made up with a view to how each component will change during the period the wine is stored on yeast lees. Each component of the blend contributes special features.
• *Chardonnay* – added to the blend to provide finesse and elegance. Great potential for long ageing on yeast lees.
• *Pinot Noir* – the backbone of many sparkling wines, providing fullness, weight and length to the palate. Great potential for long ageing on yeast lees.
• *Pinot Meunier* – added to some blends to provide fruitiness and roundness.

In the finished wine, Chardonnay and Pinot Meunier flavour sensations are apparent to the taster earlier than those of Pinot Noir, whose stronger flavours develop in the mouth with time. Both Chardonnay and Pinot Noir contribute to length and persistence. The composition of the cuvée often determines how the wine is labelled.

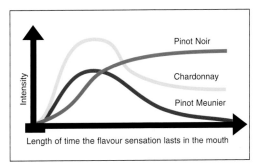

The diversity of base wines
Imagine there are ten vineyards (five Chardonnay vineyards, four Pinot Noir vineyards and one Pinot Meunier vineyard) from which grapes are sourced for sparkling wine production. If each vineyard is harvested separately and the grapes pressed to obtain three juice fractions, and if they are fermented separately into wine, thirty different base wines would be obtained in all.

Wineries producing sparkling wine may make up to a hundred (or even more) base wines, representing many varieties, vineyards, pressing fractions and winemaking variations. This gives the winemakers many options in blending their cuvée.

Secondary fermentation (creating the bubbles)

After the composition of the cuvée is decided, the selected wines are mixed with an amount of sugar (around 22 grams per litre), yeast and some other additives and then transferred to heavy-weight pressure-tested bottles. These are the bottles in which the secondary fermentation will take place and in which the wine will be sold.

Each bottle is crown sealed and stored on its side. The small amount of sugar is converted by the yeast to alcohol and carbon dioxide gas, which is trapped in the bottle giving the wine its bubbles. The alcohol content of the base wine is raised by about 1.5% v/v.

Sugar + Yeast ➜ Alcohol + Carbon Dioxide (the bubbles)

The secondary fermentation occurs in the bottle.

The secondary fermentation lasts approximately six weeks; then the yeast cells die and settle on the inside of the bottle. The bottles are then stored for a further period of time, sometimes up to three years or even longer. This period is referred to as storage on yeast lees. It is during this storage period that the wine slowly ages and the primary fruit characters of the cuvée evolve into new sensations that we call developed fruit characters. The wine can take on bread, biscuit, meat, toast, honey and nut characters. After some months the yeast cells start to break down (yeast autolysis), releasing flavour compounds into the wine which interact with those formed during the ageing process. Yeast autolysis often produces sensory characters that we associate with bread, biscuits, nuts and vegemite. Some of the words are similar to those we use for describing developed fruit characters.

The quality of sparkling wine is largely dependent on the development of fruit characters, which give subtle and complex flavours and structure to the palate. Yeast autolysis characters complement these changes in the fruit profile.

Sparkling wines made from cuvées of lower quality are usually stored for a shorter period (six months to about two years), since they do not contain a high concentration of components which will improve with age. These wines do not necessarily improve through being left on yeast lees for longer periods. Some, in fact, will be removed from the yeast lees even before yeast autolysis occurs.

High quality sparkling wines benefit from a longer time on yeast lees, since the cuvée from which they were made would have contained many desirable flavours that develop with time and benefit from interaction with the flavours from yeast autolysis. These wines may spend from two to five years or more on yeast lees, allowing greater time for the merging of aged and yeast autolysis characters. Apart from these aroma and flavour changes, the wine can take on a creamy texture, giving a very pleasing sensation of the palate.

The drives at Seppelt Great Western Winery, where the wines slowly develop their sparkling wine character under constant cool temperature conditions.

Remuage
(moving the residual yeast deposit to the neck of the bottle)

When the winemaker considers that the wine has developed the characters of the desired style, it is necessary to remove the yeast lees from the bottle to obtain a clear sparkling wine product. The bottles are shaken and transferred to either a special wooden frame or a mechanical remuage machine for the remuage (riddling) procedure. This aims to shake the yeast lees to the neck of the bottle in the minimum time and without leaving yeast lees sediment either in solution or as streak marks down the side of the bottle.

The remuage process may be carried out on an A-shaped wooden frame, which often has sixty slots on each side. The remueur follows a pattern in which each bottle is lifted, shaken, turned and replaced on the rack, normally twice a day. Each bottle is usually turned an eighth of a turn (45°) clockwise each time and is gradually raised so that its position on the rack becomes more vertical. The sediment is observed after each operation to check that it is being effectively shaken down towards the neck of the bottle. This procedure goes on for about twenty days until the sediment has moved into the neck of the bottle.

Each batch of sparkling wine requires a slightly different remuage pattern. The job of the remueurs is a very skilful one, and once experienced they can often manipulate thousands of bottles in a day. All this adds to the atmosphere and tradition of sparkling wine production. The work is very laborious, and it takes a long time to process a large number of bottles. Therefore it can be readily appreciated why some companies have moved (in part or totally) to the use of mechanical means of carrying out the remuage process, such as gyropallettes.

Yeast lees settle on the lower side of the bottle during storage.

The bottle is transferred to the frame where the remuage process occurs.

The bottle is slowly brought to the upright position.

The remuage process is completed and the yeast lees now rest in the neck of the bottle.

The cellars at Domaine Chandon in the Yarra Valley

Disgorging (removing the yeast deposit)

At this stage the bottle is fully inverted and the yeast lees have settled into the neck of the bottle, leaving clear wine above. The neck of the inverted bottle is immersed in a freezing solution (approximately minus 30°C), which has the effect of freezing the plug of yeast lees into an intact solid mass. The bottle is then turned upright and the crown seal removed. The internal bottle pressure derived from the carbon dioxide produced in the secondary fermentation is sufficient to expel the frozen plug of yeast lees out of the neck of the bottle. Because the wine is cold there is minimum loss of pressure during this operation. It can be done either manually or, more commonly, by machines which form a part of the bottling operation.

Some winemakers release the sparkling wine onto the market at various stages, eg when it has had three, five or more years on yeast lees, and to indicate that the wine has only recently been disgorged it may be labelled recently or late disgorged. This indicates that it is different from the first or previous releases.

Dosage, bottling and packaging

After disgorgement, each bottle is topped up with the same wine and is usually sweetened by the addition of a sugar/wine solution (liqueur) to a pre-determined sweetness level appropriate for the style. A sparkling wine that is labelled brut (indicating a dry style) may have up to 12 grams of sugar per litre, while other styles may have between about 15 and 30 grams of sugar per litre, depending on the particular wine. Each company has its own special recipe for this dosage addition; sometimes a touch of brandy or reserve wine may be added as well as sugar. These aid in maintaining the style of the particular sparkling wine.

The bottle is then corked, and a wire strap (muselet) is placed over the cork and tightened around the neck of the bottle. The wiring prevents the cork ejecting as the wine warms up or as the cork shrinks in the bottle over time.

The bottle is shaken to mix the dosage addition into the wine, and then the bottle is labelled and packaged.

Sparkling wine corks — before insertion into the bottle and showing how the cork can change shape over approximately two years in the bottle

Storage of the packaged wine

Sparkling wine is ready to drink when it is released on the market, as it is at this stage that the winemaker considers the wine to be at its best, reflecting the harmony of all the steps in its making. Storage after the wine is released is referred to as 'time on cork'. If stored for too long a period, the wine will slowly develop additional characters, associated with bottle age, which may or may not complement the other characters of the wine, and the wine may have reduced gas pressure. The better the wine, the longer the period it can spend 'on cork'. It is difficult to predict how each wine will be affected, but generally sparkling wine is ideally consumed soon after its release and at least within a year to two. Sparkling wines, with very few exceptions, are not wines to be stored for long periods of time in your cellar.

The styles of sparkling wine

Non-vintage
If the cuvée is made up of less than 85% of the year's vintage, the final wine must be labelled as Non vintage or without any indication of the year.

Vintage
If 85% or more of the cuvée comes from the current vintage, the final wine may be labelled as Vintage.

Blanc de blancs
If the cuvée is made up of wine made from 85% or more of Chardonnay grapes, the final wine may be labelled Blanc de blancs.

Blanc de Noirs
If the cuvée is made up of wine made from 85% or more of Pinot Noir, the final wine may be labelled Blanc de Noirs.

Rosé
If some red wine is added to the cuvée, or if some skin contact is allowed during the making of the base wine, the final wine may be labelled Rosé.

Prestige
The very best wine from each company is often referred to as their Prestige wine.

THE EVOLUTION OF SPARKLING WINE IN AUSTRALIA

The Australian sparkling wine industry began around 1850. It is reported that a Mr James King produced a sparkling wine in the Hunter Valley in 1843 for which he received gold medals in the Sydney Horticultural Show in 1850 and 1852. Around this time sparkling wine was also being produced in South Australia and Victoria. In the 1890s, Hans Irvine set up facilities for making sparkling wine in the Great Western Region of Victoria. This area remains a major centre for the production of sparkling wine, the site of Seppelt Great Western Cellars.

Whether the wine is from a Champagne House or an Australian winery, creating a distinctive style is what sparkling wine is all about. Whereas the Champenois have had hundreds of years to develop their styles, Australian producers of sparkling wine have only just commenced their journey towards the definition and refinement of their styles. It is only in the last 15 years or so that Chardonnay, Pinot Noir and Pinot Meunier, grown in cooler regions, have been used to make sparkling wine in Australia. Regions such as the Adelaide Hills in South Australia, the foothills of the alps in New South Wales and Victoria, the Macedon region of Victoria and parts of Tasmania are now the source of grapes for many premium sparkling wines. Experience is being gained with winemaking techniques and blending, and stocks of reserve wines are being accumulated. All of these factors combined will contribute to the continued evolution of Australian sparkling wine styles.

Describing the character of the wine

Appearance

The colour of sparkling wine can vary from pale straw through to deep yellow. Rosé styles are salmon pink to light red.

The bubbles should be small and form a persistent bead and mousse.

Aromas (by nose) and flavours (by mouth)

Often the feature of these wines is their subtlety. Their characters are not as immediately obvious as in some other table wines. Generally, the aromas and flavours present in sparkling wine are a mix of primary fruit, winemaking derived and developed characters. However, the contribution of each feature may vary in any particular wine. Some sparkling wines show more obvious primary fruit characters, while in others the developed characters become more pronounced.

Primary fruit characters include — *tobacco, lemon, citrus, grapefruit, apple, melon, fig, floral, fruity, perfumed, strawberry* and *confectionery.*

Developed fruit characters include — (Some of these will be developed fruit characters, others will be derived from yeast autolysis; often the descriptors represent the synergy between the two influences.) *yeast, dough, freshly baked bread, crusty bread rolls, bread, biscuit, wheaten, oyster, meatiness, cold roast lamb, savoury, toast, bonox, vegemite, marmite, cashew, hazelnut, nut, roasted nuts, dried fruit, fig, creamy, coconut, caramel, nougat, honey, honeycomb, almond, mushroom* and *truffle.*

Flavours, tastes and mouthfeel sensations

Fine sparkling wine can invoke a feeling of lightness and delicacy in the mouth. Palate structure is important. As well as showing an intensity of subtle flavours, the palate should be complex and have length and persistency. A pleasant creamy feeling in the mouth should complement the crisp, drying acidity.

Sparkling wine — style variation

Sparkling wines vary in style from the so-called apéritif (lighter bodied) styles through to fuller bodied styles.

The apéritif style is more delicately flavoured and structured. Subtle primary fruit characters are finely balanced with developed characters. The finish should be crisp and fresh. These wines, although more delicate and lighter bodied, can still be complex and have a creamy mouthfeel. Some descriptors for this style are likely to be *green apple, grapefruit, lemon, biscuit, bread, toast* and *honey.* These wines are predominantly Chardonnay based.

The fuller bodied styles have a greater impact in the mouth, with more powerful and richer flavours and often with less emphasis on primary fruit characters. They can also have a soft creamy mouthfeel. Some descriptors for these styles include *oysters, meat, cold lamb, savoury, bread, toast, nut, honey* and *mushroom.* These wines are normally a blend of Chardonnay and Pinot Noir, with Pinot Noir making up the major proportion.

The quality of each of the above styles depends very much on the intensity of the various flavours and their balance with the weight and structure of the wine on the palate. Consumer choice for any particular style varies considerably and depends on personal preference, the food that accompanies the wine, and the occasion.

Lighter bodied styles go well with appetizers and seafood. The fuller bodied styles can accompany a range of food including seafood, chicken, game and light meat dishes prepared with delicate sauces, and also light desserts.

SPARKLING WINE – *a diversity of styles from across Australia*

Some examples to try

Generally the less expensive wines show a greater emphasis on primary fruit characters and have less complexity of flavour and mouthfeel. They are well made, flavoursome, refreshing sparkling wines. These wines include Orlando Carrington, Seppelt Great Western, Seaview Brut, Omni and Yalumba Angus Brut.

The premium sparkling wines from each company are more influenced by longer time on yeast lees and show greater intensity, complexity and length of flavour and a creamy mouthfeel. They have been made from grapes sourced from cooler climates; sites such as the Adelaide Hills in South Australia, Hoddles Creek, The Pyrenees and Macedon Regions in Victoria and sites in Tasmania. The character of the grapes carries over to give a fine, tight, palate structure in the finished wine. The examples below range from light- to medium-bodied styles such as Seppelt Salinger, Petaluma Croser, Taltarni Clover Hill and Yellowglen Cuvée Victoria, through to more medium-bodied styles of Orlando Trilogy, Domaine Chandon Brut, Yalumba D, Cope-Williams Romsey Brut, Hardys Sir James and Blue Pyrenees Reserve Brut NV. In the lighter styles the flavour impact is more refined and subtle while in the other styles it will be stronger and more pronounced. Each expresses its own individuality. But in all expect to experience strength of fruit and yeast derived flavours, complexity and a creamy mouthfeel. Explore the characters of these wines and discover the subtleties of style variations in premium Australian sparkling wines.

Producers of quality sparkling wine include Petaluma, Yalumba, Orlando, Wolf Blass Wines, Hardys, Seaview, Padthaway Estate, Mountadam and Peter Rumball in South Australia; Blue Pyrenees, Taltarni, Cope-Williams, Hanging Rock, Yellowglen, Seppelt, Brown Brothers and Domaine Chandon in Victoria; and Heemskerk in Tasmania. Usually each producer makes a range of wines of different qualities and price points.

SPARKLING WINE

Experience the diversity of characters that come from the different styles of sparkling wine

THE VINEYARD

Selection is from Chardonnay, Pinot Noir and Pinot Meunier vineyards across Australia including the Yarra Valley, Strathbogie, Macedon, Mornington Peninsula, Geelong, Coonawarra, Tasmania and Great Southern (WA) regions.

To achieve the delicacy and finesse required for this style only Chardonnay grapes are used and these are sourced from vineyards in the Yarra Valley, Coonawarra, Strathbogie and Tasmania.

THE WINERY

The wine is made by the traditional méthode champenoise process. Uncompromised selection of the finest cool climate fruit generally consisting of more than 50 individual base wines in the blend. About 30 to 40% of the blend will be made up of wines that have undergone malo-lactic fermentation. The wine spends from 2.5 to 3 years on yeast lees.

The wine is made by the traditional méthode champenoise process. Produced using a selection of base wines from south eastern Australia. Current wine has a low level of malo-lactic fermentation. The wine is aged on yeast lees from 3 to 4.5 years after secondary fermentation in bottle.

THE CHARACTER OF THE WINE

The flagship of the Domaine Chandon stable. The most harmonious and complete wine. The nose has subtle fruit characters with distinct Pinot Noir development while the flavour is a complex mix of bread, biscuit, nutty and honeyed tones. These flavours are complemented by a pleasing creamy mouthfeel and a characteristic soft dry finish.

The characteristic delicacy and refined freshness of Chardonnay benefit greatly from the subtle enhancement of yeast ageing characters which evolve into biscuity and honeyed tones. The nose remains very fresh with distinct fruitiness while the palate leads with fruit into a lovely creamy and soft middle palate which finishes with refreshing dryness. A wine showing great finesse in its structure.

SOME MATCHING FOOD SUGGESTIONS

A wine which can be enjoyed as an apéritif or matched with a variety of dishes. Cooked and raw seafood, vegetarian cuisine and Asian dishes are some choices to explore.

Blanc de Blancs styles are the ultimate apéritif but also try them with delicate white flesh fish or sheep's milk cheeses.

Sparkling wines — many choices when matched with food

Here we provide some exciting choices and a selection of some of the dishes from the menu of the restaurant at Domaine Chandon Cellars in the Yarra Valley.

Vintage Brut - enjoy with 'Freshly cooked Crayfish on a Corn Fritter with a Cucumber Salad and Roasted Coriander Seed Oil'.

Blanc de Blancs - appreciate the delicate flavours with a dish of 'Fresh Asparagus with Feta, Oil and Thyme'.

Blanc de Noirs Cuvée Pinot Noir - the ultimate experience is to match Blanc de Noirs with Reggiano cheese.

Vintage Brut Rosé - match it with 'Smoked Salmon on Potato with Red Onion, Capers, Preserved Lemon and our own Virgin Olive Oil'.

Cuvée Riche NV - enjoy with a 'Thai Style Noodle Salad with Fresh Crab Meat or Blueberry and Domaine Chandon Cake'.

Only Pinot Noir grapes sourced from Yarra Valley, Strathbogie, Coonawarra, Mornington Peninsula, Macedon and Tasmania are used to craft this distinctive Blanc de Noirs style.

Fruit is sourced from a range of vineyards including those from Yarra Valley, Strathbogie, Mornington Peninsula, Geelong, Coonawarra, Tasmania and Great Southern (WA) regions.

Chardonnay, Pinot Noir and Pinot Meunier grapes are sourced from vineyards in the Yarra Valley, Strathbogie, Coonawarra, King Valley and Great Southern (WA) regions.

Made by the traditional méthode champenoise process. Yarra Valley and other cool climate viticultural regions are chosen exclusively for their complete structure as a single varietal wine. Some of the base wines (about 20%) undergo malo-lactic fermentation. After secondary fermentation, the wine spends from 4 to 5 years on yeast lees.

Made by the traditional méthode champenoise process and modelled on the Brut blend. At the blending stage 8-10% Pinot Noir red wine is added. This Pinot Noir wine is made by a normal fermentation on skins; it gives colour and strength to the blend, characters which follow through to the sparkling wine. After secondary fermentation the wine spends 2.5 to 3 years on yeast lees.

Made by the traditional méthode champenoise process. Particular base wines are chosen to carry the additional sweetness of the liqueur added in the dosage. The wine spends 18 to 24 months on yeast lees after secondary fermentation in the bottle.

More structure and texture than the other styles, typical of Pinot Noir. The nose is powerful with distinctive 'savoury', yeasty aromas. Creamy textures enhance the sustained power of the rich, complex flavours on the palate - a great match with food.

The objective with great Rosé is to include the structure of red wine while retaining the elegance of the best white sparkling wines. Typically a wine with red berry tones intermingled with complex bread and toasty developed fruit. Great length and complexity of flavours combine to a beautifully structured, dry finish.

A unique style modelled on the French champagne style 'doux'. Unmistakably sweeter, richer and more luscious - yet finishes refreshingly crisp.

The power of this wine can carry dishes with strong Asian flavours and Mediterranean influence.

The most versatile and underrated of all the styles. A wine which offers the perfect synergy with many types of food. Fantastic with Japanese or Chinese dim sum (Yum Cha). Outstanding with lamb and rare grilled salmon, while it could be argued that the ultimate match is quail.

The ideal match with desserts that are primarily fruit driven with low sweetness or foods that cry out for a richer apéritif style; dishes such as tarte tatin, rich blue cheese, sweeter Thai dishes, smoked salmon and rich patés.

Enjoy fine cuisine while taking in the picturesque backdrop of the Domaine Chandon vineyards and the distant mountains.

There is nothing quite like the crimson red, almost plasma-coloured, 'alive' mousse of a young sparkling red wine. However, the appeal of these wines lies not with the bubbles, but with the complexity they develop with age.

What you may see on the label
Many are still labelled 'Sparkling Burgundy', but with time this name will not be used, and Shiraz based wines will be called 'Sparkling Shiraz' or special brand names will be used. Wines from other varieties will be labelled as the variety or again using special brand names.

SPARKLING RED WINES
Sparkling Shiraz

These are red wines with bubbles, wines that have undergone a secondary yeast fermentation in the bottle. The process is similar to the Méthode Champenoise but the sparkling wine produced is deep red in colour and has distinctly different characters to other sparkling wines. Traditionally these wines have been called Sparkling Burgundy.

The name Sparkling Burgundy originates from the Burgundy region of France, where the wine was first produced from Pinot Noir grapes in 1820. It was first made in Australia, also from Pinot Noir wines, in 1881. Then in 1893 Edmond Mazure made a sparkling red wine using Shiraz base wines at the Auldana winery near Adelaide. This wine was intensely crimson red, richly flavoured and vastly different to the Pinot Noir based wines. Although made from Shiraz, the wine retained the name Sparkling Burgundy for many years; however these wines are now being labelled Sparkling Shiraz or special brand names. More recently this style of wine has been made not only from Shiraz, but also from other black grape varieties. In Australia the varieties of grapes used to make this style of wine include Shiraz, Pinot Noir, Cabernet Sauvignon, Merlot and Durif.

Describing the character of the wine

Appearance
The colour of young wines is deep, crimson red. They should have a fine persistent bead, forming a strong, crimson red mousse. Older wines may be garnet red with ruby hues, grading to leather brown.

Aromas (by nose) and flavours (by mouth)
Primary fruit characters include — *spice, cherry, violet, plum, pepper, plum pudding, mulberry, blackberry, licorice, sarsaparilla* and *jammy*.
Developed fruit characters include — *earthy, sweet, barnyard, slightly leather, mushroom, truffle, meaty, smoky* and *chocolate*.

Flavours, tastes and mouthfeel sensations
The palate should be rich, full-flavoured and complex, have soft tannins and length of sweet berry fruit characters. The wines should finish dry and not be overly astringent. Older wines, and particularly those that have had extensive yeast lees contact, will show greater complexity and a creamy, velvet mouthfeel.

The role of the vineyard

Grapes are picked in the later stages of ripening and need to have ripe, rich flavours. In the traditional Sparkling Shiraz, grapes are selected with intense plum, blackberry and licorice aromas and flavours.

The influence of winemaking

Each batch of grapes is harvested and processed separately into a dry red wine, using techniques that give good flavour and colour extraction but which avoid excessive tannin pick-up. After the base wines are made they are tasted and those with the right characters (normally rich flavours but soft tannins) are selected as base wines. The cuvée is then assembled.

After the composition of the cuvée is decided, the selected wines are mixed with an amount of sugar and yeast and then transferred to heavy-weight pressure-tested bottles. These are the bottles in which the secondary fermentation takes place and in which the wine is sold.

Most commercial styles remain on yeast lees for one to three years. Others, such as Seppelt Show Sparkling Shiraz, may spend seven or more years on yeast lees. During this time, the yeast autolysis characters merge with those of maturing fruit. The wine becomes more complex and can develop a creamy taste. When it is decided that the wine has spent sufficient time on yeast lees, the processes of remuage, disgorging, dosage, bottling and packaging take place.

At the dosage stage a sugar solution may be added to balance the astringency of the wine. The level of sugar addition may range from about 8 to about 40 grams per litre of residual sugar. Also at this stage there is an opportunity to add a touch of either older or younger wine to fine-tune the character of the finished product. Some wines will be left to mature in the bottle to take on more developed characters before they are released. The time in the bottle, post yeast lees removal, is termed 'time on cork'. Usually the longer the 'time on cork', the less the gas pressure within the bottle. Classic older examples (some of which may be wax sealed) frequently open without a 'pop', and provide only a tingling tactile sensation on the tongue as a reminder of an earlier sparkling past. The wine, however, is usually well preserved, soft, generous and often with a velvet texture.

Types of Sparkling Shiraz

Non vintage
The cuvée is made up of young and older base wines. The older wines may have been stored in large vats or older barrels, or even in bottles, for a number of years before they are selected. They contribute aged characters to the cuvée.

Vintage
The very best base wines from a particular year are used to prepare the cuvée.

Some examples to try
Seppelt, Rockford, Peter Rumball, Brown Brothers, Charles Melton, Temple Bruer, Barossa Valley Estates, Hardys, Majella and Andrew Garrett Wines.

Other sparkling red wines
Other black grape varieties such as Pinot Noir, Cabernet Sauvignon, Merlot and Durif can also be made into sparkling red wines. These may be made by the Méthode Champenoise process or by any of the other methods for making sparkling wine.

The aromas, flavours and taste sensations of these wines depend very much on which grape varieties they were made from and what primary fruit characters were present in the grapes at harvest, how long the base wines were aged and how long the wine was stored on yeast lees.

Some wines may show oak influence, but fruit flavours (either primary or developed) and not oak should be the feature of the wine. These wines offer a choice in sparkling red wine styles, and many are rich and flavoursome, but the flavours are different to those of sparkling Shiraz wines.

Some examples to try
Yalumba Cuvée Prestige Cabernet Sauvignon, Jim Irvine Sparkling Merlot Brut, Morris Sparkling Durif, Brand's Laira Sparkling Coonawarra, The Wilson's Hippocrene, Hollick Sparkling Merlot and St Leonards Sparkling Cabernet.

Seppelt Show Sparkling Shiraz offers complex aromas and flavours: spice, pepper, plum and prune flavours of youth in harmony with the earthy and other characters of age.
The long time that these wines spend on yeast lees provides further complexity and texture to the palate. These are wines that epitomise the taste of classic Australian Sparkling Shiraz.

Sparkling Shiraz and other sparkling reds are the perfect accompaniment to turkey, duck, kangaroo, spicy sausages and strong cheeses.

Chardonnay grapes - ready for harvesting

DRY WHITE TABLE WINES

The wines

These are wines made from varieties of grapes coloured various shades of green or yellow. Normally, they are made using only the juice of the grape.
Some are refreshing 'drink early' styles, while others are best enjoyed after some maturation in the bottle.

The grape varieties

Grape varieties used in the production of dry white wines in Australia include:

Chardonnay	Riesling
Chenin Blanc	Sauvignon Blanc
Colombard	Semillon
Frontignac	Trebbiano
Gewürztraminer	Verdelho
Marsanne	Viognier

The wine styles

There are many styles, as dry white wines are made from different grape varieties, and each variety can be grown in a range of climatic regions and then made into wine using a mixture of winemaking techniques.

Wines from the varieties Riesling, Gewürztraminer and Sauvignon Blanc are normally light- to medium-bodied, having predominant primary fruit aromas and flavours. They are dry, crisp and refreshing to taste. Normally they are not aged in oak, except for some Sauvignon Blancs. Most are 'early drinking' styles, but if you cellar some of the better Rieslings you will be amply rewarded for your patience, as they develop intriguing complexity with time.

Wines from the varieties Chardonnay, Semillon and Marsanne are normally medium- to full-bodied styles and often their character is enhanced by wine-making techniques which add complexity, texture and interest. They can be fermented and matured in oak barrels and some may undergo a malo-lactic fermentation as well. Many of these wines improve with age.

RIESLING

Riesling is characterised by small, very tight bunches with small, round, spotted berries, coloured greenish yellow through to gold when exposed to the sun and fully ripe. Normally these grapes are made into light- to medium-bodied styles. Riesling is regarded as one of the world's classic grape varieties. It has been grown in Germany for over a thousand years and is one of the main varieties of the Rhine and Mosel Valleys, where it produces highly aromatic wines of various levels of sweetness. However, the perception that all Riesling wines are sweet is misleading. Australian winemakers, as well as making sweeter styles, make a style of Riesling which is dry. Distinctively Australian, these dry Riesling wines have a natural refreshing acidity and enticing flavours which make them a drink to be enjoyed on their own or as an accompaniment to food. They are one of Australia's best kept secrets, waiting to be discovered by wine drinkers around the world.

Describing the character of the wine

Appearance

The colour of young wines can range from straw through to light yellow, often with green tinges. With age the wines take on deeper yellow colours.

Aromas (by nose) and flavours (by mouth)

Primary fruit characters include — *floral, fragrant, perfumed, rose-petal, cold tea, green apple, pear, lemon, citrus, lime, grapefruit, pineapple, fruity, peach, apricot, passionfruit* and *tropical fruit.*

Developed fruit characters include — *toast* and *honey; sometimes, a kerosene character can develop; this can add some complexity, but it is pleasing only if present in small amounts.*

Flavours, tastes and mouthfeel sensations

Normally these wines are light- to medium-bodied. The best have an intensity of flavour providing depth to the middle palate. They have crisp acidity and some can give a sensation on the palate that is often described as 'steely', relating to the crispness of the acid and other structural features such as a highly defined narrow band of flavour. Carbon dioxide may be added at bottling to prevent the wine from oxidising, and in some wines its presence can give a tingling lift to the palate. The sugar content may vary from about 2 to around 7 grams per litre. Winemakers will balance the sugar and acid levels of any wine so that they are in harmony with each other and with the flavour intensity of the wine.

The role of the vineyard

The vineyard is the key, since the flavours and other characters of Riesling wines evolve from their grapes, with little alteration due to winemaking practices. The characteristics of these wines appear to be closely linked to the climate of the vineyard and generally can be grouped into the following styles.

Cooler climates - these wines are more aromatic with delicate floral tones, green apple characters, higher natural acidity and steeliness on the palate, great potential for ageing. In some years, normally those of higher rainfall and humidity, the grapes may be slightly infected with the Botrytis mould and the wines may have some marmalade and apricot characters, which in small amounts can add complexity.

Cool to warm climates - citrus and lime flavours intensify, the steeliness may diminish, but wines retain refreshing crispness and tightness of structure. They develop into distinctively toasty, honeyed wines.

Warmer climates - these wines have more pronounced, lemon and tropical fruit characters, more softness and fullness on the palate, earlier drinking styles.

What you may see on the label
You will find the word Riesling used on labels in different ways. Varietal wines are labelled Riesling or sometimes Rhine Riesling.

The word Riesling is also used to describe a generic style of wine (a crisp, fruity, dry white wine). You will mainly find this style of wine in wine casks. These wines do not necessarily need to be made predominantly from Riesling grapes; they are made from a mixture of white grape varieties and often bear little resemblance to true Riesling wines. It is hoped that with time the word Riesling will be associated only with wines made from the grape variety Riesling.

Generally Australian Rieslings have more palate weight than many of their European counterparts, a bonus of our vineyard climates being warmer than those in Germany, allowing our grapes to reach full ripeness in most years.

Riesling grapes can be made into either dry, semi- sweet or sweet white wine styles; we discuss the sweeter styles in the section on semi-sweet and sweet white wines.

The influence of winemaking

Riesling wines are made with meticulous care. They are made from highly clarified juice, fermented at low temperatures and protected from oxidation throughout their making. The prime concern of the winemaker is to maintain intensity of primary fruit characters and freshness, so these wines do not undergo malo-lactic fermentation and are not stored in oak barrels. Although pleasing to drink soon after release, quality Riesling wines can also be enjoyed after a period of ageing in the bottle; the toasty, honey characters that develop with age add further dimensions to their taste.

Riesling — style variation

Most Riesling wines are light- to medium-bodied. Style definition is related more to the types of primary fruit characters and associated structural features. Further variation comes with ageing. The intensity of flavours and acid balance of the better wines allow them to age and develop in the bottle for long periods of time. Patience plays a large part in the appreciation of these wines, but the wait can be rewarding as the characters of aged Riesling wines can be very enjoyable.

Some examples to try

Grouping of sites into different climatic regions requires some caution and qualification, since factors such as site location and vintage variation can alter the profile of flavours and acid structure that develop in grapes during ripening. Generally the sites below are considered to be cool and cool to warm.

South Australia

The Clare Valley and surrounding areas are renowned for their Riesling wines and there are many producers, including Jim Barry, Mitchell, Paulett, The Wilson Vineyard, Crabtree, Taylors, Grosset, Pikes, Leasingham, Tim Knappstein and Tim Adams. Mountadam is situated in the area known as Eden Valley and many other producers source fruit from here, including Tollana, Wolf Blass Wines, Orlando, Henschke, Peter Lehmann, Grant Burge, Yalumba, Chapel Hill, Wirra Wirra and Richmond Grove. They all make classic cooler climate styles. Wines from Glenara and Ashton Hills wineries in the Adelaide Hills area are showing promise.

Victoria

The Goulburn Valley wineries of Mitchelton and Chateau Tahbilk have consistently produced full-flavoured Riesling, while wineries such as Knight Granite Hills in the area around Macedon and Delatite in the foothills of the Victorian Alps make delicate cool climate styles.

New South Wales

Clonakilla, Lark Hill and Doonakuna Estate in the Canberra district are good examples.

Tasmania

Refined, elegant styles come from Pipers Brook, Heemskerk, Fishburn and O'Keefe, Moorilla and Elsewhere Vineyards.

Western Australia

Good examples come from Howard Park, Plantagenet, Jingalla, Goundrey, Alkoomi, Leeuwin Estate and Capel Vale.

Young dry Riesling wines can be used as an apéritif or to accompany seafood, salads and food from the Asian regions, while aged Rieslings, because of their greater complexity, match a wider range of foods, including chicken and lighter meat dishes.

What are the characters of a good Riesling?
Simply they are intensity of fruit characters, coupled with tight, fine structure, signalling 'the wine's' potential to age.

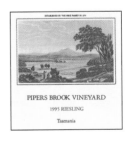

RIESLING

Experience the character of Riesling from the Barossa, Clare and Eden Valleys

THE VINEYARD

The Florita vineyard at Watervale in the Clare Valley region produces some of Australia's best Riesling grapes. The red brown earth over limestone marl and cool temperature during ripening are ideal for balanced vine growth and for developing intense flavours, coupled with high acidity in the grapes at harvest.

Fruit is sourced from vineyards in the cooler undulating hills of the southern Barossa Valley. The dry, cool to warm ripening conditions are suitable for producing grapes with plenty of flavour with lemon and citrus tones.

Grapes are sourced from a number of recognised premium districts including the Barossa Valley, Clare, Eden Valley and Coonawarra. Skilful blending of the best Riesling parcels ensures a wine of excellent varietal definition and quality.

THE WINERY

Harvesting the grapes in the cool of the night, gentle pressing, use of free run juice, cool fermentations and prevention of oxidation during processing and storage ensure retention of grape flavours. These wines are fermented in stainless steel, do not undergo malo-lactic fermentation and are not stored in wood.

Blending ensures that the wine displays consistent varietal character.

Careful selection and blending produces a wine of consistent style from year to year.

THE CHARACTER OF THE WINE

Expect classic Watervale Riesling characters; intensity and length of lime and citrus flavours finishing with refreshing crisp acidity. With time the wine will develop typical honeyed, toasty characters. A wine to enjoy when young or for long term cellaring.

Typically shows citrus and lime with melon and some tropical fruit tones, displaying a soft flavoursome middle palate while finishing with crisp acidity. A wine for immediate enjoyment or long term cellaring.

Expect to experience a flavoursome wine with plenty of lemon and lime characters with refreshing acidity. A wine that consistently shows good varietal character. An excellent wine at its price point, best enjoyed as a young wine within about two years of its making.

SOME MATCHING FOOD SUGGESTIONS

Match with prawns and lemon grass salad.

The stronger flavours go well with freshly cooked warm yabbies and with chicken dishes such as chicken and almond stir fry.

Seafood crepes with a lemon sauce enhance the lemon, limey flavours of the wine.

Some of Australia's most famous Riesling wines were made by John Vickery. Wines made in the 1960s and 1970s have aged superbly. They testify to the great potential of Australian Riesling to age when properly made and cellared.

The Eden Valley vineyards in the cooler climates of the elevated ranges above the Barossa Valley are renowned for producing grapes with high acid and intensity of elegant fruit characters.

Orlando established the Steingarten vineyard in 1962. This prestige vineyard is situated at about 200 metres on the western ridge of the Barossa ranges. The higher altitude, shallow well-drained soil and close vine planting combine to give grapes with the flavours and other elements that potentially provide wines with elegance and fine structure.

John Vickery, now at Richmond Grove Winery, is considered Australia's master craftsman of Riesling.

Hand harvesting, gentle pressing, use of free run juice, cool fermentations and prevention of oxidation during processing and storage ensure retention of grape flavours.

Early bottling retains the fresh, lemon, citrus characters of this wine.

Hand harvested and meticulously crafted. Only exceptional vintages are released and it has been, and will continue to be, a comparatively rare wine.

The Steingarten vineyard

Normally a wine with delicate floral tones intermingled with lemon and lime flavours. This elegant intensely flavoured, high acid style of Riesling can be enjoyed in its youth but has the propensity to improve with age for five or more years developing honeyed, toasty complexity.

The feature of Steingarten Riesling is the great length of fine floral and lime flavours and a structure on the palate that gives a flinty, steely mouthfeel. Offers outstanding cellaring potential and can normally be cellared with confidence for at least ten years.

The cellar door sales area at Richmond Grove Winery in the Barossa Valley

The delicate flavours and texture combine well with a calamari salad, other seafood and lamb or veal dishes.

Savour the qualities of this wine with whiting with a light mustard sauce or salmon with fresh coriander.

St Helga - an accompaniment to fine cuisine

GEWÜRZTRAMINER

You can also see this wine labelled as Traminer. The wines are light- to medium-bodied. Gewürztraminer is probably the most easily recognised varietal wine; its primary fruit characters are very distinct and descriptors include — *floral, spicy, perfume, rose, lime, passionfruit, lychee* and *lavender*.

The spicy, perfumed and lychee characters are most evident when the grapes develop in cool climatic conditions; their fragrant aromas and flavours are then coupled with crisp acidity. They are 'early drinking' styles and are an excellent accompaniment to seafood, asparagus and Asian cuisine.

Some examples to try

Brown Brothers from the King Valley in Victoria, Delatite Winery from the alpine area in Victoria, and Moorilla Estate and Pipers Brook from Tasmania.

FRONTIGNAC

Frontignac is another variety that can produce intensely fragrant, perfumed wines. It can be made into either dry or sweet styles of white wine. Descriptors include — *floral, perfume, scented, aromatic, spicy, rose* and *blossom*.

Some examples to try

Brown Brothers, at Milawa in North-East Victoria, produce a dry, aromatic style, labelled 'Muscat de Blanc'. Wines from Frontignac are mostly semi-sweet styles and are often blends with Traminer.

CHENIN BLANC

This is a grape variety that produces crisp, flavoursome white wines. Varietal descriptors include — *herbaceous, herbal, grassy, floral, apple, tropical fruit, almond, marzipan* and *honey*. Often the wines are stored in wood.

Some examples to try

Houghton in Western Australia, Broken River Wines and Best's in Victoria and Coriole, Peter Lehmann and Temple Bruer in South Australia.

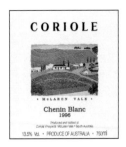

PINOT GRIS/GRIGIO

Pinot Gris is grown in the Alsace region of France. In Italy, it is called Pinot Grigio. It is a mutation of Pinot Noir, differing in that it has much less pigment in the skins of the berries. The berry colour ranges from greyish blue to brownish pink. This grape produces a dry white wine with a yellowish colour, sometimes described as coppery. We are only just beginning our experience with Pinot Gris/Grigio in Australia and it is too early to be definitive about style variation. Some descriptors that have been used to describe these wines are *hay, lightly perfumed, scent of violets, slightly nutty, minerally, savoury, pineapple, honeysuckle* and *honey*. Generally, they have a soft mouthfeel and will vary in body from light- to more full-bodied depending on the alcohol content.

Some examples to try

T'Gallant, Best's, Mount Langi Ghiran and Dromana in Victoria and Pipers Brook in Tasmania.

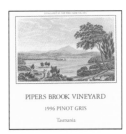

COLOMBARD

This white wine grape variety produces full-flavoured wines with fresh acidity. Its varietal descriptors include — *herbaceous, grassy, apple, citrus, lime, melon, passionfruit, tropical fruit* and *honeysuckle*. It performs well in warmer climates, as the grapes retain their acid levels and lively fruit characters during ripening.

Some examples to try
Good examples come from Primo Estate Wines and Angove's in South Australia and Deakin Estate in Victoria.

VERDELHO

Verdelho is a Portuguese variety. In Australia it is used to produce dry, sweet and fortified wine styles. It performs well in a range of climates and is gaining in popularity, this being reflected in the increased plantings over recent years. Western Australia and the Hunter Valley have been the main areas where this variety has been grown, but it is now expanding into areas such as Cowra in New South Wales.

Its varietal characters range from *herbaceous, spicy* and *grassy* through to *melon, pineapple, guava, honeysuckle, tropical fruit* and *fruit salad*, depending on where it is grown and at what stage the grapes are harvested.

Verdelho is best described as a generously flavoured style, reminiscent of tropical fruits, and balanced with crisp acidity. Wines from Verdelho are often quite high in alcohol (about 13–14%v/v), as the grapes are often picked at the later stages of maturity when they have developed these strong, tropical fruit aromas and flavours. Some wines may have been fermented or stored in wood.

Some examples to try
Western Australia
Moondah Brook, Westfield, Sandalford, Happ's, Willespie and Olive Farm all produce fine examples.

South Australia
Bleasdale at Langhorne Creek makes both a table wine and a fortified sweet wine style. Sevenhill Winery near Clare produces a blended Verdelho (with Crouchen and Chenin Blanc) labelled as St Aloysius. Fox Creek, a new winery in McLaren Vale also makes a Verdelho.

New South Wales
Lindemans, Tulloch, Wyndham Estate and Rothbury from the Hunter Valley and Richmond Grove Cowra Vineyard produce full-flavoured Verdelho wines.

MARSANNE, ROUSSANNE, VIOGNIER - The Rhône connection
Marsanne

Marsanne is one of the world's rarest grape varieties. It is a native of the Côtes du Rhône area in the south of France. The second largest plantings of Marsanne in the world are in the Goulburn Valley of Victoria. Vines sourced from St Hubert's vineyards in the Yarra Valley were established at Chateau Tahbilk in the late 1860s, and although none of the older plantings have survived, the vines that are now used to make Chateau Tahbilk Marsanne are about seventy years old, reputedly the oldest Marsanne vines in the world. The primary fruit characters of Marsanne are described as *lemon*, *peach* and *honey*, but with bottle age these change to *honeysuckle* fragrances. Generally these wines are medium- to full-bodied, with crisp acidity balancing the full array of flavours on the palate.

Some examples to try

Several wineries in Victoria produce a wine from this variety, including Chateau Tahbilk, All Saints and Mitchelton.

Viognier

Yalumba has small plantings of Viognier in its Heggies Vineyard. A crisp, dry wine is produced from this variety. Descriptors include — *lime*, *lemon*, *citrus*, *orange peel*, *orange blossom*, *apricot*, *peach* and *musk*.

The blends

Marsanne and Viognier are often blended with each other and/or other Rhône varieties including Roussanne to give a wine of greater complexity and interest of flavours and textures. Additionally, some may show some oak influence.

Yeringberg, in the Yarra Valley, produces a Rhône style wine made from a blend of the varieties Marsanne and Roussanne and which aims to emulate the wines produced at Yeringberg over a hundred years ago.

Marsanne wines, depending on their style, match a large range of foods, from lightly flavoured dishes through to full-flavoured poultry, veal, lamb and pork, and also cheeses and desserts.

ORGANIC WINE

During the last decade there has been increasing interest in and demand for organically grown food products. The aim of producing organic grapes and wines is to create and work with a balance between the vines and nature.

The procedures for growing grapes organically prohibit the use of most synthetic pesticides and manufactured fertilisers. Copper and sulphur based pesticides, bacterial insecticides and fertilisers from natural sources are permitted. The use of sprays in the vineyard to control disease is minimal, but this approach is also followed in most Australian vineyards (either organic or non-organic).

Organic wine is made from grapes which are not only grown organically, but are also processed in accordance with the standards of organic winemaking practice. These include the use of micro-organisms (yeast and bacteria) and certain chemicals, such as sulphur dioxide, carbon dioxide, natural acids and some fining agents.

Organic wine is different in that the practices required in the vineyard and the range of additives and fining agents that can be used are limited. The allowed level of sulphur dioxide is also lower than in other wines. For those people who believe in and support the philosophy of organic agriculture and food, these wines provide a guarantee that they were made in this way.

Organic wines, apart from differences in levels and types of additives and fining agents, are made in very much the same way as other wines. Chardonnay, for example, can be made according to organic standards and still be barrel fermented and stored on lees, undergo malo-lactic fermentation and be stored in wood.

We are lucky that many vinegrowing areas of Australia have warm, sunny and dry climates during the growing season, conditions which require minimal use of sprays and which favour a clean, green image for Australian vineyards.

The organic approach to making wine can produce wines that range from average to premium quality products. Organic wine, like any other wine, relies very much on the quality of the grapes and the skills of the winemaker.

Some examples to try:
Botobolar and Thistle Hill in New South Wales and Mountadam in South Australia are some of the wineries that produce organic wines.

'NO PRESERVATIVE ADDED' WINE

Some people are very sensitive to sulphur dioxide, and even the small additions that are made in making wines can cause concern to these people. Some companies such as Hardys and Botobolar Vineyard make a white and a red wine that have no sulphur dioxide added during the winemaking process. These wines are recommended for people with a low tolerance to sulphur dioxide or those seeking to avoid preservatives in their diet. However, it must be understood that although no sulphur dioxide is added during the winemaking process, there may be very small amounts present in the finished wine as the yeast can produce some sulphur dioxide during the fermentation process. Apart from no addition of sulphur dioxide, these wines are made similarly to other wines. Typically they are wines for early consumption with medium term cellaring potential.

REDUCED ALCOHOL WINES

Wines that have lower alcohol level, in the order of 6 to 7% v/v, are also available. These offer further choice to wine consumers as they select wine for different occasions.

Organic wines can be made from both white and red wine grape varieties, for example Mountadam Eden Ridge Sauvignon Blanc, and Mountadam Eden Ridge Cabernet Sauvignon.

'No preservative added' wines can be made from both white and red wine grape varieties, for example Hardys Chardonnay and Hardys Cabernet Sauvignon.

SAUVIGNON BLANC

Sauvignon Blanc has small, oval shaped, greenish-yellow berries. It produces a light- to medium-bodied wine. Sauvignon Blanc is famous for producing the refreshing, aromatic, dry white wines of the Loire Valley Region in France. It is also grown in Bordeaux, where it is used to make dry and sweet wines in combination with Semillon. In Australia, it is used to produce a dry white wine, either as a varietal wine or with Semillon and/or Chardonnay in a blended wine.

Describing the character of the wine

Appearance
The colour of these wines ranges from straw to yellow. Older wines can be deep yellow to gold.

Aromas (by nose) and flavours (by mouth)
Primary fruit characters include — *vegetal, asparagus, green bean, peas, capsicum, tomato bush, lantana, herbaceous, freshly cut grass, grassy, gooseberry, honeydew melon, passionfruit* and *tropical fruit.*
The piercingly fresh aromas and flavours of Sauvignon Blanc are often described as being zesty.
Developed fruit characters include — *spice, vanillin, honey* and *toast.*
Characters derived from winemaking include:
• barrel storage — *smoky, vanilla, toast, sawdust, coconut* and *charred.*

Flavours, tastes and mouthfeel sensations
These wines are normally light- to medium-bodied and should have a long aftertaste and a fresh, crisp finish. Good wines generally have a well balanced mixture of herbaceous, grassy, gooseberry and tropical fruit nuances. Further flavours can be apparent if the wine is stored in oak barrels.

Vegetal is a general term for *asparagus, capsicum, green pea* and/or *green bean* characters.

Herbaceous is a general term used more for the *grassy* and *herb* characters.

The role of the vineyard
Overcropped vines or vines with dense canopies, where leaves and bunches are heavily shaded, can produce grapes with lower sugar levels and unripe characters which lead to wines with intense vegetal characters (asparagus and canned green peas). These characters intensify even more when such vines are grown in very cool environments. Improving the trellis and spreading the vine's canopy, or removing leaves in the vicinity of the bunches, exposes the leaves and bunches to more sunlight. Under these improved light conditions, the ripening pattern of the grapes is modified so that these vegetal tones are lessened whilst the grassy, gooseberry and tropical fruit characters are enhanced. Wines from vines with open canopies, as well as having more of these ripe fruit characters, tend also to have an improved and fuller palate structure.

The influence of winemaking
Unwooded styles are made from clear juice, fermented at low temperature in stainless steel tanks and protected from oxidation to retain the delicate varietal aromas and flavours. For their wooded styles, winemakers often make several batches of wines. Some of the wines are totally fermented and stored in stainless steel vessels, while others may be stored in oak barrels for a number of months. Other techniques such as barrel fermentation and time on lees may also be employed. The wines are then assessed prior to blending and the winemakers decide on the various proportions of unwooded and wooded wines to make up the blend. As a rule, they are looking for a consistent style from year to year. The wine may be labelled 'Fumé Blanc'.

Sauvignon Blanc — style variation

These light- to medium-bodied wines can be unwooded, wooded or blended.

Unwooded

These wines show a range of varietal flavours, predominantly vegetal, herbaceous, gooseberry and tropical fruit accents and a fresh crisp acidity. The presence of excessive asparagus and canned green pea characters may be unpleasant in some wines, often 'over the top'. It is very much a matter of personal preference whether the degree to which these characters are present in any particular wine is perceived as an enjoyable feature. Generally wines with more grassy and gooseberry tones and weight on the middle palate are regarded as the better wines.

Some examples to try
In South Australia good examples come from Katnook, Hardys, Stafford Ridge and Shaw and Smith, in Victoria from Yarra Ridge and in Western Australia from Plantagenet.

Do Sauvignon Blanc wines age?
Generally these wines are best consumed as young wines, and seldom are they intended for long ageing. However, some wines that have an intensity of flavour and steely acidity can age for up to 10 years (or more), as exemplified by the wines of Katnook Estate, notably the 1982 and 1988. With age, the taste of some Sauvignon Blanc wines can become similar to that of aged Semillon wines.

Wooded

These wines, as well as having varietal Sauvignon Blanc characters, can show restrained smoky oak aromas and flavours, giving additional complexity and more variation to the smell and taste of the wine. The palate can have more weight than unwooded wines. The finish of these wines should be fresh and dry. Sometimes they are labelled as 'Fumé Blanc'. These styles also are best enjoyed as younger wines.

Some examples to try
Tim Knappstein in South Australia and Taltarni in Victoria.

Blended

Sauvignon Blanc wines can be blended with other varieties, typically Semillon. These wines may be wooded or unwooded. Semillon contributes extra flavours and tends to fill out the palate. Sometimes these blends are also labelled 'Fumé Blanc'. In Western Australia, they are often labelled 'Classic Dry White'.

Some examples to try
A number of wineries in Western Australia produce this style, including Evans & Tate, Capel Vale, Xanadu, Voyager, Sandalford, Cape Mentelle and Vasse Felix.

Try Sauvignon Blanc wines with oysters, smoked salmon, fresh asparagus, chicken or a plate of antipasto.

SEMILLON

Semillon berries are thin-skinned, small, round to oval and greenish coloured. They can be made into a range of wine styles. Semillon is one of the major grape varieties of Bordeaux, where it is used to produce the famous dry and sweet white wines of that region. In Australia, it is also used to make both dry and sweet wines. Dry styles of Semillon are produced in many Australian wine regions, but it is in the Hunter Valley where one of Australia's unique wine styles can be found. Here, Semillon grapes are used to make a wine that is initially subdued, but with bottle age develops into a full-flavoured, toasty, honeyed wine, a style that is now recognised as a classic Australian wine style.

Describing the character of the wine

Appearance
The wines can range in colour from straw to yellow and, in older wines, golden.

Aromas (by nose) and flavours (by mouth)
Primary fruit characters include — *pea-pod, lantana, herbaceous, green bean, grassy, flinty, straw, gooseberry, apple, quince, lemon, lime, citrus, fig, passionfruit* and *tropical fruit.*
Developed fruit characters include — *fig, toast, butterscotch* and *honey.*
Characters derived from winemaking include:
• barrel fermentation/time on lees — *creamy, yeast, vegemite, bonox, marmite, cheese, bread, toast, lanolin* and *leesy.*
• malo-lactic fermentation — *creamy, butter, butterscotch, yogurt, caramel* and *bacon.*
• barrel storage — *vanilla, toast, sawdust, cedar, olives, spicy, bacon, lanolin, coconut, pencil shavings, dusty, cashew, smoky, burnt caramel, raisin* and *charred.*

Flavours, tastes and mouthfeel sensations
The taste and texture of the wines depend very much on how they are made. They can be medium-bodied through to full-bodied, with various influences from assorted winemaking techniques, such as barrel fermentation and wood storage.

The role of the vineyard
Grapes and wines from cooler regions are more likely to have lively pea-pod herbaceous tones coupled with lemon and citrus characters and have higher natural acidity, while those from warmer regions will usually be less herbaceous and have a greater intensity of citrus and tropical fruit characters. Wineries in some areas, such as the Barossa Valley, are now sourcing Semillon from old vines.

The influence of winemaking
Some of these wines are barrel fermented with or without lees contact and/or stored in oak barrels. These techniques serve to add complexity and texture to their flavours and tastes.

Semillon grapes can also be made into sweet white wine styles, which we cover in the section on semi- sweet and sweet white wine styles.

Semillon — style variation

Semillon grapes can be made into unwooded, wooded or blended styles.

Unwooded

Unique to Australia are the classic aged Hunter Valley Semillons which we discuss on page 92.

Some producers, from areas other than the Hunter Valley, also produce unwooded styles. Normally these are from cooler regions, in which the fresh herbaceous and grassy varietal characters feature on the nose and palate and are balanced by crisp acidity. They are normally medium-bodied styles.

Wooded

Typically these wooded styles are medium- to full-bodied wines. Those from cooler climates can show more herbaceous, grassy, citrus varietal characters while those from warmer climates are more grassy, lemon and tropical fruit-like. The wines show various degrees of oak characters. Further complexity can be moulded into these wooded styles through barrel fermentation, time on lees and malo-lactic fermentation. These techniques may add creamy, buttery, nutty tones to the aroma and flavour profiles, as well as contributing texture to the palate.

Some examples to try

Semillon wines from Western Australia are usually vibrantly flavoured with subtle oak and barrel fermentation influence. Fine examples come from Moss Wood, Voyager, Evans & Tate and Xanadu Wineries.

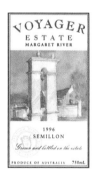

The Barossa Valley Semillons tend to be rich, fuller bodied wines with strong grassy, lemon and tropical fruit flavours balanced with complex oak and barrel fermentation characters and creamy textures. Good examples are made by Peter Lehmann, St Hallett, Basedows, Krondorf, Penfolds and The Willows Wineries.

Blended

Semillon can also be blended with other varieties, often Sauvignon Blanc or Chardonnay. You will find these blended styles from many of our wine regions. Their characters depend on the proportion of each variety in the blend.

Enjoy unwooded Semillons with seafood while wooded Semillons match chicken, veal, game birds and pasta dishes.

Classic aged Hunter Valley Semillon

Whilst some Hunter Valley producers are releasing styles similar to those described previously, the Hunter Valley is better known for developed, bottle aged Semillons. It is rare today for wine companies to age wine in the bottle prior to release, but this is exactly what happens with aged Hunter Semillons. The fruit is picked at relatively low sugar levels (10–11° Baumé). The best years are when the grapes are naturally high in acid. The grapes are crushed and the clear juice (often with the pressing component added) is fermented cool (10–12°C). After fermentation the wine is clarified, filtered and bottled. These wines do not undergo malo-lactic fermentation and are not stored in oak barrels. The wines are then aged in the bottle for up to six years (or longer) before they are released onto the market. They can continue to improve in the bottle for many years. Some of these wines are still magnificent twenty years or more after they were bottled.

When bottled, these wines are light straw in colour and may appear quite neutral, having light grassy, apple and lemon aromas and flavours. The characters of the wines gradually change as they age in the bottle. With time these subtly flavoured wines develop golden colours, build in weight and take on variations of rich, toasty, honey and fig developed characters. This interesting complexity, coupled with relatively low alcohol content (about 11% v/v), is the trademark of this style of wine. An added advantage is that they are relatively inexpensive to buy as younger wines.

A great way to experience the character of aged Hunter Valley Semillon

A rewarding tasting experience is to try Lindemans Hunter River Semillon, relatively inexpensive, and the Lindemans Hunter River Classic Release Semillon. The latter is a special selection made from the best Semillon and held back for maturation; it is released as part of Lindemans Classic Release programme after a number of years of bottle age. Previously these wines were labelled Chablis. Lindemans 1970 Hunter River Chablis Bin 3875 remains Australia's most awarded white table wine.

McWilliam's release two aged Hunter Valley Semillon wines. The Mount Pleasant Elizabeth Semillon is released about five years after its making and shows classic buttered toast, honeyed development. Relatively inexpensive, it is an excellent introduction to the taste of aged Semillon.

And then there is McWilliam's Mount Pleasant Lovedale Semillon, a wine that is only released in exceptional vintages and only when fully matured. Released at about ten years of age, it epitomises the characters of aged Hunter Semillon and testifies to the longevity of these wines.

Mount Pleasant vineyard in the Hunter Valley

Allow these wines to age and they develop wonderful nutty, toasty and honeyed aromas and flavours while still retaining their fresh acid backbone.

CHARDONNAY

The bunches of Chardonnay are small and compact with small, round, green-yellow berries. Chardonnay vines make up a major part of the plantings in the Champagne and Burgundy regions of France. In Burgundy, Chardonnay is used to make dry white wines. Interest in Chardonnay has spread all around the world. In Australia its popularity soared in the 1980s, as wine drinkers discovered the taste of Chardonnay through a range of wines that were generously flavoured with ripe fruit characters, often enhanced with sweet oak flavours and available at affordable prices. With time, as vineyards were established in cooler climates and winemaking practices fine-tuned, a diversity of styles evolved. Australian winemakers now produce quality wines, of vastly different styles, across our wine regions, while continuing the search for vineyards with those elusive special terroirs.

You will find Chardonnay wines that vary in style from medium-bodied through to full-bodied with a range of fruit flavours, coupled with various degrees of oak, malo-lactic and yeast lees contact characters. You can also find wines that are blends of Chardonnay and other varieties, including Semillon and Verdelho.

Describing the character of the wine

Appearance
The wines range in colour from straw through to deep yellow depending on where the grapes were grown, how the wines were made, and the age of the wine.

Aromas (by nose) and flavours (by mouth)
Primary fruit characters include — tobacco, cucumber, apple, grapefruit, lemon, lime, pineapple, gooseberry, melon, rockmelon, nectarine, peach, fig, tropical fruit and fruit salad.

Developed fruit characters include — toast, honey, fig, nuts, almond and cashew.

Characters derived from winemaking include:
• fermentation on solids — cheese and wax-like.
• barrel fermentation/time on lees — creamy, yeast, vegemite, bonox, marmite, cheesy, bread, toast and leesy.
• malo-lactic fermentation — creamy, butter, butterscotch, yogurt, caramel and bacon.
• barrel storage — vanilla, toast, sawdust, cedar, olives, spicy, bacon, lanolin, coconut, pencil shavings, dusty, cashew, smoky, burnt caramel, raisin and charred.

Flavours, tastes and mouthfeel sensations
Chardonnay wines range from medium- to full-bodied styles. Some may be high in alcohol (often about 13.5% v/v), a feature which contributes to their palate weight. Oak, malo-lactic and yeast lees contact characters may be apparent, these features adding to the textural nature of these wines. They can have creamy, cheesy, butter, fat and glycerol impressions on the palate.

The best wines have rich, complex, persistent flavours, fine structure and freshness, qualities that signal their potential to age superbly over many years.

The role of the vineyard

As Chardonnay grapes ripen, their flavours can change from apple, grapefruit and lemon through to lime, pineapple, melon and peach characters. In grapes that ripen in warmer climates and come from vines with moderate yields, further changes can occur and the flavours in these grapes, particularly at higher sugar levels, are often similar to peach, rockmelon and tropical fruit characters. However, the stage of flavour ripeness and the intensity of those flavours at any particular sugar level, depend very much on the climatic conditions under which the grapes ripen and the efficiency of ripening, a concept that we discuss in the viticulture section. Wines from grapes grown in cooler climates show predominantly grapefruit, lime, pineapple and melon characters and have finer structure and greater longevity. Wines from grapes grown in warm to hot climates are most likely to show more peach and tropical fruit characters and may be higher in alcohol.

The influence of winemaking

Chardonnay is a variety upon which winemakers can use their skills to the fullest. They can choose to clarify the juice to various degrees, ferment and/or store the wine in oak barrels, leave the wine on yeast lees, put it through a malo-lactic fermentation or various combinations of these techniques, leading not only to a diversity of flavours but also to different textures on the palate. Often they make different batches of wine in various ways and then blend these to produce the desired style of wine. The task of the winemaker is to balance the intensity and types of aromas and flavours that come from the grapes with the characters that emerge during fermentation and storage.

Many of Australia's early Chardonnay wines relied heavily on the use of oak and often had pronounced vanillin, toasty flavours. Today, there is a more subtle approach and the oak characters are more integrated into the taste of the wine. Phillip Shaw, winemaker of Rosemount Estate, describes the role of oak in the making of Roxburgh (Rosemount Estate's prestige Chardonnay wine) as enriching and complexing the wine. He says, 'Oak is used to give the wine extract, not oak character. It gives depth and complexity to the wine and contributes to the richness of flavour.'

Ageing is an important part in the development of flavours as it takes time for the toasty, honey and almond characters to evolve. Many Chardonnay wines will require maturation in the bottle to reach the optimum stage of development.

Oak barrels: an important part in the making of a complex Chardonnay wine

Unwooded

These wines highlight the fresh varietal fruit characters of Chardonnay, and are now being produced from a range of climatic regions. The primary fruit characters present in any one wine will depend on where the grapes were grown and at what stage of ripeness they were harvested. These unwooded styles will generally be medium-bodied, highlight the varietal fruit characters and finish fresh and crisp on the palate. They provide a greater choice in the selection and enjoyment of Chardonnay wines.

Some examples to try

Wineries producing these styles include — Mountadam, Wolf Blass Wines, Leconfield, Chapel Hill, Shaw and Smith and Hardys in South Australia, T'Gallant and Boynton's of Bright in Victoria and Pepper Tree, Montrose and Rosemount in New South Wales.

Wooded: medium-bodied

These are wines that generally have plenty of fresh melon and peach flavours, complemented in many cases by nutty, vanillin, toasty oak characters. You can rely on these wines to be consistent in style. Typically, they are made from Chardonnay or Chardonnay blends. They offer a fine fresh Chardonnay taste at an affordable price and are some of Australia's most well known and popular wines.

Some examples to try

Orlando Jacob's Creek, Lindemans Bin 65, Hardys Siegersdorf, Yalumba Oxford Landing and Woodley Queen Adelaide.

Classic Blends

These wines represent Chardonnay blended with other varieties such as Chenin Blanc, Verdelho, Semillon and Sauvignon Blanc. Typically they offer plenty of flavour and fresh acidity. Some examples include Houghton White Burgundy and Montrose Poet's Corner.

Wooded: medium- to full-bodied

Often these wines have higher alcohol content, about 13% v/v. Generally they offer a greater intensity of fruit and winemaking derived characters, which in the better wines harmonise to give balanced richness and complexity on the palate. Each winemaker crafts a style that reflects his or her winemaking philosophy and highlights the regional character of the vineyard from which the grapes were sourced.

These styles come from all the wine regions. Since winemaking practices play such a large role in structuring the taste of these wines, it is sometimes difficult to group them into styles associated with particular regions. In wines that come solely from one region, the fruit characters that you are likely to find are generally related to the climate of that region as we described previously, the intensity of the flavours depending very much on yield and viticultural practices. The characters of the wine are influenced further by the winemaking philosophy of its maker, eg how much barrel ferment, malo-lactic and/or oak treatment.

However, taking all the above into account, we can suggest two groupings that broadly separate the different styles of medium- to full-bodied Chardonnay wines, fully appreciating that there will be exceptions.

The first group, normally from vineyards in warm to hot climates, is made up of more robust, full-flavoured styles, having plenty of fruit characters (rockmelon and peach), an apparent sweetness, sometimes an oiliness or fatness, often obvious winemaking influence with buttery and oak tones and creamy textures, while some can show a warmth on the finish from higher alcohol.

Wines in the second group are normally from vineyards in cool to warm climates and are described as more elegant, refined styles, showing a richness of fruit characters but more of the lime and melon theme, freshness from higher natural acidity, fine structure and more subtle winemaking influences, all these features indicating a greater potential to age.

South Australia

Here we highlight a collection of some of South Australia's top Chardonnays —
skilfully crafted and displaying fruit richness enhanced with layers of nutty,
biscuit-like characters from barrel fermentation and yeast lees contact as well as
creamy malo-lactic tones. These premium wines come from Petaluma and
Chain of Ponds Wineries, Petaluma near Piccadilly and Chain of Ponds near
Gumeracha in the Adelaide Hills region; Normans Chais Clarendon near
Clarendon just south of Adelaide; Mountadam in the Eden Valley region;
Orlando St Hilary from vineyards in the Padthaway region; and Hardys Eileen
Hardy sourced from a number of cool climate viticultural regions.

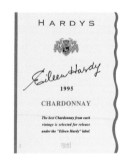

New South Wales

Rosemount's Roxburgh and Tyrrell's Vat 47, both from the Hunter Valley, are
New South Wales most renowned Chardonnay wines. Typically they are
full-bodied and with intense ripe varietal fruit characters, and barrel ferment,
malo-lactic and oak storage influences which provide complexity and texture
to the palate.

Reynolds Chardonnay comes from the new vineyard developments around
Orange, in the Central Highlands and shows the potential of the area to
produce quality Chardonnay wines; in this case a medium-bodied wine with
strength of fruit flavours balanced with soft acidity and complexity from
malo-lactic fermentation and maturation on yeast lees.

Western Australia

Vineyards in the south-west of Western Australia are the source of many premium Chardonnay wines, richly flavoured and textured. Wineries such as Killerby in the Geographe region, Devil's Lair in the Margaret River region and Wignalls and Goundrey in the Great Southern region are producing exciting Chardonnay wines.

Victoria

Wineries in the Yarra Valley have established an enviable reputation for their impressive Chardonnays — wines where the richness of cool climate fruit characters are complemented with barrel fermentation and other winemaking nuances; elegantly structured wines with excellent examples being Shantell and Yarra Burn Bastard Hill.

Miranda's High Country Chardonnay comes from fruit sourced from the King Valley, another of Australia's newer viticultural regions. Typically the wine has intense cool climate fruit characters, fresh acidity and balanced complexity from subtle barrel fermentation and oak storage treatment.

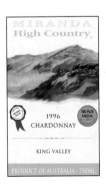

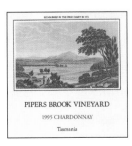

Tasmania

Pipers Brook in northern Tasmania produces superb Chardonnay wines — wines that have distinct cool climate fruit qualities, complexity, finesse and tangy acidity.

Chardonnay is an ideal seafood wine and it is also a good accompaniment to pasta, chicken and veal. Richly flavoured, textured and complex Chardonnays are suited to a range of full-flavoured dishes.

CHARDONNAY

Experience the diversity of characters that come from different vineyards and different winemaking approaches.

THE VINEYARD

Grapes are principally sourced from the Riverland in South Australia, and careful blending ensures that the finished wines have consistent desirable characters from year to year.

Selected parcels of fruit are chosen from the premium viticultural regions of Padthaway and McLaren Vale. The vines are managed to achieve lower yields, aimed at maximising desirable varietal flavours in the grapes at harvest.

Grapes come from the Padthaway region where the cool conditions during ripening are well suited for producing grapes with flavour intensity and high acid; qualities ideal for producing an unwooded Chardonnay.

THE WINERY

After crushing the must is held on skins for a short time and then pressed. The juice is fermented cool in stainless steel tanks and then stored in oak barrels for a short time.

A combination of tank and barrel fermentation, time on lees, malo-lactic fermentation and further ageing in oak barrels enhances the rich fruit characters and contributes to the complexity on the nose and palate.

The grapes are gently pressed via a tank press. Specially selected yeasts are used to conduct the fermentation at cool temperatures to retain the fresh fruit flavours.

THE CHARACTER OF THE WINE

Normally light yellow coloured with fresh citrus, melon and peach fruit characters balanced by hints of vanillin oak. Best enjoyed as a young wine.

Expect to experience plenty of fresh citrus, lime, melon and peach fruit characters with nutty, toasty and creamy complexity. Typically the wine has length of flavour and a creamy soft mouthfeel. Ageing potential two to three years.

Typically, abounding in melon, tropical fruit and some sweet peach characters giving a wine with rich flavours and a soft mouthfeel. Best enjoyed as a young wine, chilled slightly before serving.

SOME MATCHING FOOD SUGGESTIONS

Enjoy with chicken and avocado topping, sprinkled with chopped hazelnuts.

Combines well with pasta and a creamy sauce or an asparagus and scallop salad.

Seafood soufflé or a goat cheese salad match the strong fruit aromas and flavours of this unwooded chardonnay.

The making of Eileen Hardy Chardonnay

The vineyard

The premium fruit for this wine comes from two prime cool climate sites in Victoria's Yarra Valley, the Yarra Burn and Beenak vineyards. The latter is a high altitude site 400m above sea level, set on the steep slopes at the eastern end of the valley, while the Yarra Burn vineyards are situated on the valley floor east of the small town of Yarra Junction.

Fruit from three of Australia's most highly regarded cool climate viticultural regions, Padthaway, Yarra Valley and the Adelaide Hills is used for the making of Eileen Hardy, Hardys prestige Chardonnay.

The fermentation, first in stainless steel tanks and then in oak barrels

After a stringent selection process, only fruit from the best sections of each vineyard is chosen for the basis of Yarra Burn Chardonnay. Gentle pressing, cold settling with retention of some solids, barrel fermentation in new and one year old French oak barriques and partial malo-lactic fermentation techniques are used to skilfully craft the wine.

After crushing and pressing the free run juice is partially fermented in stainless steel and then transferred to new French oak barrels where the fermentation is completed. The wine is then aged on yeast lees for up to nine months. Approximately 50% of the wine is put through a malolactic fermentation to add complexity. The wines from individual barrels are tasted and the best are selected for the Eileen Hardy blend.

Further storage in oak barrels

A wine of elegance and finesse— the array of lemons, limes, melon, nuts, cream, malt and oak flavours and high acidity provides the wine with freshness, elegance, complexity and exquisite mouthfeel. Ageing potential three to five years.

Fine elegant flavours of lemon, citrus, melon and hints of grapefruit and peaches are well integrated with creamy maltiness, buttery, cashew nut, barrel fermentation and malo-lactic fermentation characters. An intensely flavoured wine with great mouthfeel and balance of fruit, oak and acid. A wine to cellar for five or more years to enhance its richness and complexity.

The wine is sampled and tasted regularly to follow its development.

Pan fried tuna with anchovy sauce is a great accompaniment to this elegant and complex wine.

Veal medallions with macadamia nut herb crust or poached trout with a creamy mushroom sauce are delicious choices for Eileen Hardy Chardonnay.

The wine served, ready to be enjoyed with food.

Not all the descriptors are found in any one wine. The combination of these vary from wine to wine depending on where and how the grapes were grown. The aroma and flavour characters that you experience when the wine is smelt and when it is in the mouth are described in some wines by one or two descriptors, while in others a combination may be more appropriate.

Remember, that the presence and intensity of the various varietal characters, although an important part of the appeal of a wine, are only part of the overall character. The balance between the basic tastes and other features of the wine, as well as its textural nature are equally important when assessing the character/quality of a wine.

Examples of varietal character descriptors for white wines

Riesling
Primary fruit characters — *floral, fragrant, perfumed, rose petal, cold tea, green apple, pear, lemon, citrus, lime, grapefruit, pineapple, fruity, peach, apricot, passionfruit* and *tropical fruit*.
Developed fruit characters — *toast* and *honey*; sometimes, a *kerosene* character can develop; this can add some complexity, but it is pleasing only if present in small amounts.

Gewürztraminer
Primary fruit characters — *floral, spicy, perfume, rose, lime, passionfruit, lychee* and *lavender*.

Frontignac
Primary fruit characters — *floral, perfume, scented, aromatic, spicy, rose* and *blossom*.

Chenin Blanc
Primary fruit characters — *herbaceous, herbal, grassy, floral, apple, tropical fruit* and *honey*.
Developed fruit characters — *almond, marzipan* and *honey*.

Pinot Gris/Grigio
Primary fruit characters — *hay, perfumed, violets, pineapple, savoury, nutty, honeysuckle* and *honey* (*some latter terms may also be associated with developed characters*).

Colombard
Primary fruit characters — *herbaceous, grassy, apple, citrus, lime, melon, passionfruit, tropical fruit* and *honeysuckle*.

Verdelho
Primary fruit characters — *herbaceous, spicy, grassy, melon, pineapple, guava, honeysuckle, tropical fruit* and *fruit salad*.

Marsanne
Primary fruit characters — *lemon, peach* and *honey*.
Developed fruit characters — *honey* and *honeysuckle*.

Viognier
Primary fruit characters — *lime, lemon, citrus, orange peel, orange blossom, apricot, peach* and *musk*.

Sauvignon Blanc
Primary fruit characters — *vegetal, asparagus, green bean, peas, capsicum, tomato bush, lantana, herbaceous, freshly cut grass, grassy, gooseberry, honeydew melon, passionfruit* and *tropical fruit*.
Developed fruit characters — *spice, vanillin, honey* and *toast*.

Semillon
Primary fruit characters — *pea-pod, lantana, herbaceous, green bean, grassy, flinty, straw, gooseberry, apple, quince, lemon, lime, citrus, fig, passionfruit* and *tropical fruit*.
Developed fruit characters — *fig, toast, butterscotch* and *honey*.

Chardonnay
Primary fruit characters — *tobacco, cucumber, apple, grapefruit, lemon, lime, gooseberry, melon, rockmelon, pineapple, nectarine, peach, fig, tropical fruit* and *fruit salad*.
Developed fruit characters — *toast, honey, fig, nuts, almond* and *cashew*.

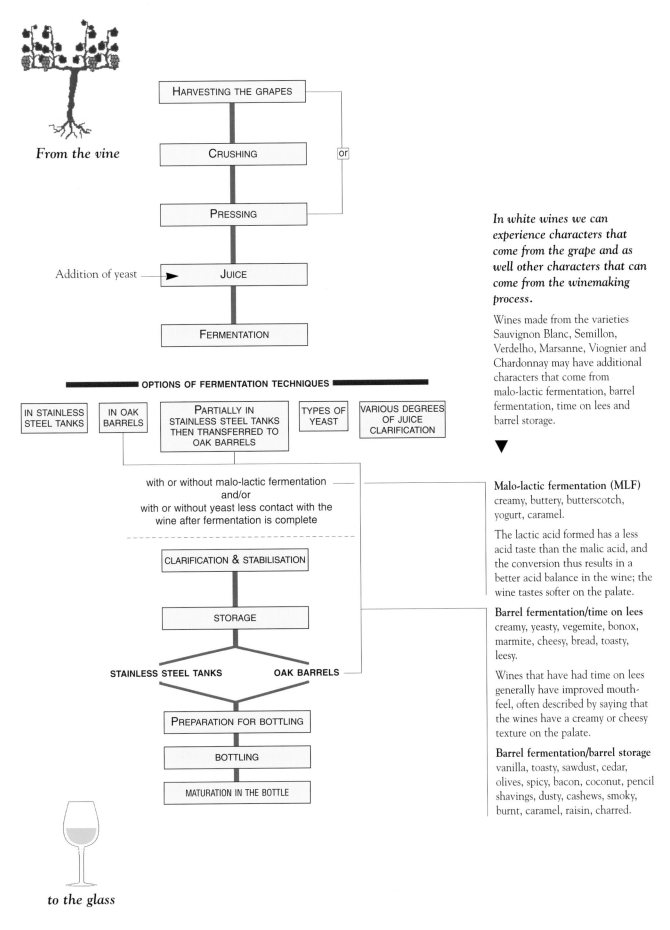

From the vine

HARVESTING THE GRAPES

CRUSHING   or

PRESSING

Addition of yeast → JUICE

FERMENTATION

OPTIONS OF FERMENTATION TECHNIQUES

| IN STAINLESS STEEL TANKS | IN OAK BARRELS | PARTIALLY IN STAINLESS STEEL TANKS THEN TRANSFERRED TO OAK BARRELS | TYPES OF YEAST | VARIOUS DEGREES OF JUICE CLARIFICATION |

with or without malo-lactic fermentation
and/or
with or without yeast less contact with the
wine after fermentation is complete

CLARIFICATION & STABILISATION

STORAGE

STAINLESS STEEL TANKS   **OAK BARRELS**

PREPARATION FOR BOTTLING

BOTTLING

MATURATION IN THE BOTTLE

to the glass

In white wines we can experience characters that come from the grape and as well other characters that can come from the winemaking process.

Wines made from the varieties Sauvignon Blanc, Semillon, Verdelho, Marsanne, Viognier and Chardonnay may have additional characters that come from malo-lactic fermentation, barrel fermentation, time on lees and barrel storage.

▼

Malo-lactic fermentation (MLF) creamy, buttery, butterscotch, yogurt, caramel.

The lactic acid formed has a less acid taste than the malic acid, and the conversion thus results in a better acid balance in the wine; the wine tastes softer on the palate.

Barrel fermentation/time on lees creamy, yeasty, vegemite, bonox, marmite, cheesy, bread, toasty, leesy.

Wines that have had time on lees generally have improved mouth-feel, often described by saying that the wines have a creamy or cheesy texture on the palate.

Barrel fermentation/barrel storage vanilla, toasty, sawdust, cedar, olives, spicy, bacon, coconut, pencil shavings, dusty, cashews, smoky, burnt, caramel, raisin, charred.

Botrytis cinerea — growing on Semillon grapes

SEMI-SWEET AND SWEET WHITE WINES

The wines

Semi-sweet and sweet white wines are made in a range of styles. As their names suggest, they are wines that give an impression of sweetness on the palate, varying from just a suggestion through to a lusciousness in the sweeter styles. Some are wines made from grapes affected by a mould, *Botrytis cinerea*.

The grape varieties

Grape varieties used in the production of semi-sweet and sweet white wines in Australia include:

Frontignac   Riesling
Gewürztraminer   Semillon
Muscat Gordo Blanco

The wine styles

Semi-sweet styles

Generally, the semi-sweet styles contain between about 10 and 30 grams of sugar per litre and have enticing, fragrant aromas and flavours and noticeable sweetness on the palate. They can be light-bodied or more medium- to full-bodied. Normally they are drink-early styles.

Sweeter styles

Sweet white table wines are full-bodied styles containing from around 30 to 100 or more grams of sugar per litre and with an assortment of rich, complex flavours and luscious sweet tastes. These are wines best enjoyed after a period of bottle maturation. Some can age superbly for many years.

They can be further sub-divided into —
• sweet wines made from grapes *not affected* by *Botrytis cinerea*; and
• sweet wines made from grapes *affected* by *Botrytis cinerea*.

What you may see on the label
The words 'late harvested' and 'special late harvested' often appear. Other names that you may see are Moselle and Spätlese. These generic terms have been borrowed from Germany and are used to describe wines that are moderately sweet. However, they should only be used as a guide, as sugar levels can vary considerably. In time, Australian wines will no longer use the word Moselle on their labels, since this term relates to a wine from the area along the Mosel River in Germany.

Semi-sweet and sweet white wine styles (non-botrytis-affected)

These wines often provide a good introduction into the world of wine as their sweet, fruity tastes can be reminiscent of previous experiences with food. Many wine consumers, having tasted these wines, have been enticed to try different wine styles and have discovered all the diversity and interest that wine has to offer. These styles are made from a range of grape varieties including Riesling, Gewürztraminer, Frontignac and Muscat Gordo Blanco. They vary from light-bodied fruity styles through to more intensely flavoured and complex full-bodied styles.

Describing the character of the wine

Appearance
These wines range in colour from light yellow through to gold. Deeper yellow, golden colours are associated with the sweeter styles, particularly when they have aged.

Aromas (by nose) and flavours (by mouth)
The sensory characters associated with any wine depend on the variety/varieties from which it is made. Typically semi-sweet and sweet wines are intensely *floral*, *fragrant* and *fruity*, while the sweeter styles may be more complex, with *honey* and *marmalade* characters.

Flavours, tastes and mouthfeel sensations
The light-bodied styles contain lower sugar levels and generally have a fragrant, flavoursome palate. The finish should be clean and fresh. The medium- to full-bodied styles contain higher sugar levels and may have more intense and complex aroma and flavour profiles. The palate of the sweeter styles should be rich and luscious and have palate weight, good mouthfeel and a long finish. Even though these wines are sweet to very sweet they should not be cloying, but rather should finish with a crispness in the mouth due to balanced acid.

The role of the vineyard

Late harvest

To achieve these higher sugar levels naturally, the grapes are left on the vine beyond the normal harvest period, sometimes up to 4 weeks. °Baumé levels of up to about 15 may be achieved naturally, but this depends on the climatic conditions prevalent during the later stages of ripening. In addition, at these later stages of ripening, the berries can lose water and shrivel. The sugar, acids and flavours present in the berries are concentrated, making the grapes more suitable for the sweeter styles. Wines made from these grapes are referred to as being *late harvested*.

Cane-cut

However, to reach the even higher grape sugar levels required for the sweet to very sweet styles, techniques other than natural ripening and berry shrivel are normally required. A technique sometimes used at the later stages of ripening to induce berry shrivel is to cut the canes of the vine and allow them to hang on the trellis wire. This encourages berry shrivel to occur at a stage when desirable flavours are present and often avoids the development of overripe characters. Wines made from these grapes are sometimes referred to as *cane-cut*.

The influence of winemaking

One way to produce semi-sweet and sweet white wines is to make the wine in a similar manner to dry white wine and to interrupt the fermentation part way through, before all the grape sugars are converted to alcohol. This leaves unfermented sugar (residual sugar) present in the wine. The suitability of any batch of grapes for a particular style relies very much on the sugar content and flavour profile of the grapes at harvest. For example, if the grapes are harvested at about 12° Baumé, and the fermentation is stopped after 11 of these units have been converted to alcohol, the wine will contain about 11% v/v alcohol and about 20 grams per litre of sugar. However, if the grapes are harvested at about 15° Baumé and the fermentation is stopped after 11 of these units have been converted to alcohol, the wine will contain about 11% alcohol and about 70 grams per litre of sugar. When the grapes do attain higher sugar levels, there is usually also a greater intensity of flavours in the grapes and the wines should be more flavoursome and luscious.

Prior to fermentation, some winemakers hold the juice in contact with the skins for a short period before pressing to increase the colour and flavour of the final wine. The juice is fermented with specially selected yeasts to the stage when the winemaker considers the balance of alcohol and sugar is appropriate for the particular style of wine. The fermentation can be stopped by chilling the wine (which reduces yeast activity and also helps to retain fresh fruit characters), by the addition of sulphur dioxide (which prevents microbiological activity) and by filtration (to remove the yeast). After fermentation ceases the wine is clarified, stabilised and bottled.

Another method of making semi-sweet and sweet styles of white wine is to allow the juice to ferment to dryness and then add concentrated grape juice to sweeten the wine to the desired sugar level. Traditionally, the sweet wines from the Hunter Valley, such as Lindemans Hunter River Porphyry, are made this way. The juice is fermented to dryness and then a concentrated and very sweet grape juice is added to increase the sugar level to about 100 grams or more per litre. Although these sweet wines can be enjoyed as fresh young wines, they are better when left to mature in the bottle for a number of years. In time these wines develop lovely apricot, toffee, honey, caramel and marmalade characters to complement their luscious, lingering tastes.

Some examples to try

Several companies including Wolf Blass Wines, Grant Burge, Yalumba, Peter Lehmann and Angove's in South Australia, Brown Brothers in Victoria and Ballandean Estate in Queensland produce semi- sweet and sweet wines from varieties such as Riesling, Gewürztraminer, Frontignac, Muscat Gordo Blanco and Sylvaner.

Semi-sweet styles are normally made to be enjoyed as young wines, while the sweeter styles may benefit from maturation.

Semi-sweet styles complement the spicy cuisine from Asian regions. Sweeter styles match rich desserts.

Sweet white wine styles (botrytis-affected)

Botrytis cinerea is one of the many moulds which occur wherever fruit and vegetables are grown. In most cases, it is unwanted, but for the production of sweet white wines, the growth of this mould on Riesling or Semillon grapes can be highly desirable. As the mould grows, the grapes shrivel and are transformed into constricted packages, highly sugared and flavoured. Picked at just the right time, these grapes make rich, complex, luscious wines. *Botrytis cinerea* plays a role in the sweet Semillon based wines of the Sauternes and Barsac regions of France and the sweet Riesling wines of the Rhine and Mosel vineyards of Germany. Botrytis infection can be found in vineyards all around the world. In Australia it occurs mainly in our cooler, more humid vineyards, but surprisingly the climate of the Riverina region of New South Wales is also very favourable for the growth of botrytis, and wineries from this area produce outstanding botrytis-affected Semillon wines.

Describing the character of the wine

Appearance
The colour of these wines ranges from yellow to deep golden. After being swirled in the glass these wines, being quite viscous, may adhere to the sides of the glass forming syrupy tears.

Aromas (by nose) and flavours (by mouth)
These wines have a mixture of botrytis derived characters and primary and developed fruit aromas and flavours; the intensity of each depends on the degree of botrytis infection, the ripeness of the grapes when they are harvested and the age of the wine. The apricot and marmalade characters are typical of the flavours that come from botrytis-affected grapes. In some wines volatility may be obvious, but should not be regarded as a fault if it is in balance and not too noticeable. It can add lift and complexity to the powerful fruit and botrytis-derived flavours of these wines.

Some descriptors for the mix of aromas and flavours include :

Riesling

citrus, lime, pineapple, quince, crab-apple jelly, floral, perfume, passionfruit, mango, tropical fruit, fruit salad, cumquat, apricot, dried apricot, honey, toffee, caramel, golden syrup and *treacle*. Various combinations will be present in different wines.

Semillon

herbs, spice, cloves, orange peel, mandarin peel, marmalade, apricot, dried apricot, honey, toffee, butterscotch, nutty, almond and *marzipan*. Various combinations will be present in different wines.

Flavours, tastes and mouthfeel sensations
The palate, like the nose, should be rich and complex. Textural features are often described by terms such as *viscous, luscious, rich, oily* and *unctuous*.

Although these wines are luscious and sweet they should finish crisp, the sweetness balanced by refreshing acidity and/or the contribution of phenolics from oak storage, as is the case with Semillon.

The role of the vineyard

Botrytis is one of the many moulds that can grow on grape berries. There are two forms of *Botrytis cinerea*: the desirable form, often called *noble rot*; and the undesirable form, *grey rot*. Infection with noble rot may occur in either spring or autumn. In spring, flower parts can be infected, while in autumn during the later stages of berry ripening, the infection occurs through the intact skin. When climatic conditions are just right, the botrytis spores form on the outside of the berry. To continue their growth they need to get to the sugars and acids in the juice inside the berry. To do this, the roots of the germinating spores pierce the skin, forming a tangled mass in the juice beneath the skin of the berry. As the mould grows, it extracts water from the berries and they shrivel; the skin takes on a purplish colour and the juice becomes more yellow.

While the berries are shrivelling, some extraordinary changes are occurring in the berry. A range of chemical transformations happen. Glycerol, acetic acid, gluconic acid, new flavour compounds and an oxidative enzyme called laccase are produced. Some of the sugar and acids of the berry are broken down as the mould uses them for its energy source. As well, water is lost from the berry. The overall effect is that the juice becomes very viscous, luscious and enriched with complex flavours. Wines made from these grapes have distinctive apricot, marmalade, caramel and honey characters.

The berry may lose up to 50% of its original weight and one berry may produce only a few drops of golden juice with a sugar content of 20° Baumé or greater. The greater the level of infection, the greater the degree of shrivelling and the higher the concentration of sugar and other compounds. Once the desired stage of botrytis infection is reached, judged by the degree of berry shrivel and sugar concentration, the grapes are hand harvested. Not all berries or bunches are affected to the same extent by the botrytis growth, and it may be necessary to pick bunches at different times. Each time only those bunches that have reached the desired stage are selected. Harvesting the vineyard may take place in stages over three or four weeks. This selection and picking of bunches can be very time consuming, but it is necessary if the winemaker aims to make the best wine possible.

It is important that the berry remains intact during the growth of the botrytis, since if the berry splits the undesirable form of botrytis, grey rot, and other infections can grow. As well, juice from split berries can be infected with wild yeast and bacteria (present on the grape skin) and the juice can become volatile. These conditions occur if the humidity is too high or if excessive rain falls during the period of botrytis growth and the berries take up water and split. The bunches are then not suitable for the production of quality botrytis-affected wines.

Mother nature plays a large part in the making of these botrytis style wines. In some vineyards the right conditions will occur every year, whereas in others they may only occur once every few years. It is only in favourable years that this style of wine can be produced naturally.

Yalumba's Heggies vineyard, source of their Botrytis Riesling.

Optimum conditions for desirable botrytis infection and growth are cool, moist, misty mornings followed by warm, dry afternoons. Optimal temperatures are about 15 to 20°C, with humidity around 90%.

Botrytis infection, while highly desirable in white grapes, can be a disaster on red or black grapes, as the enzyme laccase can destroy their colour.

Possible changes in the appearance of the bunch during Botrytis cinerea growth

The golden brown juice oozing from the press.

Botrytis-affected styles are usually sold in half bottles. The production of these wines is quite costly. Not only does the winemaker lose about half the weight of the grapes as they shrivel on the vine or on the trays, but making these wines is also risky and very labour intensive.

The influence of winemaking

The grapes are either crushed and pressed or whole bunches are pressed without initially being crushed. The enzyme laccase can cause oxidation of the juice, and higher than usual additions of sulphur dioxide to the juice may be necessary to inhibit the laccase activity.

The viscous liquid that oozes from the press is clarified by settling and/or filtration. The juice, when free of solids, is pumped to a fermentation vessel and yeast added to initiate the fermentation. The process requires specially selected yeast that can tolerate and ferment these high-sugar juices. Even then the fermentation will be very slow, sometimes taking several weeks or longer to reach the correct balance of alcohol and sugar level required in the final wine.

In the production of these styles of wine the yeast can produce high levels of volatile acidity, as well as fermenting the sugar. It is difficult to make these styles without this influence, but it should not be overpowering. In fact, certain levels can add complexity to the nose and palate. Once the fermentation has reached the desired stage it is stopped and the wine is clarified and cold stabilised. Botrytis-affected grapes contain large polymeric compounds (called glucans) which can block filter pads, and so clarification of the wine can be difficult. Clarification may be achieved by allowing the wine to settle over a long period of time. Some producers use equipment such as centrifuges in combination with various filtration systems to clarify the wine.

Wines made from Riesling grapes are stored in stainless steel tanks, while those made from Semillon grapes may be matured in oak barrels prior to being bottled. These wines are often aged in the bottle before being released.

In regions where natural botrytis infection does not occur, some winemakers make this style of wine by artificially inducing botrytis. Here the grapes are carefully picked and any grapes showing the slightest sign of splitting are rejected. The grapes are laid out in trays in a room with high humidity. They are then sprayed with a solution containing botrytis spores that has been prepared in the laboratory. The high humidity simulates the ideal conditions and encourages the botrytis spores to grow and infect the grapes, causing them to shrivel. At the desired degree of infection, the grapes are crushed and/or pressed and the winemaking commences.

Try these botrytis-affected Riesling and Semillon wines with strongly flavoured cheeses, rich liver patés, dried fruit and nuts, and rich desserts.

BOTRYTIS-AFFECTED RIESLING WINES

Some examples to try

Climatic conditions suitable for the growth of *Botrytis cinerea* regularly occur in vineyards in Coonawarra, Padthaway, Eden Valley and the hills surrounding the Barossa Valley. Yalumba, Hardys, Tollana and Bethany Wineries produce excellent examples of this style. Bethany Select Late Harvest Riesling is produced from grapes where the canes of the vine have been cut and in this year where they have also been affected by *Botrytis cinerea*.

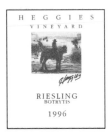

BOTRYTIS-AFFECTED SEMILLON WINES

Some examples to try

The humid, misty mornings followed by drier afternoons, that prevail in late autumn in the Semillon vineyards in the Riverina district are ideal conditions for infection and growth of *Botrytis cinerea*. Highly flavoured, very sweet grapes are used to craft the complex, luscious botrytis-affected Semillon wines. Wineries within the Riverina district, and also some other wineries outside the district who own or source grapes from these vineyards produce these botrytis-affected styles - wines that are acclaimed world wide.

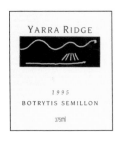

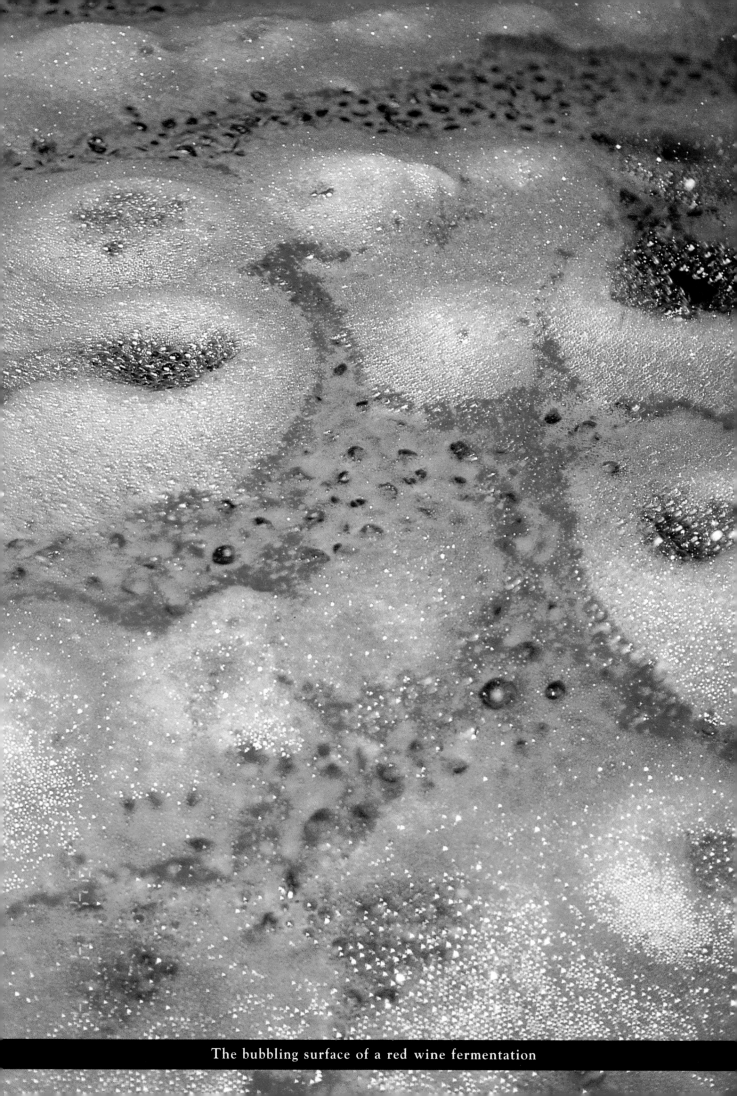

The bubbling surface of a red wine fermentation

DRY RED TABLE WINES

The wines

These are wines made from varieties of grapes coloured red, purple or black. The mixture of juice, skins and seeds is kept together after crushing and during fermentation, until the winemaker decides that sufficient colour, tannin and flavour have been extracted from the skins. Some are ready to drink when young, while others can be enjoyed over many years.

The grape varieties

Grape varieties used in the production of dry red table wines in Australia include:

Barbera
Cabernet Franc
Cabernet Sauvignon
Chambourcin
Durif
Grenache

Malbec
Merlot
Mourvèdre
Nebbiolo
Petit Verdot
Pinot Noir

Ruby Cabernet
Sangiovese
Shiraz
Tarrango
Zinfandel

The wine styles

Australian red wine styles range from light-bodied through to full-bodied wines. They are made from a single variety or a blend of different varieties, and with many different winemaking philosophies.

Light- to medium-bodied styles are normally made from the varieties Grenache and Pinot Noir, but they may also be produced from Shiraz, Cabernet Sauvignon and other varieties if extraction from skins is limited during fermentation. Generally, these wines are low in tannin, do not exhibit strong oak characters and are refreshing, drink-early styles.

Medium- to full-bodied and full-bodied styles are normally made from the varieties Cabernet Sauvignon, Shiraz, Cabernet Franc, Merlot, Malbec, Durif and sometimes from Pinot Noir and Grenache. These wines may show complexity due to the influences of oak storage, racking and age. They are more tannic and may be astringent when young. Most have potential to improve with age. They are often made as blends of the different varieties.

LIGHTER BODIED RED WINES

Rosé styles

In Australia this style of wine is made from a number of grape varieties, but most often from Grenache, Cabernet Sauvignon or Shiraz or sometimes Pinot Noir. The grapes are picked at lower sugar levels (about 10-11° Baumé). Typically they have higher amounts of acid and cherry and raspberry flavours — features necessary for the production of crisp, fruity, light-bodied wines. After crushing, fermentation is conducted at cool temperatures and skin contact is minimal: just one or two days depending on the desired level of flavour, colour and tannin extraction. After transferring the wine to the press, the free run juice is fermented just as if it were a white wine. There is no malo-lactic fermentation or oak contact. The finished wine is normally a bright crimson colour with a light, soft, fruity palate and a crisp acid finish. It is ideal for drinking when young and soon after bottling.

Another method is to drain off part of the fermenting juice at an early stage of a normal red wine fermentation. The lightly coloured run-off juice is fermented and processed similarly to a white wine to produce a rosé style.

The 'Carbonic Maceration' process

A Frenchman, Professor Michael Flanzy, developed a winemaking procedure which has become known as the Carbonic Maceration Process. It is used in the Beaujolais region of France to produce light-bodied, brightly-coloured, fruity styles of red wine from the grape variety Gamay. Bunches of grapes are placed in a container which is then filled with carbon dioxide gas to exclude air. An enzymatic fermentation occurs in the berry. After the bunches of grapes have been stored under these conditions for a number of days, they are crushed, yeast is added and a normal fermentation with short skin contact time is conducted. The aromas and flavours produced during the carbonic maceration stage, often described as cherries, cinnamon and perfumed, become mixed with those of the normal fermentation and a more appealing wine results.

In the mid 1980s the process was adopted by Australian winemakers to produce attractively coloured and fruity light reds from the varieties Shiraz, Cabernet Sauvignon and Grenache. A young Australian winemaker, the late Stephen Hickinbotham, developed a system which greatly improved the handling of grapes during the initial storage period. The grapes are picked by hand and placed directly into plastic bags packed into specially designed boxes. All this occurs in the vineyard. This way there is little damage to the berries and they remain intact. The boxes are transported back to the winery and stored for up to two weeks, allowing the carbonic maceration process to take place inside the berries. The grapes are then crushed and fermented on skins for a short period. The final result is a light, flavoursome red wine.

In the classical method, as practised in France, the bunches of grapes are placed in large fermentation vessels for storage. However, the weight of the bunches crushes some of the grapes at the bottom, producing juice, and some normal fermentation can occur during the storage period. This is referred to as partial carbonic maceration. In practice, winemakers normally process some of the grapes by the carbonic maceration process, some by partial carbonic maceration and others by traditional fermentation. The final wine is made up of a blend of these components.

Other light-bodied red wines

Generally, any variety which has low levels of colour and tannins is likely to produce a lighter bodied wine as long as the alcohol level is not excessively high, regardless of the production technique. Light- to medium-bodied wines are often made from the varieties Tarrango, Chambourcin and Sangiovese.

Some examples to try

Below we highlight some light- to medium-bodied styles that come from different grape varieties and from wineries across Australia.

Houghton Cygnet is a fresh, crisp, lively wine made from early picked Cabernet Sauvignon grapes from vineyards in Western Australia. Consistently one of the best Rosé styles in Australia. Enjoy with lighter meat dishes, salmon and Asian stir fried dishes.

Novello Rosso, from the Chain of Ponds Winery near Gumeracha in South Australia, is a light- to medium-bodied style red wine with fragrant cherry-like aromas and a soft flavoursome palate crafted from a blend of Grenache and Sangiovese grapes - great for summer picnics and alfresco dining.

Chambourcin is a rare variety in Australia. It is a French hybrid variety - a cross between a *Vitis vinifera* grapevine and an unknown species. Cassegrain Reserve Chambourcin from Cassegrain Winery in the Hastings River region of New South Wales is produced from 100% bio-dynamically grown fruit. Typically it is medium-bodied in style with cherry, plum and spicy characters. A portion of the wine is stored in oak barrels before blending. Its concentrated fruit flavours match well with lamb dishes or char-grilled tuna.

Tarrango is an uniquely Australian grape variety, developed by CSIRO scientists in 1965 by crossing the Portuguese red grape variety Touriga with the versatile white grape Sultana. It ripens late and is well suited to warm to hotter regions because ripening then occurs in the cooler months of late March to April. Under these cooler conditions the grapes develop fresh cherry, red berry and spicy flavours while still retaining their acidity. Brown Brothers Tarrango has a vibrant cherry colour with lifted berry aromas and flavours and some hints of spice which lead into a fresh, flavoursome palate. A portion of the wine is made by the carbonic maceration technique. A good accompaniment to an antipasto dish or lighter meat dishes.

PINOT NOIR

The bunches are fairly small and compact, with small round berries coloured dark violet to black. There are many clones of Pinot Noir, and berry size and colour can vary immensely across these clones and further due to site and cultural practices. But even with the best clones, ripened under ideal conditions, Pinot Noir grapes generally have lower amounts of colour and tannin than varieties such as Shiraz and Cabernet Sauvignon. Because of this genetic trait, Pinot Noir grapes tend to produce light- to medium- and medium-bodied red wine styles.

Pinot Noir is one of the world's most ancient varieties. It is likely that a clone of Pinot Noir was brought to Australia by Captain Phillip with the First Fleet in 1788, and it would also have been part of the Busby collection established at Kirkton in the Hunter Valley in the early 1800s. About 150 years later, interest in Pinot Noir was rekindled as consumer interest turned to table wines and especially varietal wines, including Pinot Noir. With Pinot the task was not easy. Nevertheless, a small but ever-growing group of Australian winemakers has taken up the Pinot challenge, and we are now beginning to see premium Pinot Noir wines, coming mainly from our cooler viticultural regions.

Describing the character of the wine

 ### Appearance
The colours of young wines can vary from cherry red to medium plum red. These change to brown tones with age.

 ### Aromas (by nose) and flavours (by mouth)
Primary fruit characters include — *herbs, spice, strawberry, red cherry, raspberry, black cherry, violet, perfume, black pepper, plum, stewed plum, rhubarb, beetroot, blackcurrant* and *prune.*
Developed fruit characters include — *earthy, cowyard, barnyard, gamey, leather, tobacco, bacon fat, mushroom, the smell of forest floor, humus* and *truffle.*
Characters derived from winemaking include:
• barrel fermentation/barrel storage — *spicy, coconut, smoky, chocolate* and *mocha.*
• carbonic maceration — *spicy, cinnamon* and *fruity.*
• addition of whole bunches/stalks — *stemmy, hay* and *stalky.*

 ### Flavours, tastes and mouthfeel sensations
Pinot Noir styles vary from light-bodied wines with more strawberry and red cherry characters through to wines with more body and a higher intensity of raspberry, plum and other richer characters. Generally, these medium-bodied styles are more complex and have more tannin. Their mouthfeel is frequently described as sappy, silky and velvety. The taste of the wine should be soft, have persistency of flavour and finish fresh.

The characters derived from winemaking may be present to varying degrees. Carbonic maceration characters are more likely to be obvious in the lighter styles. Any stemmy or oak characters should not dominate the expression of the primary and/or developed fruit.

The role of the vineyard

As the grapes ripen, the aromas and flavours usually change from strawberry through to raspberry and finally into plum and boiled beetroot characters, the flavours of truly ripe Pinot Noir being somewhat elusive to describe.

Pinot Noir is extraordinarily sensitive to climate. It does not perform well in hotter climates. Yet grown in cool and cool to warm conditions, it can produce grapes with lifted fresh raspberry and plum aromas and flavours and enough acid and tannin to provide structure and texture in the wine. However, even when the right climate is found, this must be coupled with sound vine management, since Pinot Noir is also very sensitive to overcropping. Vines laden with excessive crops struggle to ripen their grapes and generally produce wines that are lightly coloured and lacking in mouthfeel and flavour, sometimes described as strawberry cordial. With time Australian vignerons have come to appreciate the finicky nature of Pinot Noir. They now select their sites more carefully and manage their vines more thoughtfully. Well managed vines grown in cool climates generally produce softly textured medium-bodied wines with fully ripened flavours, some vineyards showing hints of those nebulous fruit characters that ultimately produce great wines.

Of the many clones of Pinot Noir, some have small berries while others have large; some berries have thick skins, others thin. Clones that produce smaller berries are the most sought after. Often a mixture of clones is planted in the same vineyard, the complexity of characters being carried over into the wine. Only in the last few years have some of the top Burgundian clones been available in Australia. Their performance and their wines will be followed with interest; perhaps they will bring us closer to the elusive Pinot experience.

The influence of winemaking

There are many ways to make Pinot Noir wines. Some winemakers use a whole bunch fermentation technique, where the grapes are picked and placed in a tank for a few days prior to crushing. Crushing is sometimes carried out by treading and breaking the grapes with the feet. The fermentation progresses gradually as the juice is released; it is essentially partial carbonic maceration.

Some winemakers only partially crush the grapes, the ferment being a mix of whole and crushed bunches. Others use a technique where the grapes are crushed and then the mixture held at cold temperatures for up to a week prior to the start of fermentation. Other makers crush the grapes, removing the stalks in the process, but then add back varying proportions of stalks to the must. Some drain off a portion of the juice prior to fermentation; the flavours, colour and tannins extracted from the skins are then concentrated in the smaller volume of wine obtained. Often a large parcel of grapes is processed in several different ways to give the winemaker greater blending options in preparing the final wine.

The ferments are typically conducted at higher temperatures (often about 25 to 30°C). These conditions aid in the extraction of colour and tannins, as well as inducing further complexity in the finished wine. After, and sometimes towards the end of, fermentation the wines are transferred to oak barrels, normally of French origin and of varying ages. This process may incorporate subtle barrel ferment as well as desired oak characters to the wine. Although the above techniques can increase complexity, they should not be a major feature. It is the primary and developed fruit characters that give these wines their personalities, those fresh raspberry, violet and plum characters that gradually interweave with the intriguing earthy and gamey expressions that develop with time.

Pinot Noir — style variation

Wines produced from grapes that lack intensity of fruit character and/or wines more influenced by the carbonic maceration technique tend to be more light-bodied. They may have pleasant cherry, strawberry and spice characters but generally lack interest on the palate.

However, most Australian Pinot Noir wines are more medium-bodied, variation in style coming from firstly the vineyard and then the intricacies of winemaking.

Styles of Pinot Noir can be broadly classified as:

• those wines showing more lifted fruit (fresh raspberry and plum characters) and which have round, sappy and silky mouthfeel sensations;
• those wines showing a greater intensity of raspberry, plum, stewed plum and beetroot characters with more complexity derived from winemaking, a round, velvety mouthfeel, but with more weight and tannin texture — bigger, more complex Pinots; and
• aged Pinot Noir wines (the real taste of Pinot?) — with time the primary fruit flavours gradually change to, amongst others, gamey, barnyard and truffle characters and the sweetness of developed fruit and alcohol become more apparent on the palate.

Many companies are now releasing reserve or special wines, which they consider to be their premium examples of Pinot Noir. They may be more expensive but they have more of the quality features that you look for in a good Pinot. While the Burgundians have had centuries to grapple with the intricacies of Pinot Noir, Australian winemakers are only at the beginning of unravelling the Pinot puzzle. There are so many factors involved — clones, climate, soil, yield, canopy management and winemaking approaches, that it will take time to fully appreciate their interactions and to discover the special terroirs within Australia that make great Pinots.

Pinot Noir and Shiraz - many similarities

There may be obvious differences in the palate weight but their characters can be tantalisingly similar. Both can show a spiciness and fresh berry fruit and plum flavours, satiny textures on the palate and seductive gamey characters of age. With maturity their characters become even more similar, although Shiraz, particularly the more powerful and full-bodied styles, can take longer to reach the optimum maturity. Furthermore, aged Sparkling Shiraz, Australia's unique sparkling wine style, can have characters very similar to aged Pinot Noir.

PINOT NOIR — *exciting flavours and velvety textures*

Some examples to try

South Australia
The Adelaide Hills is fast developing a reputation as an area to produce quality Pinot Noir. Good examples are Lenswood, Henschke, Pibbin, Ashton Hills and Hillstowe.

Tasmania
Tasmania's cool climate vineyard areas seem well suited for growing Pinot Noir. Some good producers include Pipers Brook, Delamere, Freycinet, Moorilla and Meadow Bank.

Western Australia
Some fine producers are Leeuwin Estate and Moss Wood from the Margaret River Region, while Wignalls in the Great Southern Region, has a reputation for producing strongly flavoured, complex Pinot Noir wines.

Victoria
The areas spanning Port Phillip Bay (Geelong, the Yarra Valley and Mornington Peninsula) are described by James Halliday as the 'Cool Climate Dress Circle around Melbourne'. It is here that some of Australia's best Pinot Noir wines are produced. Diamond Valley, Yarra Ridge, Coldstream Hills, Long Gully, Tarrawarra, Bannockburn, Scotchmans Hill, Main Ridge and Stoniers are some of the best to try. In the Gippsland area, Bass Phillip is a leading example of the art of making Pinot Noir. Some wineries eg Stoniers produce two labels - their reserve label is a special selection for that vintage.

What are the characters of a good Pinot Noir?
As young wines they are likely to have an intensity of the riper fruit characters (perfumed and with fresh raspberry and plums), some complexity, a round, velvet mouthfeel and freshness. But, allowed to age, these wines have more to offer. With time, the gamey, truffle flavours and apparent sweetness evolve and are more readily discernible and the character of these wines become more intriguing. In the best wines, as well as these aged characters, there are still some reminders of the rich primary fruit, that pleasing textural nature is still there and they retain a freshness belying their age. In tasting Pinot Noir wines, you need to remember that Pinot is not, by nature, a big wine. A feature of premium Pinot is its delicacy, yet with length of flavour. The harmony of its flavours and mouthfeel can give an impression on the palate some tasters describe as seamless, ie perfectly integrated.

Pinot Noir wines, depending on their styles, can complement cold meats, pasta dishes, veal, lamb and a range of game such as duck and pheasant.

GRENACHE

The bunches are short and broad with plump berries varying in colour from reddish pink to blue-black. The wine can be medium-bodied through to full-bodied, often with an array of spicy, berry fruit flavours. Large areas of Grenache vines are planted in Spain and the Rhône Valley of France. It was Australia's most planted black grape variety prior to the mid 1960s, used to produce rosé, dry red and tawny port styles. After that time, plantings of Shiraz and Cabernet Sauvignon became more significant as consumer tastes changed from fortified wines to table wines. Grenache was mainly used in blends, but rarely did its name appear on the wine label. Now it is possible to find labels where Grenache (usually from very old vines) is featured either as a varietal wine or as a major part of the blend. You can discover most of these wines at wineries in the Barossa Valley, Clare Valley and McLaren Vale districts of South Australia.

Describing the character of the wine

Appearance
Typically the wines are light to medium plum red in colour.

Aromas (by nose) and flavours (by mouth)
Primary fruit characters include — spice, floral, perfume, boiled lolly, cherry, raspberry, blackberry, black pepper, plum, stewed plum, prune and *licorice.*
Developed fruit characters include — earthy, meaty, savoury, barnyard and *gamey.*

Flavours, tastes and mouthfeel sensations
Normally the tannin levels are not high and these wines have a soft, fleshy mouthfeel. The alcohol level can be high, this often adding apparent sweetness and viscosity to the palate and also warmth on the finish. Higher alcohol can also add weight to the palate, contributing to the more full-bodied nature of some wines; however, it should not overpower the subtle fruit flavours of the wine.

The role of the vineyard
Many of these vines are very old and grown in warm to hot regions. Grenache vines seem to thrive in these conditions provided they are not cropped too heavily. Many are dry grown bush vines supported by a simple trellis, if any at all.

The influence of winemaking
These wines are made by traditional red winemaking methods with an emphasis on gentle extraction. Some batches may be processed by partial (or full) carbonic maceration techniques and the wines later blended. Normally oak characters are quite subtle as most wines are stored in older oak barrels and/or larger oak vats.

GRENACHE • SHIRAZ • MOURVÈDRE • DURIF

The Rhône connection

The wines from the southern Rhône Valley in France are blends of wines from different grape varieties including Grenache, Syrah and Mourvèdre, the most famous being those from Châteauneuf-du-Pape, where thirteen varieties are used to mould the structure of the final wine. In Australia, Syrah is known as Shiraz and Mourvèdre is also known as Mataro. These varieties formed a large part of the plantings in early Australian vineyards and very old vines, in some cases over a hundred years old, can still be found growing in the Riverland, Barossa Valley and McLaren Vale districts. Wines from these varieties, blended in various combinations, offer a range of flavours from spice and cherries through to plums and chocolates, and often with a touch of earthy development woven in. Typically they have a soft, silky texture. Grenache is added for its spicy and berry fruit flavours and to reduce the weight of the wine in the mouth. The addition of Mourvèdre can provide perfumed and anise flavours and gritty tannins. The structuring of these wines, although following a theme, can result in considerable diversity of style; different flavours will be more pronounced depending on the contribution of each variety to the blend. The proportions of each variety in the blend may vary from year to year due to vintage variation.

Durif is also a Rhône Valley variety. In Australia it is mainly planted in the north-east area of Victoria. It produces wines with intense colour, abundant spice and plum fruit flavours and plenty of tannins, wines that have longevity and require cellaring. You can discover wines from this variety at wineries in the Rutherglen district of Victoria.

Some examples to try

Several wineries are now making varietal wines or blend of these varieties — enjoy the abundant flavours and silky textures of Temple Bruer Cornucopia, a varietal Grenache from Langhorne Creek in South Australia and Penfolds Barossa Valley Old Vines, a blend of Shiraz, Grenache and Mourvèdre. Morris Winery in the Rutherglen Region produces a powerful, rich wine from the variety Durif.

Another way to experience the characters of these varieties is to try the range from d'Arenberg including the Custodian Grenache, The Twenty Eight Road Mourvèdre and d'Arry's Original, a Shiraz Grenache blend.

The wines made from these rustic varieties readily complement the flavours of Mediterranean food.

MERLOT

Merlot is characterised by loose bunches with thin-skinned, small to medium, blue-black berries. As a wine, it is normally used in blends with Cabernet Sauvignon to soften its firmer tannins. On its own, Merlot tends to produce medium-bodied wines with roundness and softness on the palate yet with structure and strength of flavours.

Merlot vines make up a major part of the plantings of Bordeaux. It can be used to make a varietal wine, the most famous being from Chateau Petrus, but most often it is used in blends with Cabernet Sauvignon. In the New World the popularity of varietal Merlot is a more recent phenomenon, its berry and plum flavours and approachable softness on the palate appealing to a wide range of consumers seeking something different to Cabernet Sauvignon or Shiraz.

Describing the character of the wine

Appearance
The colour of young wines is medium red; with age, brown hues become more apparent.

Aromas (by nose) and flavours (by mouth)
Primary fruit characters include — *herbaceous, leafy, fruity, aromatic, perfume, violets, sappy, spice, cherry, raspberry, plum, beetroot, fruitcake, blackcurrant, blackberry, mulberry,* and *rhubarb.*
Developed fruit characters include — *earthy, meaty, truffles, chocolate,* coffee and *tobacco.*
Characters derived from winemaking include —
• barrel fermentation/barrel storage — *spice, coconut, smoky, chocolate, vanilla, pencil shavings, sawdust, toast, cedar, black olives, bacon, dusty, nuts, cashew, burnt* and *toffee.*

Flavours, tastes and mouthfeel sensations
Typically, these wines are soft with supple silky tannins, giving a fleshy mouthfeel, coupled with plenty of berry, plum and fruitcake flavours and a fresh acid finish. Some wines, often from lower yielding older vines, can be more full-bodied with stronger fruit characters; these wines are more tannic when young, only softening after a few years in the bottle.

The role of the vineyard
Merlot appears to grow best in cool to warm climates. Lower yielding vines, soundly managed, tend to produce grapes (and wines) with higher natural acidity and with a greater intensity of riper fruit characters and more tannins.

The influence of winemaking
Merlot is made in a similar way to Cabernet Sauvignon. Some makers use rotary fermenters to extract the flavours and tannins gently. Careful use of oak is required so that the oak characters do not dominate the expression of fruit. Many wines from Merlot are generally lower in flavour and tannins than Cabernet Sauvignon and tend to mature more quickly.

Merlot — style variation

For some time now, Australian winemakers, including those from Irvine, Yarra Yering, Petaluma, Henschke and Capel Vale Wineries have produced wines from Merlot. Other winemakers are now exploring the potential of this variety in a range of areas across Australia. Most wines follow the Merlot theme - round and soft with fleshy texture and plum-like fruit characters and vary mainly in the intensity of fruit, tannin strength and contribution of oak characters.

Some examples to try

The award winning Merlots from Irvine Wines, a small family winery in the Eden Valley region, highlight the quality of the Merlot fruit grown in this area; while Petaluma Coonawarra Merlot has also established a reputation as one of Australia's leading Merlots. The successful Henschke Abbott's Prayer, a wine made from a blend of predominantly Merlot and some Cabernet Sauvignon, from Henschke Lenswood vineyards in the Adelaide Hills justifies their choice of this area for growing Merlot. Vineyards in the hills around the McLaren Vale region are also proving to be good sources of Merlot fruit, with wines from Shottesbrooke and Tatachilla Wineries being softly textured, highly flavoured styles; while in the Geographe region of Western Australia, the winemaking team from Capel Vale Winery draw on over 10 years of experience to craft a richly flavoured, finely structured Merlot.

Merlot wines can match strongly flavoured fish dishes, pasta and most white and lighter red meat dishes - try with baked salmon or roast lamb.

ITALIAN GRAPE VARIETIES

Wine companies such as Brown Brothers, Best's, Coriole and Montrose have been making wine from Italian grape varieties for 10 years or more. As wine consumers become more accepting and knowledgeable of the diversity of wine and the enjoyment that this brings to drinking wine, there is a growing interest in wines made from Italian grape varieties. There are about 2000 grape varieties in Italy, many being native varieties grown in regional areas. The most well known red wine grape varieties are Nebbiolo, Barbera and Sangiovese, while others include Dolcetto and Teroldego. In the Piedmont region of Italy, Nebbiolo is used to make the famous Borolo and Barbaresco styles, full-bodied and richly flavoured wines. In the Tuscany region Sangiovese is used to make medium-bodied fruity styles known as Chianti. Currently in Australia there are only small areas planted with Italian varieties, but this is changing as these vines are being planted in a range of regions. You can expect to see a diversity of styles emerging as Australian winemakers investigate the sites and winemaking practices that best suit these varieties. Typically they are great food wines; their intriguing characters, ranging from spice and berry fruit through to complex savoury tones, with softer tannin structure, complement the flavours of a range of foods and particularly Mediterranean style dishes.

Below we provide a guide to some of the characters that you may experience in the different styles. Wines may have varying influences of oak treatment, but here we concentrate on the fruit derived characters, primary and developed, which are the attractive features of these wines.

Some of the characters of wines made from Italian grape varieties —
Barbera — light- to medium-bodied.
Descriptors: *spicy, nutmeg, berry fruits, cherry, plums, licorice, savoury* and *earthy*.
Typically wines with higher acid giving freshness with berry fruit characters.
Wines with medium-term ageing potential.

Dolcetto — light- to medium-bodied.
Descriptors: *spicy, cinnamon, cherry, fruity, fragrant, tobacco* and *almonds*.
Generally a fruity, early drinking style of wine.

Nebbiolo — medium- to full-bodied and full-bodied.
Descriptors: *perfumed, violets, roses, raspberry, plums, fruitcake, licorice, truffles, tar, nutmeg* and *savoury*.
Wines can be highly coloured and tannic when young, but age superbly, when their developed characters enhance those of roasted meat dishes.

Sangiovese — medium-bodied.
Descriptors: *fruity, cherry, spice, raspberry, blackberry, plums, earthy, nutty* and *savoury*. Typically the wines have subtle but complex flavours.
Some examples to try
As a guide to these emerging styles we suggest you try the wines from Montrose in New South Wales, Brown Brothers, Best's and Dromana Estate in Victoria and Coriole in South Australia.

OTHER VARIETIES
Cabernet Franc
A variety typically used in structuring blends. As a single varietal wine it is generally a medium- to full-bodied style but lighter in colour, flavours and tannins than Cabernet Sauvignon. Its characters can be described as *spice*, *raspberry*, *pepper*, *plum* and *dusty*.

Knappstein Wines in the Clare Valley produce a good example of a varietal Cabernet Franc with spicy, cherry and raspberry flavours and some dusty oak characters supported by firm tannins.

Zinfandel
A red grape variety predominantly planted in California and produced in a range of styles from a White Zinfandel through to more robust reds. In Australia, Zinfandel is used to make a medium- to full-bodied dry red wine style with *herbal*, *spicy*, *cherry*, *rhubarb* and *ripe berry* flavours. Cape Mentelle in Western Australia and Thistle Hill in New South Wales are wineries that make a varietal Zinfandel.

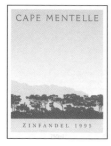

The Cape Mentelle Zinfandel is normally a powerful wine, full of concentrated spice, berry and charry oak flavours intermingled with powdery tannins.

CABERNET SAUVIGNON

The bunches are small and conical with small, bluish, thick-skinned berries. In these smaller berries the ratio of skin to juice is high; thus in berries with plenty of colour when extraction occurs during winemaking, the wines can be highly coloured and some can also be quite tannic.

Regarded by many as the most noble of red wine grapes, Cabernet Sauvignon is one of the major grape varieties in Bordeaux. It is planted in most wine producing regions of the world, including Australia. By the 1860s, Cabernet Sauvignon vines were planted in the Yarra Valley. Around this time the vineyards of Yering, Yeringberg and St Hubert's were established. It is rumoured that Paul de Castella, who set up Victoria's first vineyard at Yering, obtained vine cuttings from the famous Chateau Lafite in Bordeaux. Regrettably, the Yering vineyard did not survive, but the site was replanted in 1988 and now all three original Yarra Valley vineyards are once more producing wines. Some of Australia's best Cabernet Sauvignon wines come from locations as geographically diverse as Coonawarra in South Australia, the Yarra Valley in Victoria and Margaret River in Western Australia.

Grown in the right climate and soundly managed, it can produce wines that are medium- to full-bodied with powerful flavours and great structure. As is the practice in Bordeaux, Australian winemakers often blend Cabernet Sauvignon with other varieties including Merlot, but additionally they have created a unique Australian blend, a partnership of Cabernet Sauvignon and Shiraz.

What you may see on the label
Wines are labelled Cabernet Sauvignon and/or Cabernet Sauvignon blends. Where the wine is a blend of a number of varieties, all the varieties may be shown on the label or the wine may be labelled as a 'brand name' for example Orlando Jacob's Creek, Mildara Jamiesons Run and Lindemans Pyrus. Some of these wines may still be labelled 'Claret', a generic term usually used in Australia to describe a medium- to full-bodied red wine with a firm finish. With time this term will disappear from labels of Australian wine, according to the agreement between the Australian Wine Industry and the EEC.

Describing the character of the wine

Appearance
The colour can vary from intense red with purple tinges in young wines through to brick red as the wine matures, and finally to the brown hues of aged wine.

Aromas (by nose) and flavours (by mouth)
Primary fruit characters include — *capsicum, tomato leaf, vegetative, herbaceous, cinnamon, menthol, eucalyptus, leafy, minty, violet, perfumed, dusty, berry, plum, stewed rhubarb, cooked beetroot, blackcurrant (cassis), black olive, prune, licorice* and *inky.*
Developed fruit characters include — *earthy, dusty, cigar-box, cedar, chocolate, tobacco, coffee* and *mocha.*
Characters derived from winemaking include:
• barrel fermentation/barrel storage — *spice, coconut, smoky, chocolate, vanilla, pencil shavings, sawdust, toast, cedar, black olives, bacon, dusty, nuts, cashew, burnt* and *toffee.*

Flavours, tastes and mouthfeel sensations
The tannins impart firm astringency to the palate. Young wines with large amounts of tannin can give a huge mouth puckering sensation, which is not necessarily unpleasant but can mask the other features of the wine. As the wine ages, the impact of the tannins diminishes and the tannins, especially in the better wines, give a fine grainy feeling in the mouth. Most Cabernet Sauvignon wines would have been stored in oak barrels, and oak characters may be present on the nose and palate. Such characters should be well-integrated with the other features of the wine. An 'apparent sweetness' may be perceived on the palate. This may come from the developed 'ripe' fruit characters and/or glycerol and/or alcohol. This impression may be more obvious in older wines.

The role of the vineyard

As the grapes ripen, the aromas and flavours generally change from herbaceous through to perfumed, dusty, minty, then to licorice, blackcurrant and black olive characters.

Herbaceous (grassy) and vegetal (capsicum-like) characters are most pronounced in wines that come from vines grown in cold to cool sites, with high yields and shaded canopies. The intensity of these characters can be lessened by manipulation of the vine's canopy to increase the amount of sunlight within the canopy through improved trellising and/or practices such as removing leaves around bunches, but generally Cabernet Sauvignon is not particularly suited to colder sites. Often, even if the vines are well managed, the wines are high in acid, low in alcohol, colour and body and noticeably herbaceous.

Grapes grown in cool to warm and warm climates produce medium- to full-bodied wines with mainly mint, berry and blackcurrant characters. Not only do wines made from these grapes normally have more naturally balanced acidity, but they are also more richly coloured and flavoured. The tannins are also more finely structured. However, it is important to appreciate that in cooler regions, vintage variation can be quite pronounced and varietal characters may change from year to year. Generally, wines from lower yielding vines have greater intensity of blackcurrant characters and finer palate structure. Wines from grapes grown in hot conditions and with sound vine management generally have attractive berry characters but often have less intensity of flavour and colour than wines from warm regions.

The influence of winemaking

The finer points of making Cabernet Sauvignon wine lie in the art of the wine-maker to balance the power of the fruit with the extraction of colour and tannins and additional characters derived from the winemaking process. During their making some wines are left on skins for an extended period after the completion of fermentation, whilst others are barrel fermented. Racking can also play an important part in modifying the structure of these wines. Most winemakers prefer to ferment/store their Cabernet Sauvignon wine in French oak barrels. Because Cabernet Sauvignon wines are frequently blended with other varieties, the flavours and structure of the final wine depend on the proportion of the different varieties and where they are grown.

Many of these wines require ageing to allow the tannins to mature and soften, to make the wine more pleasurable on the palate, and to enable the full enjoyment of the flavours that develop with time.

The art of blending

Some wines made from Cabernet Sauvignon have a structural dip or 'hollow centre', often referred to by tasters as a 'doughnut effect'. In these wines the flavour weight is obvious when the wine enters the mouth and on the finish but there is little depth in the middle of the palate. Often winemakers blend Cabernet Sauvignon with various proportions of other varieties to improve the weight of the middle palate and to soften the impact of the tannins. Merlot is used to give a more rounded mouthfeel and to add softness to the palate. Often Shiraz is added to the blend to add richness and strength and to fill out the middle palate. At other times Malbec is used. Sometimes Petit Verdot is added, normally in small amounts, to strengthen the tannin structure. The wines can be blends of different varieties from either the same or different regions. The flexibility to blend across varieties and regions gives our winemakers the opportunity to craft a wine of a desired style and quality.

Methoxypyrazines
Scientists have identified the chemical group called methoxypyrazines as the compounds responsible for many of the herbaceous and vegetative aroma and flavour characters. You may hear some tasters refer to wines with these vegetative characters as having strong pyrazine character.

These compounds are present in grapes and wines at very low concentrations (parts per billion) but are very potent and easily detected. Generally they are not seen as desirable compounds, hence the need to minimise them with good site selection and canopy management.

Medium-bodied

Normally these wines are blends of varieties and regions. They are wines which have attractive flavours with a soft mouthfeel and some oak influence. Each year they are made to a consistent style and offer an appealing introduction to the flavours of Australian wine at an affordable price. These represent some of Australia's most popular and top selling red wines.

Some examples to try

Hardys, Tyrrell's, Orlando and Penfolds are some of the producers of this range of wines. Sometimes Cabernet Sauvignon is the major component, while in others Shiraz is the dominant variety.

Jacob's Creek Vineyard in the Barossa Valley - one of the vineyards that contributes to the Jacob's Creek blend

Medium- to full-bodied

Across the style range you will find wines made from either 100% Cabernet Sauvignon or blends of Cabernet Sauvignon and other varieties. The make-up of the blend will depend mainly on how the winemaker wishes to structure the palate profile of his/her wines.

Capsicum-like characters may be more obvious in wines from cooler regions and seasons. Generally though, these medium- to full-bodied styles show leafy, minty, dusty and distinctive blackcurrant characters. Typically these wines have length of flavour and firm astringency from the tannins. Cabernet Sauvignon wines are usually complemented with French and/or American oak flavours.

Broadly these wines can be grouped into two styles
• medium- to full-bodied wines with rich, complex primary fruit flavours, more of a leafy, minty, dusty, plum and licorice nature, with a touch of blackcurrant, fine grain tannins — finely structured, elegant wines with further complexity coming from oak (usually French) and age; and

• bigger wines with a richness of fruit character similar to the above but generally towards the plum, licorice and blackcurrant tones. They may be more extracted and when young the tannin sensation can be quite mouth puckering. Oak characters (often American as well as French) may be obvious in the flavours of the wine; however, in the better wines the power of the fruit can well match the greater oak emphasis.

Some examples to try
In the medium- to full-bodied style bracket you will find good Cabernet Sauvignon wines and/or blends of various styles from all our wine producing regions. Expect to see differences in the characters of these wines not only between regions, but also within a region from year to year due to vintage variation. Australian winemakers are now making their wines to be softer and more approachable when young, and many of these wines can be enjoyed either as young wines or when more matured.

Western Australia
Many wineries in the south-west corner of Western Australia produce quality Cabernet Sauvignon wines. The wines from the Margaret River region often being outstanding - beautifully balanced with freshness, rich fruit characters and fine grained tannins; Cullen, Moss Wood and Cape Mentelle consistently producing fine examples.

What are the characters of a good Cabernet Sauvignon and/or a Cabernet Sauvignon Blend?
Different wines will have characters that appeal to different people. In younger wines look for rich varietal character, particularly those flavours towards the riper end of the flavour spectrum (minty through to blackcurrant) and layers of additional flavours from oak and age influence. The feel of the tannins will be firmer but should still be approachable. Look for persistence of flavour and freshness on the finish. The appeal of more mature wines is the greater complexity as the chocolate, cigar box, coffee and 'sweet fruit' flavours of maturity build along with mellow tannins that coat the mouth, coupled with fresh balanced acidity and long lingering flavours on the finish. In the best wines, these come together in such a way that the overall impression is a harmony of all their characters.

New South Wales

The climate of the Mudgee region seems to be well suited for growing grapes for red wines. Cabernet Sauvignon is a top performer here, typified by the elegant, intensely flavoured wines from Huntington Estate - wines that offer great cellaring potential. Lake's Folly Winery has produced many fine Cabernet Sauvignon wines from its Hunter Valley vineyard and is regarded as one of the leading producers. Tyrrell's Old Winery Cabernet Merlot represents a blend of fruit from a range of premium regions including McLaren Vale and Coonawarra. There are also exciting examples from new wineries and new regions in this state, such as Bluegrass Cabernet Sauvignon from Saddlers Creek Winery in the Hunter Valley and McWilliam's Barwang Cabernet Sauvignon from their new vineyards around Young.

Victoria

Classic examples are made in the Yarra Valley and the Mornington Peninsula regions. Oakridge Estate, a long standing producer of premium Yarra Valley wines, crafts its Cabernet Sauvignon and Merlot blend from grapes from low yielding vines to give an elegantly structured wine with pleasing fine grained tannins. Vineyards that span the central-west area, around Bendigo, Ballarat, Avoca and Kyneton are the source of many premium Cabernet Sauvignon wines and we feature the Balgownie Estate Cabernet Sauvignon on page 133.

South Australia

The areas around Reynella, McLaren Vale and Langhorne Creek, just south of Adelaide, are highly regarded for their premium wines from this variety, for example fruit sourced from Langhorne Creek is used in structuring Wolf Blass Grey Label Cabernet Sauvignon. Wineries in the Clare Valley district also produce some top Cabernets - wines that are often densely coloured and with flavours that are rich and concentrated. Taylors is one of the wineries in the Clare Valley Region to have established a large following for its flavoursome, well balanced Cabernet Sauvignon wine. Hardys Insignia is a blend of Cabernet Sauvignon and Shiraz, reflecting the art of blending, not only between different varieties but of fruit from a range of regions, including the Riverland, Padthaway, Coonawarra and McLaren Vale.

Coonawarra is Australia's most famous red wine producing region and it is here that you discover some of the best Cabernet Sauvignon wines, not only in Australia but in the world. Wineries located in other parts of Australia also source grapes from this premium area. Many excellent wines are consistently produced from vineyards in this small but special vineyard area and here we highlight the wines from Hollick, Balnaves, Orlando, Penfolds and Leconfield Wineries. These wines show the diversity of style from this region and offer a great introduction to the taste of Coonawarra.

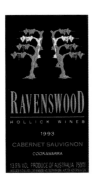

Cabernet Sauvignon wines match a large range of full-flavoured foods including duck, game, lamb and beef.

Experience the character of Cabernet Sauvignon from Coonawarra, Langhorne Creek, Clare and Bendigo

THE VINEYARD

Grapes are sourced from Mildara's vineyards located in the famous strip of 'terra rossa' soil in the Coonawarra region in South Australia. The cool ripening conditions of this area lead to grapes with intensity of flavours and balanced acidity.

Only the best vineyard sites from the 'terra rossa' strip in Coonawarra are selected for sourcing grapes for Robertson's Well. Vineyard practices aimed at achieving more open canopies and lower yields ensure full ripening, developing strong mint and blackcurrant characters in the grapes at harvest.

Langhorne Creek in South Australia, the source of grapes for the Grey Label, is one of Australia's top red wine grapegrowing regions. The warm ripening temperatures and relief of vine stress from cooling breezes from Lake Alexandrina are ideal for producing grapes with powerful fruit flavours and sturdy tannins.

THE WINERY

Grapes from separate sections of the vineyards are fermented separately in stainless steel tanks; regular mixing of the cap ensures full colour and flavour extraction. After fermentation the wine is transferred to French and American oak barrels for maturing for about twelve months. The wines are then tasted and the final blend components determined. Wine from the blend is then stored in oak for a further three to four months prior to bottling.

Initially the wine is fermented in stainless steel tanks and then part way through the fermentation it is transferred to French and American oak barrels to complete the fermentation. After this process the wine is racked into new barrels and matured for about eighteen months before bottling. Only the best oak barrels are used to match the power of the characters of this wine.

The grapes from different vineyards are fermented separately. Part way through the fermentation the wines are assessed and those with intensity of eucalypt and mint characters are selected to finish their fermentation in new American and French oak barrels. After completion of fermentation the wines are stored in barrels for a further twenty four months maturation prior to bottling.

THE CHARACTER OF THE WINE

Typically a medium- to full-bodied wine. Expect to experience strong mint and berry flavours intermingled with distinct smoky, vanillin oak characters, coupled with a soft puckering tannin sensation. Medium term (four to eight years) cellaring potential.

A premium quality wine. A full-bodied wine with intense mint and blackcurrant fruit characters complemented with well integrated oak features and plenty but pleasing mouth coating tannins. A well structured wine with potential to cellar up to ten years or more.

A full-bodied style showing depth and complexity of flavour, typically regional fruit characters of eucalypt, mint along with vanillin oak tones. With time the wine will develop chocolate, tobacco tones of age and the initially firm tannin sensation will soften. Cellaring potential is normally six to ten years.

SOME MATCHING FOOD SUGGESTIONS

Enjoy with fresh tomato and egg plant pasta.

Full-flavoured meat dishes such as roast fillet of beef or kangaroo match the flavours and texture of Robertson's Well.

A range of dishes complement the characters of this wine — venison, pasta dishes and seasoned rack of lamb.

The stories behind the labels

Annie's Lane

Annie Wayman was a legend in the Clare Valley. She often supplied sandwiches and a warm drink to the workers who pruned and harvested the vines in the early days of the development of the Clare region, about the turn of the century. One evening Annie's horse and cart got bogged in a lane adjacent to one of the valley's best vineyards. There was great activity as the vineyard workers helped Annie restore her cart to firm ground. Thereafter the locals referred to the lane as Annie's Lane. The wine from these vineyards, is made in the magnificent century old cellars at Quelltaler Winery.

Balgownie Estate is situated near Bendigo in Central Victoria. This cool to warm temperature during ripening are ideal for the accumulation of colour and flavour as well as retained higher acid levels in the grapes at harvest. The grapes from which the wine is made are 100% estate grown.

The Cabernet Sauvignon grapes are sourced from Annie's Lane vineyard at Polish Hill and other selected Clare Valley vineyards. The Merlot component comes from low yielding old wines sited around the historic Quelltaler winery.

Regular but gentle plunging and pumping over of the cap during fermentation provides good extraction of colour and flavour and helps build the tannin structure. After fermentation the wine is stored in French oak hogsheads for about twelve months prior to bottling.

The wine is fermented (sometimes up to two weeks) in small 4 tonne open fermenters with regular plunging and pumping over. It is then stored in new and older French oak barrels for a period of about fifteen months prior to bottling.

Quelltaler Winery

Robertson's Well

John 'Poor Man' Robertson, was one of the most illustrious pioneers of the Coonawarra region and at one time ran 60,000 sheep on his property. In the 1840s Robertson commissioned the sinking of a large well deep into the hard layer of limestone in search of water. Part of the station was then called Robertson's Well; a name which has now become the trademark of the premium Cabernet Sauvignon wine produced each year from Coonawarra by Mildara.

An elegant medium- to full-bodied style normally with mint and blackcurrant primary fruit characters, balanced with pleasing oak tones. These flavours are complemented by supple tannins and fresh acidity, features which contribute to its fine structure and high quality. Suggested cellaring potential — five to ten years.

A wine of genuine class and structure showing great depth and length of fruit characters intermingled with fine grained tannins and with the oak playing a subtle supporting role. Cellaring potential — three to eight years.

Enjoy with a dish of Osso Bucco Milanese or Kangaroo fillets with bush tomato sauce.

Fillets of spring lamb with shredded beetroot or Pheasant with morel and wine sauce blend perfectly with the characters of Annie's Lane.

Robertson's Well and vineyard

SHIRAZ

Characteristically the bunches are long and cylindrical and are made up of small to medium oval berries, variously coloured from light purple to intensely purple black. The berries are prone to decrease in size (through water loss) towards the end of ripening and may shrivel.

The French and Americans call it Syrah and in Australia we call it Shiraz. Its most likely origins are in the Rhône Valley area of France where it has been grown for hundreds of years. Australia is the only other country with significant plantings of this variety. Shiraz cuttings were probably first brought to Australia in 1832 by James Busby as part of the collection of vines that he gathered during his European tour. Shiraz is a very versatile variety and produces a myriad of styles ranging from light-bodied through to big full-bodied wines.

Describing the character of the wine

Appearance
The colour of young wines varies from medium red through to deep rich purple/red, almost black, in the bigger wine styles. As these wines mature, they progress through various shades and intensities of red to red brown and then the distinctly tawny colour of age.

Aromas (by nose) and flavours (by mouth)
Primary fruit characters include — *herbs, spice, menthol, cinnamon, raspberry, dark cherry, mint, eucalypt, mulberry, blackberry, black pepper, plum, aniseed, licorice, blackcurrant, black olives, sarsaparilla, stewed plum, chocolate, jammy* and *raisin.*
Developed/mature fruit characters include — *chocolate, earthy, barnyard, cowyard, prune, feral, cigar-box, coffee, gamey, meaty, salami, savoury* and *leather.*
Characters derived from winemaking include:
• barrel fermentation/barrel storage — *spice, coconut, smoky, chocolate, vanilla, pencil shavings, sawdust, toast, cedar, black olives, bacon, dusty, nuts, cashew, burnt* and *toffee.*

Flavours, tastes and mouthfeel sensations
These wines generally have an abundance of flavour, often with a perceived mid-palate sweetness derived from ripe fruit and/or high alcohol. Complexity comes with time, as the primary fruit characters slowly mature. Oak characters may be incorporated in the flavour and structure of these wines. Often the mouthfeel is described as silky, velvety or smooth. Most wines give a firm tannin impression on the palate, which varies from big, but soft, chewy, furry, mouth puckering sensations in young wines, to a more supple feeling in older wines. Some wines will be high in alcohol (greater than 13%v/v) and may impart a spicy, hot feeling at the back of the mouth when swallowed, sometimes seen as a fault. However, these higher alcohol levels may not be as obvious in well flavoured and balanced wines, with the fruit intensity well able to handle such levels of alcohol.

What you may see on the label
Sometimes Shiraz based wines are labelled Hermitage, a name used by some producers because the variety Shiraz originally came from the Hermitage area in the Rhône Valley of France. On other labels of Shiraz, you may still see the word 'Burgundy,' a generic term sometimes used in Australia to describe a medium- to full-bodied red wine with a soft finish. With time the names Hermitage and Burgundy will not be used on labels of Australian wine.

The role of the vineyard

In well managed vines, as the grapes ripen the aroma and flavour compounds generally change from herbal, spice, red cherry and raspberry through to mint, plum, black pepper, blackberry, licorice, mulberry, black olives, chocolate and jammy in very ripe grapes. The combination of these flavours and their intensity vary from vineyard to vineyard.

Bunches of Shiraz grapes showing various stages of shrivel

Shiraz grapes grown in cooler climates, typically produce wines with distinctive black pepper tones, along with berry fruit and licorice characters and with higher natural acidity. The mouthfeel of the wines is more medium-bodied. Wines from grapes grown in warmer climates may show blackberry, mulberry, plum and licorice, as well as spice and earthy characters. Wines from well managed vines in these climates (and where the grapes ripen to sugar levels around 13° Baumé or more) can be more full-bodied and have plum, stewed plum, licorice and chocolate types of aromas and flavours. These grapes, fully ripened and picked 'at just the right time', can produce richly flavoured and textured full-bodied wines. Grapes grown in hotter climates generally have lower acidity and lower intensity of flavour and colour than grapes grown in cool to warm climates. Grapes from hotter climates typically produce wines with more raspberry but also with blackberry and plum characters.

Towards the end of ripening, and particularly in hotter climates, the grapes may start to shrivel; this is a finely balanced stage in the ripening process. If grapes are left too long on the vine, the nature of the fruit characters may change and the overwhelming aromas and flavours in the wine can be described as jammy and raisin. It is better to pick the grapes before this stage, and this is why the grape composition is closely monitored during ripening. In some situations, where the acid level of the grapes has decreased significantly during ripening, tartaric acid may need to be added to juice prior to winemaking to adjust the titratable acidity and pH. Often winemakers taste the grapes, so that they can more readily decide when to harvest the vineyard.

Shiraz grapes at various stages of shrivel

The intensity of flavours that develop in grapes in any one vineyard depends very much on the vineyard management practices. Lower yielding vines (often less than 10 tonnes per hectare) with well managed canopies and often with limited, but regulated irrigation can produce grapes with concentrated flavours, giving wines with rich, intense and complex characters. Higher yielding vines can produce excellent wine if the vines are well managed; however, grapes from vines with excessively high yields generally produce wines lacking in colour, flavour intensity and structure.

The influence of winemaking

Shiraz wines are made in a variety of ways, but generally with techniques that give medium to high extraction of colour and flavour from the skins. The big, full-bodied styles are often made from riper grapes (about 13° Baumé), are 'worked a lot more' (pumped over, plunged, etc) during fermentation and may be partially barrel fermented. Some wines are still fermented in open fermenters. Many wines are matured in American oak and thus may show vanillin and other oak characters along with their intense berry flavours.

Medium-bodied

These medium-bodied wines typically have spicy, cherry and raspberry aromas and flavours of moderate intensity. Generally they are clean, well-made wines with attractive flavours with some oak influence and moderately priced. Often they are wines blended from Shiraz, Cabernet Sauvignon and other red wine varieties and labelled as brand names. They include some of the wines described under this category in the Cabernet Sauvignon section on page 128.

Medium- and medium- to full-bodied

Typically these medium- and medium- to full-bodied styles have ripe berry fruit characters with distinctive black pepper tones; the cooler the climate, generally the more overt the peppery character, and the higher the natural acidity. Wines from grapes grown in cool to warm climates have more palate weight and stronger fruit characters (blackberry and plum) and spice apparent with the peppery tones. In quality wines, the spice, mint and peppery characters should be only part of the flavour spectrum and should complement ripe berry fruit, plum and licorice characters. Typically these are finely structured wines with moderate tannin levels. Oak characters may form part of the make-up of the wine but should be well integrated.

Some examples to try

It is difficult to be specific as to the characters in any one district because of vintage variation and differences in vineyard management practices. The intensity of particular varietal tones may vary from vineyard to vineyard and from year to year. As a general theme, along with rich berry flavours, Shiraz wines from Coonawarra can have mint and finely ground pepper tones, those from Great Western can have distinctive black peppercorn expressions and wines from Margaret River and the Great Southern regions can also show a spiciness and pepperiness, while those from Padthaway often have more licorice-like characters.

Victoria

Some of Australia's best cool climate Shiraz wines come from western and central Victoria. Good examples are the wines from Knight's Granite Hills, Best's, Seppelt, Mount Langhi Ghiran, Jasper Hill, Dalwhinnie, Mount Avoca, Mitchelton, Taltarni and Tisdall Wineries. In the wines below expect to see distinctive pepper tones and rich, berry flavours supported by silky tannins.

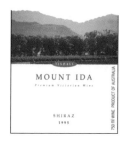

South Australia

Although Coonawarra may be well-known for wines from Cabernet Sauvignon the region also produces excellent Shiraz wines including those from Wynns, Bowen Estate, Hollick, Redman, Brand's, Leconfield and Majella. Majella Shiraz exemplifies the combination of elegance and power that can come from premium Coonawarra Shiraz. Although you do not see many wines labelled as regional wines from the Padthaway district, vineyards here produce Shiraz grapes that contribute to high quality wines such as Hardys Eileen Hardy and Orlando Lawson. In the Barossa Ranges near Kyneton, very old Shiraz vines provide fruit for Henschke's famous Mount Edelstone single vineyard Shiraz wine.

Western Australia

Wineries in the south-west corner of this state typically produce wines with spice, pepper and strong berry fruit characters. Reliable producers include Cape Mentelle, Killerby, Evans & Tate, Plantagenet, Moondah Brook, Goundrey and Alkoomi. Killerby Shiraz is packed full of complex flavours, mulberries, blackberries, plums, cloves, pepper and some chocolate tones while being balanced with firm yet soft tannins and subtle oak characters.

New South Wales

Traditionally Shiraz wines from the Hunter Valley are medium- to full-bodied styles with spice, cherry, raspberry and plum primary fruit characters; with age, these wines develop rustic, earthy, barnyard and light leathery tones and a soft, velvet mouthfeel. Some wines develop what is called 'the Hunter character' described variously as savoury, leathery and 'sweaty saddle'. Tyrrells, Tulloch, Lindemans, Pepper Tree, Arrowfield, Rothbury, McGuigan Brothers, Hunter Ridge, Brokenwood and Rosemount are some of the Hunter Valley wineries where you can try Hunter Valley Shiraz. The McGuigan family have many years experience with Shiraz in the Hunter Valley - their Millennium 2000 is a medium-bodied wine with plenty of rich cherry flavours and a soft round mouthfeel, a good introduction to Hunter Valley Shiraz.

Hunter Valley producers also source fruit from other regions in structuring some of their wine. Brokenwood Shiraz is a blend of Hunter Valley, McLaren Vale and King Valley Shiraz. The contribution of McLaren Vale fruit adds richness and body to the wine. Viticulture is expanding rapidly in New South Wales with new regions opening up in many parts of the state including the areas in the central highlands around Young, Orange and Forbes. McWilliam's Barwang Shiraz displays cool climate fruit characters of spice, cherry and violet tones combined with dusty, vanillin, oak characters. A new label from a well established area is Rosemount Estate's Mountain Blue, crafted from grapes sourced from their recently acquired vineyards in Mudgee - a powerfully flavoured Shiraz, Cabernet Sauvignon blend with underlying rich but soft tannins.

Queensland
Shiraz performs well across a range of climatic conditions and in the vineyards sited in the higher altitudes surrounding Stanthorpe, grapes are produced that lead to wines with a richness of berry fruit and spice and pepper tones. Good examples to try include Ballandean Estate, Bald Mountain and Preston Peak.

Full-bodied styles
These mainly come from vineyards in warmer climates. Typically they are packed with a range of flavours including spice, plum, mulberry, blackberry and licorice, and with maturity earthy and chocolate characters develop. Expect to see plenty of mouth puckering tannins giving a soft furry sensation in the mouth in young wines, but with time these mature to give a supple, silky texture. Often, these wines have complex aromas and flavours coming from the array of primary and developed fruit characters intermingled with expressive American oak flavours, which in some wines can be quite pronounced.

Victoria
Wineries in the Rutherglen area are famous for their big, richly flavoured mouth filling Shiraz wines; from wineries such as Stanton and Killeen, All Saints, Baileys, Campbells, Morris and Chambers.

 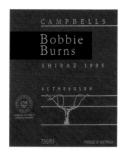

South Australia

Full-bodied Shiraz wines are produced in many of South Australia's wine regions. Typically the wines from the Murray Valley have plenty of berry fruit flavours and are soft and approachable when young and Kingston Estate Shiraz is a good example. Some wines are blends from different regions, eg Saltram Classic Shiraz, a wine with rich berry fruit flavours, soft tannins and integrated oak, is made from fruit sourced from across several South Australian regions.

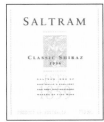

The Clare district produces Shiraz wines across the style spectrum. The full-bodied styles are packed full of flavour and tannins; they are produced at wineries such as Wendouree, Leasingham and Jim Barry Wines. Leasingham Classic Clare Shiraz shows depth and richness of flavours with mature soft tannins. 'The Armagh', from Jim Barry Winery, combines intense spice and mulberry fruit with strong American oak characters. It is one of Australia's most famous red wines and the grapes are sourced from low yielding old vines.

The area around McLaren Vale is one of the best and most consistent areas in Australia for growing grapes for the making of full-bodied Shiraz wines. Award winning wines are regularly produced at wineries such as Haselgrove, d'Arenberg, Kay's, Richard Hamilton, Pirramimma, Coriole, Seaview, Chapel Hill, Wirra Wirra, Tatachilla, Scarpantoni, Fox Creek and Woodstock. Many of these wines come from very old vines. In the wines below expect great depth of ripe fruit characters matched with powerful tannins and well integrated oak features.

Enjoy Shiraz wines with a range of full-flavoured foods including duck, lamb, beef and kangaroo.

Dotted throughout the Barossa Valley and the surrounding ranges, patches of very old Shiraz vines produce grapes which are crafted into a unique Australian style of wine — wines that show concentrated fruit flavours all wrapped up in plenty of ripe tannins. Vineyards have been passed down through the generations, and in one such vineyard, Henschke's Hill of Grace, situated close to the winery at Keyneton in the Barossa Ranges, some of the vines are 130 years old. Prue and Stephen Henschke are the current custodians of this living history. 'It's more than just growing grapes,' says Prue, the viticulturist of the partnership. 'It is a labour of love, as some of these vines span five generations of the Henschke family. It is all about maintaining tradition.'

These older vineyards are generally low yielding, as low as 2 to 5 tonnes per hectare. Grown on simple trellis systems or as bush vines, they receive little or no irrigation and are often referred to as 'dryland grown'. Many of these vines are between 50 and 100 years old. However, without the foresight of some of the Barossa producers, many of these old vines would have been pulled out in the 1980s. Robert O'Callaghan of Rockford, Bob McLean of St Hallett and others mounted a rescue operation and not only encouraged but rewarded growers to keep these parcels of old vines. These provided valuable material for them to craft their big, richly flavoured wines — wines that express the terroir of the Barossa. For a taste of 'Barossa Terroir', try the wines from Peter Lehmann Wines, Elderton, Rockford, St Hallett, The Willows, Grant Burge Wines, Penfolds and Henschke.

Henschke's Hill of Grace Vineyard (Keyneton, South Australia) - Shiraz vines over a hundred years old

The story of Grange

(Partly extracted from a paper delivered by M Schubert at the first Australian National University Wine Symposium in Canberra in September 1979 and reprinted in '*The Rewards of Patience*', Penfolds, Third edition, 1994.)

Grange Hermitage has always been a controversial and individual wine. After it was first made in 1951 it was generally not well received. Simply, no one liked this new style of wine. However, as this wine and the '52, '53 and other early Granges matured in the bottle and progressively became less astringent and more refined, people began to take notice of the qualities of these richly flavoured, full-bodied wines. The acceptance of Grange continued and its reputation grew such that today it is recognised as Australia's most famous wine — a wine of quality with individuality and character. Grange is a powerful wine, the impact of the flavour, the oak and tannin in the mouth can be overwhelming, especially in young Granges. But it was always Max Schubert's intention to make a wine that would age and last for 20 years or more, with the taste of the grapes from which it was made remaining in the wine.

The first Grange was made from a mixture of Shiraz grapes from two vineyards, the Magill vineyard in Adelaide and another vineyard just south of Adelaide. After crushing, the grapes were fermented in small, waxed concrete, open fermenters fitted with heading down boards, the rate of fermentation being carefully controlled to assist in obtaining full extraction of colour and flavour from the skins. During the fermentation, the fermenting juice was separated from the skins by completely draining the juice from the tank. Then the juice was pumped back over the top of the skins and other solids so that it would percolate through the skins, thus extracting further essentials of colour, flavour and character. In the later stages of fermentation, a portion of the fermenting wine was transferred to five new oak hogsheads. After completion of fermentation, the wines were stored in oak barrels for 18 months, then bottled and stored in underground bins.

The Kalimna Vineyard, source of the fruit which forms the backbone of Grange.

Although the vineyard sources may have changed, the selection of fruit and the winemaking philosophy have remained very much the same and over the years the style has been maintained very similar to that of the pioneering wines of Max Schubert.

The three winemakers who have crafted Grange over the years - Don Ditter, John Duval and Max Schubert.

THE VINEYARD

Grapes are sourced from the Kalimna vineyard in the Barossa Valley and from McLaren Vale, Langhorne Creek, Clare, Padthaway and Coonawarra.

Grapes are sourced from various vineyards across the Coonawarra region.

The grapes come from a single 6 ha vineyard (Magill Estate), in the eastern suburbs near the foothills of Adelaide. It is non-irrigated and the vines range in age from 30 to 50 years.

THE WINERY

The winemaking technique for both of these wine styles is similar. Grapes are crushed and transferred to stainless steel fermenters of 10 to 35 tonne capacity, fitted with heading-down boards. These boards hold the cap of skins and seeds (that rise during the fermentation) below the fermenting liquid, ensuring that the skins are always kept moist. The fermentation temperature is maintained at about 20°C. Throughout the fermentation the fermenting liquid is completely drawn off from the skins and then returned by spraying back through the boards and over the cap of skins (racked and returned). This procedure is carried out each day. Towards the end of fermentation the wine is pressed. On completion of fermentation the wine is racked. A blend is prepared from the various wines and then stored in oak barrels. Kalimna Bin 28 is matured in American oak barrels, at the twelve o'clock position, for an average period of 12 to 15 months. Coonawarra Bin 128 is stored in French oak barrels (20% new), at the twelve o'clock position for an average period of 15 months. All barrels are regularly topped. At the end of the storage period the wines from the different barrels of each wine style are separately blended.

Grapes are crushed and transferred to 6 tonne open fermenters with heading-down boards. The must is initially maintained at higher temperatures until fermentation commences and then dropped slowly to a fermentation temperature less than 20°C. The wine is racked and returned daily. On completion of fermentation it is pressed, racked and then transferred to a combination of new American and French oak barrels at the twelve o'clock position for about fifteen months.

THE CHARACTER OF THE WINE

The wine has warm, ripe berry (often mulberry) and smoky oak aromas. The palate is rich and flavoursome with sweet berry fruit, vanillin oak and solid tannins. A firm, full-bodied ripe Shiraz style. Can be enjoyed on release and should age well for at least ten years.

Lifted peppery, Coonawarra Shiraz varietal fruit and subtle French oak characters on the nose. Soft and complex palate, featuring a harmonious spicy fruit and dusty oak combination. Medium- to full-bodied the wine finishes with a soft lingering tannin finish. Enjoy on release or over a ten year period.

A complex bouquet featuring spicy Shiraz fruit characters and integrated oak. A more refined style compared to Penfolds traditional red wines; on the palate it displays rich and spicy Shiraz fruit, distinctive oak and a soft tannin finish; potential to develop great complexity over a ten to fifteen year period.

SOME MATCHING FOOD SUGGESTIONS

Try with pasta dishes, pizza or with a barbecue.

Match with a fillet of beef with a green peppercorn sauce or a dish of beef and black bean sauce.

Enjoy with lamb fillets and fresh rosemary or baked chilli snapper.

Grapes are sourced from a selection of premium low yielding South Australian vineyards, with Penfolds Kalimna vineyard and selected Barossa vineyards forming the backbone. Average yields are normally less than 5 tonnes per hectare.

Grapes are crushed and transferred to fermenters of 10 to 20 tonne capacity, fitted with heading-down boards. The must is initially maintained at higher temperatures until fermentation commences and then the temperature of fermentation does not exceed 25°C. The fermentation is worked regularly, with the rack and returns (described on the opposite page) conducted daily. When the fermentation is nearly finished the wine is drawn off (free run) and the remaining mass of skins is transferred to the press. Each portion is transferred to new American oak barrels, where the fermentation is completed. This imparts barrel fermentation characters to the wine. After a short period on yeast lees in the barrel the wine is racked, blended and transferred back to new American oak barrels. The wines mature in these barrels which are stored at the twelve o'clock position for eighteen months or more. They are regularly racked and/or topped during this period to craft the required style and to expose it to some air, enhancing the maturation. After storage in barrel, the different barrels are tasted and the appropriate blend is assembled; only those wines with the flavour intensity and other characters of Grange are selected

The wine is intensely deep, red coloured as a young wine. The bouquet is complex, featuring opulent, Shiraz berry fruit characters, varying from spice, cherry and plum fragrances through to soft, earthy nuances combined with new barrel fermentation characters and vanillin oak complexity. A wine with firm astringency, balanced acidity and integrated distinctive oak features. A full-bodied, richly flavoured and complex wine with a sweet middle palate and with spice, berry fruit and ripe plum flavours complemented with plenty of mouth-filling tannins. The wine becomes more complex with time. A full-bodied wine, structured with a capacity to develop in the bottle and mature over a long period of time. Most Granges develop superbly over a twenty year or more period.

Savour the flavours of Grange with a fillet of beef or kangaroo and sun dried tomatoes or duck with a ginger glaze.

The story of Magill Estate

When Dr Christopher Penfold first planted and tended his vines at Magill in 1844, he began a tradition of winemaking which Penfolds have preserved to this day. On arrival with his family in Adelaide he set up residence in a cottage which they called Grange, in the foothills just outside Adelaide, near what is now known as Magill.

The Grange Cottage

He brought with him some cuttings from France and Spain, which he planted around the cottage. His medical practice flourished, as did the vines. The vineyard grew in size and became a significant part of the lives of Dr Penfold and his wife Mary, and a thriving wine business began. About 100 years later, Shiraz vines in this vineyard provided Max Schubert with a major source of grapes that were used to make the first 'Grange'. The vineyard now is used to make a single estate wine, Magill Estate.

The Magill Estate complex houses winemaking facilities for the Penfolds group, and recently has been spectacularly restored, blending modern architectural themes with the atmosphere of tradition. On the site is the new Magill Estate Restaurant where you can experience fine cuisine and a range of Penfolds wines, including many rare wines by the glass.

The Magill Estate Complex

Not all the descriptors are found in any one wine. The combination of these vary from wine to wine depending on where and how the grapes were grown. The aroma and flavour characters that you experience when the wine is smelt and when it is in the mouth are described in some wines by one or two descriptors, while in others a combination may be more appropriate.

Remember, that the presence and intensity of the various varietal characters, although an important part of the appeal of a wine, are only part of the overall character. The balance between the basic tastes and other features of the wine, as well as its textural nature are equally important when assessing the character/quality of a wine.

In red wines the astringent sensation (due to the tannins) can be described as being light, medium or high and their 'feel in the mouth' by words such as *powdery, talc, grainy, gritty, silky, satin, velvet, gentle, soft, smooth, pleasing, supple, round, furry, dusty, drying, grippy, puckering, persistent, adhesive, aggressive, hard* and *rough*.

Again, as with aroma and flavour descriptors, the tannin sensation is described often by a combination of terms, eg soft and velvety, grainy and drying or furry and mouth puckering. A warm, sometimes hot sensation can also be sensed when tasting red wines that have alcohol levels that are out of balance with the levels of the other components of the wine.

Examples of varietal character descriptors for red wines

Pinot Noir
Primary fruit characters — *herbs, spice, strawberry, red cherry, raspberry, black cherry, violet, perfume, black pepper, plum, stewed plum, rhubarb, beetroot, blackcurrant* and *prune*.
Developed fruit characters — *earthy, cowyard, barnyard, gamey, leather, tobacco, bacon fat, mushroom, the smell of forest floor, humus* and *truffle*.

Grenache
Primary fruit characters — *spice, floral, perfume, cherry, boiled lolly, raspberry, black pepper, blackberry, plum, stewed plum, prune* and *licorice*.
Developed fruit characters — *earthy, meaty, savoury, barnyard* and *gamey*.

Sangiovese
Primary fruit characters — *spice, cherry, fruity, raspberry, blackberry, plums, nutty* and *savoury*.
Developed fruit characters — *nutty, savoury, earthy, barnyard* and *gamey*.

Barbera
Primary fruit characters — *spice, cherry, berry fruits, plums, licorice, nutmeg* and *savoury*.
Developed fruit characters — *nutmeg, savoury,* and *earthy*.

Nebbiolo
Primary fruit characters — *perfumed, violets, roses, raspberry, plum, fruitcake, licorice* and *savoury*.
Developed fruit characters — *truffles, tar, nutmeg, savoury, gamey* and *earthy*.

Cabernet Franc
Primary fruit characters — *spice, raspberry, pepper, plum* and *dusty*.
Developed fruit characters — *truffles, tar, nutmeg, savoury, gamey* and *earthy*.

Zinfandel
Primary fruit characters — *herbal, spicy, cherry, rhubarb* and *ripe berry*.
Developed fruit characters — *truffles, tar, nutmeg, savoury, gamey* and *earthy*.

Merlot
Primary fruit characters — *herbaceous, leafy, fruity, aromatic, perfume, violets, sappy, spicy, cherry, raspberry, plum, beetroot, fruit cake, blackcurrant, blackberry, mulberry* and *rhubarb*.
Developed fruit characters — *earthy, meaty, truffles, chocolate, coffee* and *tobacco*.

Cabernet Sauvignon
Primary fruit characters — *capsicum, tomato leaf, vegetative, herbaceous, cinnamon, menthol, eucalyptus, leafy, mint, violet, perfumed, dusty, berry, plum, stewed rhubarb, cooked beetroot, blackcurrant (cassis), black olive, prune, licorice* and *inky*.
Developed fruit characters — *earthy, dusty, cigar-box, cedar, chocolate, tobacco, coffee* and *mocha*.

Shiraz
Primary fruit characters — *herbs, spice, menthol, cinnamon, raspberry, dark cherry, violets, eucalypt, mint, blackberry, black pepper, plum, mulberry, aniseed, licorice, blackcurrant, black olives, sarsaparilla, chocolate, stewed plum, jammy* and *raisin*.
Developed fruit characters — *chocolate, earthy, barnyard, cowyard, prune, feral, cigar-box, coffee, gamey, meaty, beef stock, salami, savoury, leather* and *iodine*.

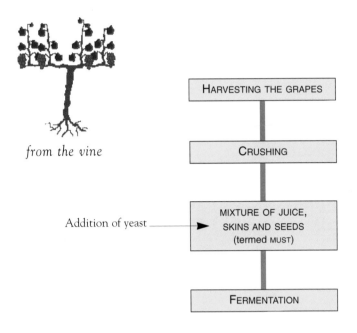

from the vine

HARVESTING THE GRAPES

CRUSHING

Addition of yeast → MIXTURE OF JUICE, SKINS AND SEEDS (termed MUST)

FERMENTATION

DURING THIS PERIOD COLOUR, TANNINS AND FLAVOUR COMPOUNDS ARE EXTRACTED FROM THE SKINS

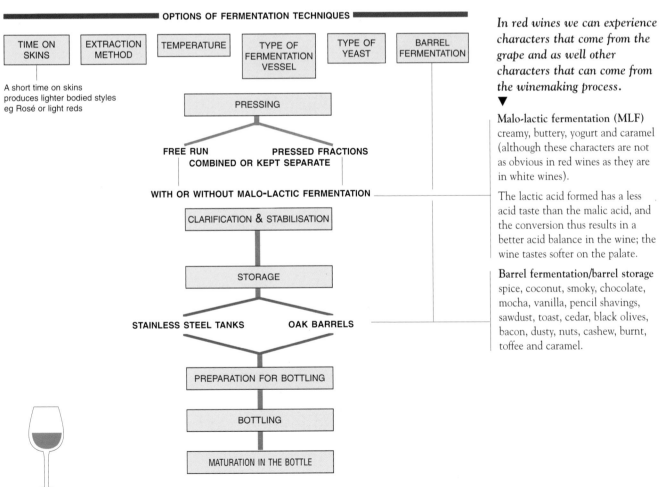

OPTIONS OF FERMENTATION TECHNIQUES

TIME ON SKINS	EXTRACTION METHOD	TEMPERATURE	TYPE OF FERMENTATION VESSEL	TYPE OF YEAST	BARREL FERMENTATION

A short time on skins produces lighter bodied styles eg Rosé or light reds

PRESSING

FREE RUN   PRESSED FRACTIONS
COMBINED OR KEPT SEPARATE

WITH OR WITHOUT MALO-LACTIC FERMENTATION

CLARIFICATION & STABILISATION

STORAGE

STAINLESS STEEL TANKS   OAK BARRELS

PREPARATION FOR BOTTLING

BOTTLING

MATURATION IN THE BOTTLE

to the glass

In red wines we can experience characters that come from the grape and as well other characters that can come from the winemaking process.
▼

Malo-lactic fermentation (MLF) creamy, buttery, yogurt and caramel (although these characters are not as obvious in red wines as they are in white wines).

The lactic acid formed has a less acid taste than the malic acid, and the conversion thus results in a better acid balance in the wine; the wine tastes softer on the palate.

Barrel fermentation/barrel storage spice, coconut, smoky, chocolate, mocha, vanilla, pencil shavings, sawdust, toast, cedar, black olives, bacon, dusty, nuts, cashew, burnt, toffee and caramel.

Large vats used to store fortified wines

FORTIFIED WINES AND BRANDY

These are wines to which spirit has been added, raising the alcohol level of the finished wine to between 17 and 20% v/v. The spirit is an alcoholic solution, ranging from high strength (about 95% v/v) to lower strength (about 80% v/v, often called *brandy spirit*). Because the wines have been strengthened with alcohol, they are referred to as *fortified*, the word originating from the Latin 'fortis' meaning strong. Apart from being a high strength alcohol solution, which simply raises the alcohol level, each spirit has its own distinctive character that contributes to the finished wine. High strength spirit imparts little extra character, while brandy spirit can often add significant nutty and almond tones. Producers of fortified wines normally have a preference for the type of spirit they add, depending on the style of fortified wine they intend to make.

In Australia, fortified wines include *sherry-* and *port-like styles*, *muscats* and *tokays*. We have chosen to refer to these wines as sherry- and port-like as with time the use of the names sherry and port will be discontinued on the labels of Australian wine. These names belong to the sherry wines of Spain and the port wines of Portugal.

Making fortified wines requires many skills, but pre-eminent is the art of blending, a skill which is frequently passed down through generations; some of the wines that the winemakers use to craft their blends have been made by their fathers or grandfathers. These older wines often form part of a solera system, from which many of our great fortified wines are assembled.

Fortified and sparkling wines — many similarities in their making
The making of these wines revolves around the skill and the art of the blender. Both types of wine can be made from wines stored as 'reserve' wines for long periods of time, and the maker needs to be able to predict how each wine will develop by the time it is released many years later.

The solera system

A solera system is used for storing casks of wines of different ages. Generally, the oldest wines are stored in the bottom barrels and the youngest at the top. At various times of the year a quantity of wine is drawn off from the barrels on the bottom row of the solera. This portion of wine is then replaced with a younger wine from the next highest layer of barrels, and so on.

This process of adding a portion of younger wine to older wine is called 'refreshing the wine'.

This system of storing wines can be used in the production of sherry- and port-like styles, muscats and tokays. This 'dynamic ageing process of fractional blending' ensures that the wines in the bottom barrels are of a consistent style and quality. It maintains freshness and consistency of 'house style'.

Fortified wines were the major part of the Australian wine industry up to about the 1970s. Since that time, table wines have become more popular and fortified wine production has somewhat declined. Fortunately for devotees of these fortified styles, many wineries have carried on the tradition.

A solera system at McWilliam's Winery

SHERRY-LIKE STYLES

Spain is the birthplace of sherry. The term 'sherry' is historically derived from the name Jerez, the region in the south of Spain where the wine is produced. Although there seems little connection between the words now, historians believe that the spelling and pronunciation of Jerez changed over the years so that sherry became the accepted English form. The history of sherry is closely linked with the English wine trade. In view of the wide popularity of sherry in the 1800s and 1900s, it is not surprising that the production of this style of wine formed part of the emerging Australian wine industry, particularly since the climates of many of our earlier established vineyards were similar to that of Jerez. Palomino is the major grape variety, while Pedro Ximines grapes are also used. In Australia, there are three main styles: *fino*, *amontillado* and *oloroso*. The first two styles are made using a special yeast called '*flor yeast*'. All three styles are produced via a solera system and ageing and blending are important aspects in creating their characters.

What you may see on the label
These wines are labelled fino, amontillado or oloroso. Often they have special names or codes, eg Seppelt D.P.117 Fino Sherry. Many are labelled as Show or Show Series, eg McWilliam's or Seppelt Show Series, indicating that these are special wines and are available commercially in small volumes. With time the name sherry will disappear from Australian wine labels; consumers will need to be familiar with the special names and codes that identify Australian sherry-style wines.

Describing the character of the wine

Appearance
Fino - The colour can vary from pale straw through straw to pale gold.
Amontillado - The colour can be yellow to deep golden.
Oloroso - The colour can be deep golden or golden amber with olive green tinges.

Aromas (by nose) and flavours (by mouth)
Some words used to describe the characters that come from the growth of the flor yeast are *nutty*, *almond*, *oxidised*, *aldehyde* and *marzipan*. Additional characters that develop with long maturation include — *walnut*, *orange-peel*, *marmalade*, *butter*, *caramel* and *rancio*. It is difficult to separate the descriptors, as flor growth and maturation are often happening at the same time.

Flavours, tastes and mouthfeel sensations
Fino styles are the lightest in body and have the driest finish. They should be fresh and show distinctive aldehydic (sometimes nutty) characters. *Amontillado styles* are fuller and richer and show more aged characters (more rancio) than fino styles. Although some sweetener may have been added prior to bottling, they should finish dry. *Oloroso styles* do not undergo the flor growth stage and thus do not show flor character. They are the fullest, richest and most complex, are fruity and aromatic and normally have higher alcohol content than flor sherries. Sweetener is added prior to bottling, and oloroso styles are semi-sweet to sweet full-bodied sherries.

The descriptor Rancio
Rancio is a difficult term to describe. It is used to describe the smell that comes from fortified wines deliberately aged with some air contact and/or from wines that have spent a long time in oak casks. The term rancio encompasses *nutty, vanillin, almond, walnut* and *musty walnut* aromas and flavours. It is a very positive feature and is a part of the character of fine sherries, tawny ports, muscats and tokays.

The role of the vineyard

For the production of fino and amontillado styles the grapes are harvested early, between 10° and 11° Baumé, to conserve natural acidity and balance.
For oloroso styles the grapes may be picked riper, when they have more fruity aromatic characters.

The influence of winemaking

Fino style

The grapes are processed into a dry wine according to normal white winemaking procedures. Spirit is added to the finished wine to increase the alcohol content to approximately 15.5% v/v and the wine is transferred to the upper stage of a solera. Sometimes the finished white wine is stored for a number of years before fortification and transfer to the solera.

The flor yeast grows on top of the wine in a partially filled barrel.

Each barrel in the solera is only partly filled with wine. The wine in each barrel is seeded with a special yeast (flor yeast) and then stored in the barrels for a number of years. It is this stage of the production process that is critical in creating the unique characters of fino and amontillado sherries. Because the barrels are only partly filled, the upper surface of the wine is exposed to air, providing conditions that are conducive to oxidation and to the growth of the flor yeast, which grows over the surface of the wine forming a film.

The flor yeast develops and the wine matures during the years the wines are stored in the barrel. The chemical changes associated with the oxidation and the growth of the flor yeast impart new flavours to the wine. During this period it is important to keep the conditions just right for flor yeast growth: the surface must not be disturbed; the temperature must be kept between 15 and 20°C; and the alcoholic strength must be maintained at between 15.0 and 15.5% v/v. In a solera, where the wine is continuously refreshed, the flor growth continues almost indefinitely. The longer the wine spends on flor, the greater the development of nutty and almond characters. When the winemaker decides that the characters of the wines in the lower stages of the solera match the desired style, the wines are removed and blended, and further spirit is added to increase the alcohol content to about 18% v/v. The wine may then be stored for a further period of time in large barrels. These fino style sherries are not sweetened.

Normally wines spend from one to two years on flor, but special wines are kept in contact with the flor for up to seven years or more before being blended and bottled.

Amontillado style

This is initially made in the same way as a fino sherry. An amontillado sherry has two distinct maturation periods, the first as a fino 'on flor' and then 'off flor' to develop into an amontillado style. Wines that have been stored in the 'fino solera' for a number of years are removed, fortified to 18% v/v alcohol and then transferred to a new solera stack specifically for amontillado style sherry. At this alcohol level no further flor growth occurs but the wine continues to mature; it becomes more golden in colour and fuller and richer on the palate.

Oloroso style

Oloroso styles of sherry should not be influenced by flor growth. They are produced by fortifying dry white wine to 18% v/v and then storing it in barrels or in a solera system for many years. Often the dry white wine has been produced from riper grapes with more fruity, aromatic characters.

Wines may be stored in the oloroso solera for 10 to 30 years, or even longer. They develop rich, complex flavours to complement the aromatic primary fruit characters. The longer they are stored, the more complex and richer they become. When removed from the solera they are normally sweetened before being bottled.

Some examples to try

The main companies producing sherry-style wines are Seppelt, Lindemans, Mildara Blass, McWilliam's, Berri Estates and Yalumba.

Some wine companies now produce these wines with lower alcohol levels, about 16% v/v, while still retaining all the complexity of aromas and flavours and tastes that are part of the character of these wines.

Start the meal with a fine fino or amontillado. Fino styles can complement consommés or green olives. Oloroso styles can be matched with creamy blue cheeses.

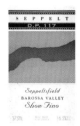

Seppelt Show Fino D.P.117 is a blend of wines that have been 'on flor' for a minimum of 7 years and then further matured in large oak barrels for some months prior to bottling. The flavours are intense, nutty and complex, showing classic flor character. The palate is fresh, the flavours lingering and the finish dry. Enjoy it slightly chilled. The alcohol level of this wine is now lower than previously, being about 16.5%.

Seppelt Show Amontillado Sherry D.P.116 is a blend of wines, of an average age of 16 years. It shows excellent aged flor sherry characters with intense, complex and rich almond aromas and flavours and a dry lingering finish. Enjoy it slightly chilled.

Seppelt Show Oloroso Sherry D.P.38 comes from a blend of wines which have an average age of 18 years. This wine shows rich, complex, ripe fruit, old oak and rancio characters. The palate is luscious but still has a drying finish.

PORT-LIKE STYLES

Port is the fortified red wine style produced in the Douro region of Portugal. The practice of adding spirit to wine began as a means of preserving the wine during its transportation from Portugal to England. Prior to the 1700s, only a small addition of spirit was made, but during the 1800s this changed and it became standard practice to fortify the wine to around 20% v/v alcohol. Other winemaking countries followed this practice when they began to make port styles of wine. Australia's pioneering wine companies built their businesses around fortified wine production. The warm to hot climates of their vineyards provided ideal conditions for ripening grapes to the high sugar levels required to make these styles of wine. In Australia, the grape varieties used are Shiraz, Grenache, Touriga, Mataro and Cabernet Sauvignon. There are two main styles, *tawny* and *vintage*.

Tawny style

Tawny style refers to a fortified wine which has been aged in wood for a period of time and which has lost its youthful colour and taken on an amber brown colour.

Describing the character of the wine

Appearance
Generally the colour is rusty brown. Older wines can show khaki and olive green tinges.

Aromas (by nose) and flavours (by mouth)
The harmonious combination of aged wine, oak and spirit is the feature of these wines; usually words such as *nut, walnut, dried fruit, prune, coffee, caramel, toffee* and *rancio* are used to describe the characters. The older the wine, the greater the development of rancio characters. The spirit that has been added during the fortification can also add to the complexity of the aromas and flavours. Some oak characters may also be present, such as *vanillin*.

The styles of tawny ports range from those which are more youthful and fruity and have less age emphasis, to the very complex styles that develop through long ageing.

Flavours, tastes and mouthfeel sensations
The palate, although sweet, should not be cloying, with sweetness balanced by the drying sensations that come from long ageing in oak barrels. Typically the palate is smooth and complex, with lingering flavours and a dry finish. The higher alcohol level may be obvious on the finish: a spicy, warming, spirit sensation at the back of the palate.

The role of the vineyard

The grapes are picked at about 15° Baumé; some berry shrivel normally occurs, concentrating the sugars and flavours. Warm to hot climates are most suitable for growing grapes for port-style wines, since such conditions are favourable for producing higher sugar levels.

The influence of winemaking

The grapes are crushed and fermented on skins to extract some of the colour and flavour. Excessive extraction is avoided. The fermentation on skins is conducted for only a few days; then the mass of skins, pulp and partially fermented wine is transferred to the press. The mixture of free run and any pressings, if added, is transferred to a tank where it continues fermenting. It is normally only the free run and light pressings that are used in the production of higher quality tawny ports. When the fermentation reaches the desired sugar level, the appropriate amount of spirit (alcohol) is added to increase the alcohol content to about 18% v/v. Sometimes brandy spirit is used in the fortification step, and some producers may add the spirit while the wine is still on skins. The addition of spirit to 18% v/v stops the fermentation.

Port-style wines have high sugar content; the actual level depends on the stage at which the fermentation is stopped by the addition of spirit, but it is normally well over 100, and often greater than 150 grams of sugar per litre. Wines that are fortified earlier in the fermentation contain more sugar.

After fortification the wine is clarified, transferred to old oak barrels and left to age for many years. The colour gradually changes from red to tawny brown. During this time the aromas and flavours also change and the wine takes on the characters that are derived from long ageing in barrels; they become more complex. Good tawny ports develop distinctive rancio characters. The flavours and acids become concentrated as water slowly evaporates through the barrels. The characters of the wine integrate over time, and the sweetness is balanced by the acids of the wine and the astringency of the oak extracted during the long period of oak storage. Many producers use a solera system to age their tawny ports, thus maintaining the consistency and quality of the style of wine they produce. At each bottling stage, wine is removed from the solera, blended, stabilised and bottled. Some of the components of the blend may be very old, especially in the more expensive wines.

Some examples to try

Some special tawny ports to try include: Yalumba Galway Pipe, Hardys Show Port, Penfolds Grandfather and, Seppelt D.P. 90. Luscious, rich and full-flavoured these fine old tawny ports, representing blends of wines of fifteen or more years average age, show pronounced nutty rancio tones.

Ruby Port

Ruby port is essentially a young tawny port. It has been aged for only a few years and will be ruby in colour, exhibiting a greater intensity of fruit type rather than aged characters.

Enjoying a tawny port

Once a tawny port is bottled it is ready to be consumed. It does not need further ageing in the bottle; all its ageing has been carried out previously in oak barrels. Once opened it should be consumed over a period of a few days, as after this time the wine in the partially filled bottle may lose its freshness.

Tawny ports can be enjoyed with cheeses and rich desserts.

Vintage style

These are wines from a single vintage that spend about two years in wood storage before being bottled. They are then aged for many years in the bottle before reaching their peak.

Describing the character of the wine

Appearance
The colour is normally ruby red. Young wines can be purple/black, while older wines are light ruby red with some amber tones.

Aromas (by nose) and flavours (by mouth)
These wines generally show rich, ripe berry fruit aromas and flavours. Descriptors include *violet*, *raspberry*, *black cherry*, *spice*, *blackberry*, *blackcurrant*, *plum*, *anise*, *chocolate*, *marzipan* and *licorice*, and depending on their age these wines may additionally show *chocolate*, *coffee*, *nut* and *walnut* characters. They should not show any oak characters.

Flavours, tastes and mouthfeel sensations
Generally vintage port has a rich, full-flavoured mid-palate and a firm, drying astringency from the tannins, leaving minimal lingering sweetness on the finish.

The role of the vineyard

Grapes for this style of port should attain high sugar levels (about 14° Baumé) but must also have strong varietal aromas and flavours.

The influence of winemaking

The grapes are fermented on skins to obtain maximum extraction of colour, tannin and flavour, and pressings are usually added back to the free fun. The wine is fortified when the desired sugar level is reached, spirit being added to raise the alcohol level to about 18% v/v. After completion of fermentation the wine is settled and stored separately until bottled. Because the wine is a vintage style, it is not blended with any aged wine. The wine is normally stored in large oak barrels for one to two years and then bottled.

Vintage ports are made to develop in the bottle for many years, 10 to 20 years or more, before being consumed. They are normally produced only in years when the grapes ripen with all the right characters for extended ageing in the bottle. The wine is not necessarily stable or finely filtered when bottled and will normally throw a crust in the bottle. Indeed some vintage ports receive no filtration once they are removed from wood storage. Vintage ports require careful decanting before being served.

The range of vintage ports is not as great as that of tawny ports, however, luckily some producers still make superb examples of this style of port. Australian styles tend to be sweeter than the classic Portuguese styles, however, there is now a trend for Australian producers to made a drier style. Characteristically the Australian style has concentrated berry and licorice flavours, smooth, velvety mouthfeel and warmth of spirit on the finish; with age they develop chocolate and coffee characters. Consumers who enjoy vintage ports need to be patient, as these wines should be cellared for about fifteen years or more to soften and develop their aged characters. Only with time can the wonderful complexity, that comes from the intermingling of primary and developed characters, be fully appreciated.

Some examples to try

Hardys Chateau Reynella VP, d'Arenberg Fortified Shiraz, Seppelt Show Vintage Shiraz, Pfeiffer Christopher VP and Stanton and Killeen.

The chocolate, walnut and coffee characters of aged vintage ports combine well with dried nuts and fruits and hard and blue cheeses.

Muscat and tokay are luscious, richly flavoured sweet fortified styles. Frontignac grapes are used to make muscat, while tokay is made from Muscadelle grapes. The wines are high in sugar and alcohol and are often crafted from blends of very old wines.

Describing the character of the wine

Appearance
These wines can range in colour from reddish gold with amber tinges through to tawny and deep browns with olive or khaki green hues.
Swirl the wine in the glass and note how the wine slowly slides down the inside of the glass, leaving so-called tears or legs as the viscous liquid clings to the side.

Aromas (by nose) and flavours (by mouth)
Muscat – the distinctive character is *raisin* but also with *prune, toffee, honey, caramel, butterscotch, nut, walnut, dried fruit, fruitcake* and *rancio* characters.

Tokay – the distinctive character is *cold tea* but also with *fish oil, raisin, toffee, caramel, butterscotch, nut, orange peel, dried fruit, fruitcake* and *rancio* characters.

Flavours, tastes and mouthfeel sensations
The palate should be fresh and lively with luscious, concentrated, complex, lingering flavours. Even though these wines have a high sugar content, the sweet taste should be balanced by acid and oak components to give a dry finish. A warming sensation may be present at the back of the palate due to the higher alcohol content. Tokay often seems to taste less sweet than muscat. Muscat and tokay wines are at their peak when bottled.

The role of the vineyard

Frontignac

The official name for Frontignac is 'Muscat à Petit Grains', meaning Muscat with small berries. There are three forms: white, red and brown. Grapes from the various forms of Frontignac are used to make muscat style wines in a number of the warm to hot and hot grapegrowing areas of Australia, including the Barossa, the Murray Valley, Milawa and Corowa. But it is in the Rutherglen area in north-eastern Victoria that the brown form (Muscat à Petit Grains Rouge, known locally as Brown Muscat) produces Muscat of Rutherglen.

Muscadelle

The name tokay originates from a case of mistaken identity. The early vignerons of the Rutherglen area thought that particular vines growing in their region were a variety that grows in the Tokay-Hegyalja district of Hungary. They called these vines and the wines made from them tokay. However, in 1976 these vines were identified as the white grape variety Muscadelle. Although the true identity of these vines is now known, the wine continues to be called tokay.

What you may see on the label
These wines are labelled muscat and tokay. The word 'liqueur', which sometimes appears on the label, loosely means that the wine is very sweet and luscious. Other names such as special, museum, old, very old and aged are also currently used. However, the use of these terms by the different producers can be somewhat confusing to the consumer — eg how does the style of a muscat labelled museum compare to one labelled special or old? Realising this, the winemakers of Rutherglen have come together to form the Muscat of Rutherglen Network. At present there are seven wineries in the Network: All Saints Estate, RL Buller & Son, Campbells Winery, Chambers Rosewood Winery, Morris Wines, Pfeiffer Wines, Stanton and Killeen Wines. This group has started to develop a system which will more clearly distinguish between the different styles, particularly in terms of their aged characters. Names such as Premium, Old and/or Rare may be used and it will be clearly defined as to what the characters will be of wines labelled this way. As yet the names to be used for the different styles have not been finalised, however you can expect that soon the labels of Muscats of Rutherglen will be more standardised. This will be a helpful guide to understanding and enjoying this unique Australian wine style.

Enjoy muscat and tokay wines with sweet desserts, rum and raisin ice cream, fruit cake, cheese, nuts and dried fruit.

In the warm autumn climate the grapes ripen and shrivel (raisin) on the vines, producing natural sugar levels in the range of 17 to 20° Baumé. In exceptional years this shrivelling effect produces raisined grapes which give a juice of about 25° Baumé.

The influence of winemaking

The grapes are picked and crushed and yeast is added. Crushing produces a mixture of juice, skins, seeds and whole raisins. The sugar level of the juice may be in the order of 20° Baumé. The mixture is allowed to stand for a few days, and extra sugar is leached from the raisins; the sugar level of the juice may increase to about 25° Baumé. During this time the yeast is slowly fermenting the sugar. Just as the sugar level starts to drop, spirit is added to increase the alcohol level to about 18% v/v and the fermentation ceases. Because the spirit is added so early in fermentation, these wines are very high in sugar, about 300 grams or more of sugar per litre. This contributes to their luscious tastes. But the wines are also complex. The fortified juice is stored and matured in large oak barrels (up to 2000 litres) for many years, gaining complexity as the components of the juice are slowly modified with time. The result is a luscious, complex, intensely flavoured wine. Many producers use a solera system to store their wines and some wines in these systems are many years older than the winemaker preparing the blend, the older wines having been laid down by previous generations. These older wines are more complex and are often used in the very special blends prepared by the different producers.

A tasting experience

Muscat – many producers make a range of products varying in the proportion of aged wine contained in the blend. An example of this is the range currently available from Campbells.

Campbells Rutherglen Liqueur Muscat – fresh and lively with lingering Muscat fruit, contains some base material twenty years old.

Campbells Rutherglen Muscat – a modern classic Muscat containing some base material forty years old.

Campbells Merchant Prince Muscat – their flagship. Very old, very special Muscat with some base material going back sixty years.

Tokay – for a very special occasion, indulge yourself with a memorable experience with *Chambers Old Liqueur Tokay*.

MUSCAT OF RUTHERGLEN — *the flavours of history*

Some examples to try

Experience the character of Muscat of Rutherglen from wineries in the Rutherglen region.

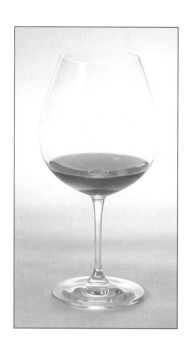

BRANDY

Brandy — the spirit of the grape

Although not strictly classified as wine, brandy is closely linked with the story of wine. Brandy, the name being a corruption of the Dutch 'brande-wijn' meaning 'burned-wine', is the alcoholic solution obtained by distilling a natural wine and then storing the distillate in oak casks, for at least 2 years and often for up to 20 years or more.

Describing the character of brandy

Appearance
Generally the colour is described as *tea-like*, *light golden* or *amber*. The older the brandy, the deeper the colour.

Aromas (by nose) and flavours (by mouth)
The descriptors include — *aromatic*, *spicy*, *vanilla*, *floral*, *toast*, *caramel*, *nutty*, *almond* and *spirity*. But the aromas and flavours of brandy are difficult to describe; they reflect the complexity derived from the marriage over many years of the characters of the distilled spirit and those of the oak that it has been stored in.

Flavours, tastes and mouthfeel sensations
The sensations on the palate are rich and smooth, with lingering flavours and a warm finish from the high alcohol content.

The role of the vineyard
In Australia, the grape varieties used for the production of distillation wine include Sultana, Trebbiano, Palomino, Doradillo and Grenache. These varieties are mainly grown in warmer to hot climates and are more suitable than other varieties as when they are made into wine they produce a neutral, clean wine suitable for spirit production. The grapes are picked early in sugar development, at about 10 to 11° Baumé, so as to retain high acid levels.

The production process
Making the distillation wine
The aim is to produce a clean wine with high acid and no off-characters. The grapes are crushed and pressed. There is little or no skin contact as the skin components can impart undesirable characters to the wine and the subsequent distillate. The pressed juice is made into wine by the normal method.

The distillation process
As soon as possible after the wine is made, it is transferred to the stills for distillation. Traditionally, these are pot-stills modelled on those that are used in the Cognac area of France and those that are used to produce Scottish malt whisky. The wine is heated by injecting steam into the still. The ethanol and other volatile components are boiled off in the form of a vapour. These boil at a lower boiling point than the water in the wine and thus rise up the column at a faster rate than water vapour. The vapour is condensed to a liquid. The solution obtained still contains many of the volatile aromas and flavour compounds originally present in the wine, but now it is much higher in alcohol concentration, in the order of 30 to 45% v/v. The solution obtained by this first distillation is called 'low wine'.

The 'low wine' is then redistilled by returning it to the cleaned pot and then reheating. This process is called *double distilling*. At this second distillation stage, three separate distillation fractions are collected: *the heads, the heart and the tails*.

The heads contain the highly volatile components such as acetaldehyde and ethyl acetate while the last fraction contains less volatile components including what is called the fusel oils. The middle portion (the heart) which contains most of the alcohol, and more of the desirable components is the 'brandy spirit'. It is about 80% v/v. This spirit is collected and later transferred to oak casks. The task is highly skilled, as the distiller makes the separations between the different fractions based on sensory evaluation of the distillate as it distils over.

The pot-stills at Angove's Renmark Distillery

The maturation

The brandy spirit is usually broken down to an alcohol concentration of about 60% v/v with pure water prior to maturation in oak casks. The size of the oak casks can vary from hogsheads to very large casks. During storage the clear liquid extracts components from the oak cask and gradually deepens in colour. It increases in aroma and flavour intensity and in complexity, and the mouth-feel becomes more mellow and rounder as the liquid is transformed into brandy. Brandy that has been stored for long periods of time is fuller in body and has greater complexity. When it is decided that the brandy has the desirable characters for the appropriate style, the brandy is removed from the oak casks, blended with components of either the same or older age, broken down to an alcohol concentration of about 40% v/v and then bottled.

Some examples to try

South Australia is the home of brandy with Angove's at Renmark and Hardys at Berri producing a range of styles, their premium products being some of the best brandies in the world.

Angove's selection
St Agnes 3 Star Brandy – a medium-bodied aromatic, spirity brandy with good depth of flavours and complexity.

St Agnes 5 Star Old Liqueur Brandy – a more complex, richer, full-bodied brandy.

St Agnes 7 Star Very Old Brandy – their flagship brandy, a full-bodied, deeply coloured extremely complex brandy with lingering nutty flavours. The components of the blend are at least 20 years old, with portions being 50 years of age.

Hardys Black Bottle Brandy – a very distinctive Australian brandy - superb flavour and smoothness. This wine displays a fullness and roundness typical of its pot-still production. Soft, attractive oak characters complement the inherent fruit qualities of the blend producing a well balanced, superior Australian brandy.

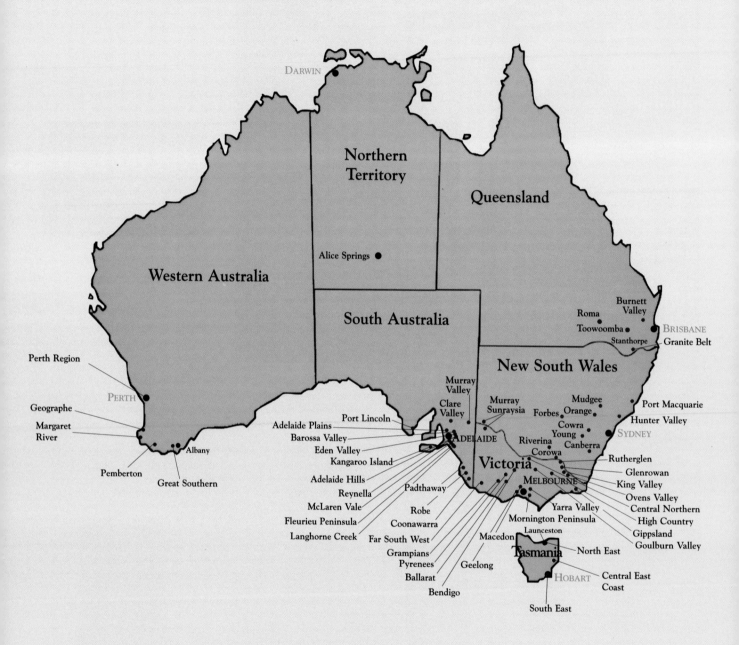

Wine areas of Australia

VINEYARDS & WINERIES OF AUSTRALIA

Vineyards are located in every Australian state and territory. The map opposite gives a guide to the location of vineyards within Australia. We refer to these locations by their commonly known names. With time each location will be allocated to a geographic zone and/or a region. The regions that form part of each zone are currently being determined. As well as new regions with new names appearing in the future, there may be changes in the naming and distribution of the boundaries of some of the established regions. This is all part of the plan to define clearly the geographic locations of Australia's wine regions as Australia becomes a more significant part of the world wine scene. Australia is a large continent; the regions in which our grapes grow cover a wide climatic spectrum with a range of soil types, and thus our winemakers produce many different types and styles of wines.

There are about 900 wineries in Australia. The major companies include Southcorp Wines, BRL Hardy, Orlando Wyndham, Mildara Blass, McWilliam's Wines and De Bortoli Wines, all crushing over 40,000 tonnes each in 1996. Medium size wineries with crush sizes between 10 and 30,000 tonnes include Miranda, Normans, Angove's, Kingston Estate, Brown Brothers Milawa, Rosemount and Yalumba. Many smaller wineries make up the remaining number.

The major wine producing regions are found in South Australia, Victoria and New South Wales.

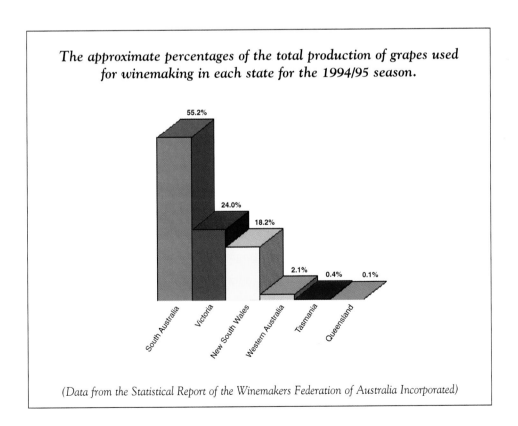

The approximate percentages of the total production of grapes used for winemaking in each state for the 1994/95 season.

55.2%
24.0%
18.2%
2.1%
0.4%
0.1%

South Australia
Victoria
New South Wales
Western Australia
Tasmania
Queensland

(Data from the Statistical Report of the Winemakers Federation of Australia Incorporated)

In this chapter we introduce the history, present and future of the Australian wine industry, and then journey through the grapegrowing and winemaking areas to discover Australian wine — the vineyards, the wineries and the wine styles.

*The Tyrrell winemaking family —
past, present and future*

AUSTRALIAN WINE — *yesterday, today and tomorrow*

The beginning of wine, about 7000 years ago, can be traced to sites in the Middle East. From there, the culture of the vine gradually spread to most parts of Europe, where wine has been made for about 2000 years. By comparison, Australians have been growing grapes and making wine for just over 200 years.

Vines were part of the cargo when the First Fleet arrived in Sydney in 1788, and were planted on land now the site of the Sydney Royal Botanic Gardens. From these beginnings in Sydney, the culture of the vine spread throughout Australia. By the 1890s, regions that we now know as the Hunter Valley, the Barossa Valley and the Yarra Valley were well established.

Before 1950 wine production in Australia focussed on fortified wines, but since then the emphasis has shifted steadily towards table wines. In the 1960s the sales of red table wine boomed, and a swing to white table wine followed in the 1980s. Red and white table wines are the major areas of production today.

European influence is everywhere in our wine industry. Many of our wine regions were developed by settlers of French and German ancestry. More recently, post World War II immigrants, also of European background, brought an ethos of wine to our country. Australians became aware and appreciative of the possibilities for enjoying wine with food and as part of their lifestyle.

The historic cellars of Chateau Tahbilk

The clock tower of Yalumba Winery

Many wineries were established as family enterprises, their winemaking philosophy being passed down through the generations. The story of S. Smith & Son's Yalumba Winery at Angaston in the Barossa Valley began in 1849 and now spans six generations; it is the oldest family owned winery in Australia. The Tyrrell family has been producing wines in the Hunter Valley since 1858, maintaining a tradition which is now in its fourth generation. In central Victoria you will find some of Australia's oldest living viticultural history in the vineyards of Chateau Tahbilk. Vines were first planted here in 1860, and some vines growing today are over a hundred years old.

In the Rutherglen area of Victoria, many winemaking families, including Chambers, Campbells, Morris, Bullers, Stanton and Killeen, have carried on the tradition of making Australia's most famous fortified wine — *Muscat of Rutherglen*.

We can only speculate about whether the early vignerons could have imagined the Australian wine industry of today. It is an industry characterised by technological excellence, where innovative approaches in the vineyard and winery have revolutionised grapegrowing and wine production.

One of the major advances in wine production, particularly in making white wines, has been the use of refrigeration throughout the winemaking process. Its widespread application in the Australian wine industry ensures that our wines are full of flavour, just like the grapes from which they were made.

But it is not just in the winery that changes have taken place; much has also happened in our vineyards. Australia has led the way in methods of pruning and harvesting grapes which lower the cost of producing wine. Many wine companies have research and development programmes aimed at improving the quality of grapes: studies on improved planting material, innovative trellis designs and irrigation scheduling, to name a few.

The last twenty years have seen great growth in the Australian wine industry, with the revival of many of the original sites (particularly in Victoria) and the discovery and establishment of many new areas as the culture of the vine spreads all around Australia. Most people will be familiar with regions such as the Hunter Valley, the Barossa Valley, Coonawarra and the Yarra Valley, but nowadays there are many new areas where grapes are grown, areas such as Gumeracha, Bicheno, Manjimup, Robe, Tumbarumba, Lenswood and Murrumbateman. The expansion of vineyard development into cooler climatic regions, by both large and small wine companies, has contributed to the quality image of Australian wine.

Approaches such as those taken by Brown Brothers of Milawa in north-eastern Victoria exemplify the willingness of the Australian wine industry to take on new ideas. John Francis Brown planted vines here in 1885 and crushed his first vintage in 1889. Subsequent generations have continued the tradition. The area is renowned for its fortified wines, but the Brown family realised that the surrounding areas offered a range of climatic conditions for growing grapes.

Brown Brothers' vineyard at Whitlands, in the King Valley, is one of Australia's more recent vineyard developments.

Brown Brothers planted vines in a range of sites, and set about finding which grape varieties were best suited to each site. One of their vineyards is Whitlands, established in 1982; at 800 metres altitude (in the foothills of the Alps), it provides ideal conditions for growing aromatic white wine grape varieties such as Riesling and Gewürztraminer. Full-flavoured red wines from varieties such as Shiraz come from vines grown in warmer, lower altitude sites. As well as focussing on 'understanding the vineyard', Brown Brothers have built an experimental winery (called 'The Kindergarten Winery') where winemaking approaches are trialled before their adoption in the larger winery.

The fact that wineries can source grapes from a range of climatic sites is important for understanding the diversity of wine styles that are made by any winery. Wine companies will source grapes from a number of regions, and make either regional wines or wines that represent blends of different regions. The great choice of Australian wine is made possible by this diversity of vineyard sites, winemaking options and blending possibilities.

The Kindergarten Winery — cradle of Brown Brothers' future wines

A traditional basket press in Rockford's Winery in the Barossa Valley

Some of Australia's best known brand names, including Jacob's Creek, Clancys and Kalmina Bin 28, are made in the BarossaValley.

Some interesting small wineries to visit include Bethany, Burge Family Winemakers, Charles Melton, Jenke, Turkey Flat, Veritas and the Willows.

A great way to find out about these areas is to visit the Barossa Wine and Visitor Centre at Tanunda, where the story of the region, its people and its culture is told through informative displays.

SOUTH AUSTRALIA

Within a radius of about one and half hours' drive from the city of Adelaide, the wine areas of the Barossa Valley, Eden Valley, Adelaide Hills, Adelaide Plains, Clare Valley, McLaren Vale and Langhorne Creek offer the wine consumer an exciting choice of world class wines.

Barossa Valley and Eden Valley

The Barossa Valley and Eden Valley, with over 150 years of grapegrowing and winemaking tradition, are situated about an hour's drive north of Adelaide. These two valleys are home to over 1,000 grapegrowers, who supply fruit to about 50 large and small wineries. They are the base of some of Australia's larger wine companies, such as Chateau Yaldara, Miranda Rovalley, Orlando, Penfolds, Saltram, Seppelt, Wolf Blass Wines and Yalumba, and also many smaller wineries including Elderton, Grant Burge, Henschke, Krondorf, Mountadam, Peter Lehmann, Rockford and St Hallett. The Barossa Valley traditionally produces medium- to full-bodied table wine, principally from Chardonnay, Semillon, Shiraz and Cabernet Sauvignon, and fortified wines. The cooler climatic conditions of the higher districts around Eden Valley are more suitable for fine Chardonnay, Cabernet Sauvignon and dry and sweet Rieslings.

The Shiraz vineyards, some over 100 years old, that dot the Barossa floor and the surrounding ranges provide fruit for wines such as Penfolds Grange, Henschke Hill of Grace, St Hallett Old Block, Peter Lehmann Stonewell, Rockford Basket Press, Yalumba Octavius and Grant Burge Meshach. Some Grenache vines have also survived many decades and their wines can be found as either a varietal Grenache or as blends with Shiraz and/or Mourvèdre.

Stocks of sherries and tawny and vintage style ports are slowly maturing in many wineries, and some great treasures can be discovered when visiting both large and small wineries. A tour of Seppelt Winery in Seppeltsfield brings to life some of this history; it is here that the famous 100 year old Para Liqueur Ports are matured.

The entrance to the Saltram Winery in the Barossa Valley

Seppeltsfield Winery in the Barossa Valley

Adelaide Hills

Vines were grown and wines made in the Adelaide Hills area as early as the 1830s. It is reported that Australia's first exported wine came from Echunga, sent as a gift in 1845 to Queen Victoria. Activities appeared to cease about 1920, but were rekindled in 1971 when the Glenara Vineyard was established by Leigh Verrall, followed in 1978 by Brian Croser, who established the first central hills vineyard of the new era and built the Petaluma Winery at Piccadilly. The Adelaide Hills is fast becoming recognised as one of Australia's premium wine regions. Its vineyards are located in the Mount Lofty Ranges at altitudes between 400 and 600 metres above sea level, from Mount Pleasant in the north to Kuitpo in the south and from Woodside, Hahndorf and Echunga in the east to the Hills face zone of Adelaide in the west. This patchwork of meso-climates varies from cool to warm, and this helps to explain why the vineyards of this region produce Chardonnay and Pinot Noir for both sparkling and table wines in the coolest parts; Riesling, Semillon, Sauvignon Blanc and Merlot in the slightly warmer areas; and Cabernet Sauvignon, Cabernet Franc and Shiraz in the lower altitudes. Presently there are ten cellar door sales outlets in the hills, including Ashton Hills at Ashton, Chain of Ponds at Gumeracha, Petaluma at Bridgewater and Pibbin at Balhannah. Other labels from wineries that have vineyards in this area include Henschke Lenswood, Shaw and Smith, Stafford Ridge and Knappstein Lenswood, while other wineries such as Penfolds and Hardys source fruit from the area.

Petaluma's vineyards in the Adelaide Hills

Vineyards at Gumeracha in the Adelaide Hills and the sign at Chain of Ponds Winery

The Murray Valley

Around the towns of Barmera, Berri, Loxton and Renmark you will find some of Australia's largest vineyards and wineries such as Angove's, Berri Estates, Renmano Wines and Normans. Other wineries source fruit from this area, often to make their large blends of popular commercial wines and fortified bases. Chardonnay and Shiraz dominate the plantings but there are also significant plantings of Grenache and Mourvèdre.

Ample sunshine coupled with sound viticultural practices ensures a consistent supply of clean, well flavoured grapes to produce diverse styles, from medium-bodied whites and reds through to fortified wines. Arguably, many of these wines are the best in the world in their price range and clearly demonstrate how the use of innovative modern viticulture and winemaking techniques can produce clean, fresh, flavoursome, enjoyable wines at affordable prices. But there are also many higher quality wines produced, where winemakers source fruit from select patches of vineyards and craft these into individual wines, from wineries such as Kingston Estate, Renmano and Angove's.

Berri Estates Winery in the Murray Valley

Bill Moularadellis on top of the Kingston Estate Winery building, with the vineyards in the background

Adelaide Plains

North-west of the city of Adelaide are the vineyards and wineries of Primo Estate near Virginia and Barossa Valley Estate near Angle Vale.

McLaren Vale

The vineyards of the Fleurieu Peninsula, scattered in the rolling hills amongst olive groves and forests, are about an hour's drive south of Adelaide. McLaren Vale is the major region, with a mix of wineries, large and small, some steeped in tradition while others are relatively new. The region's ironstone, sandy loam soils, coupled with a warm, dry Mediterranean climate and cooling breezes from the neighbouring Gulf of St Vincent, play an important role in producing high quality fruit for the production of intensely flavoured table wines. McLaren Vale has a long standing recognition for rich, full-bodied reds from Shiraz and Cabernet Sauvignon, while more recently Chardonnay, Grenache and Merlot are coming into prominence. Many companies source fruit from this region, taking advantage of the palate richness that these wines contribute to blends. A visit to the McLaren Vale region can be much more than the enjoyment of its quality wine: absorb the history at Tintara winery, which dates back to 1876; at Kay's Amery, vines from the famous Block Six, planted in 1892, still produce excellent Shiraz; at d'Arenberg you can see its old basket press in operation.

There are many opportunities to match wine and food at wineries including Woodstock, Haselgrove, d'Arenberg and Andrew Garrett. Other wineries well worth visiting include Coriole, Shottesbrooke, Wirra Wirra, Ingoldby, Pirramimma, Normans, Richard Hamilton, Scarpantoni, Ryecroft, Tatachilla, and Chapel Hill.

McLaren Vale and Fleurieu Visitor Centre at the entrance to McLaren Vale provides an opportunity to taste wines of the area as well as information on visiting wineries and other attractions. A demonstration vineyard called Stump Hill is planted with Shiraz, and visitors will be able to observe different approaches in viticultural management practices.

The sign to Coriole Winery

Shottesbrooke Winery

The Coterie at Woodstock Winery

Chardonnay vines on the Lyre Trellis system at Richard Hamilton's 'Hut Block' vineyard

Reynella

Just north of McLaren Vale is the township of Reynella, where you can visit Chateau Reynella, established by John Reynell in 1838 and now the head office and white winemaking centre of Hardys. Near Reynella you will also find Mount Hurtle Winery and Normans and Saint Francis wineries. Wine styles are similar to those of the McLaren Vale district.

Langhorne Creek

East of McLaren Vale are the vineyards and wineries of Langhorne Creek. Sited near the shores of Lake Alexandrina, the vineyards benefit from the moderating influence of cool breezes from this large expanse of water. Superb red wines from Shiraz and Cabernet Sauvignon grapes are produced from this area. As well as some smaller wineries, many large wine companies including Rosemount, Mildara Blass and Orlando Wyndham have interests in or are developing vineyards here. The largest winery in the area is Bleasdale Vineyards, an historic family owned winery founded in 1850. It is classified by the National Trust and contains an old red gum lever press made in 1892. Other wineries producing quality wines include Tonkins Currency Creek, Temple Bruer and Lake Breeze.

The vineyards in Langhorne Creek use a unique 'flooding system' to apply water to their vineyards. Flooding is carried out by utilising the winter flow of the Bremer River, through a system of floodgates and banks which divert water onto the vineyards. It remains there until the soil is saturated and is then released on to the neighbouring vineyard.

Clare Valley

About one and a half hours' drive north of Adelaide is the Clare Valley, one of Australia's most picturesque wine districts with a great range of quality wines. The vineyards are scattered in the countryside around the towns of Auburn, Leasingham, Watervale, Mintaro, Penwortham, Sevenhill and Clare. You can try fine Rieslings, distinctively lime flavoured, at wineries such as Jim Barry, Grosset, Mitchell, Taylors, Paulett, Crabtree, Quelltaler, Tim Knappstein and the Wilson Vineyard. It is interesting to compare the subtle differences in wines from neighbouring areas such as Polish Hill and Watervale. The Clare Valley is a patchwork of mesoclimates; as well as some sites being ideal for growing Riesling and each expressing slightly different tones of Riesling flavours, other locations produce superb Shiraz with varying stamps of individuality. The Shiraz wines of Mitchell and Pikes have distinctive cool climate pepper characters, while the Shiraz wines from Jim Barry, Leasingham and Wendouree wineries are big, rich and intensely flavoured. In many cases these Shiraz wines are made from grapes from very old vines. The wineries of the Clare Valley also produce other table wine styles, and exciting examples of Cabernet Sauvignon and blends can be found at Taylors, Sevenhill, Grosset and Wendouree. Absorb a sample of the region's history at Sevenhill Cellars, established in 1851 by the Jesuits, and where today Brother John May continues the long line of Jesuit winemakers making quality table wines and sacramental wine for religious purposes. And then there are the newer, often quite small, wineries just starting to build their history but also offering excellent table wines typical of the quality of Clare Valley, wineries such as Tim Adams, Waninga, Pikes Polish Hill River Estate, Paulett and Stephen John Wines.

Jim Barry in front of Jim Barry Winery at Clare

Taylors Winery at Auburn in the Clare Valley region

Padthaway

North of Coonawarra, about 45 minutes' drive, is the Padthaway district, where many of the large wineries have extensive plantings, mainly of white wine varieties. Some excellent Chardonnay wines are made from fruit grown in this district. Chardonnay and Pinot Noir grown here are also used for sparkling wine production. At Padthaway Estate in the Woolshed Winery, you can see a traditional Champagne press in operation during vintage.

The Woolshed Winery at Padthaway Estate

Coonawarra

Viticulture has long been part of the tradition of the south-east corner of South Australia. In the 1860s, John Riddoch purchased 35,000 acres of land around Penola. He established the 'Coonawarra Fruit Colony', which included fruit trees and vines. In 1890 he built the 'Gables' winery (now Wynns Coonawarra Estate), which is still in use today. His energy and efforts provided the foundation for today's Coonawarra. The predominantly maritime climate, coupled with patches of the famous 'terra rossa' soil, provides ideal conditions for growing vines. Many of Australia's premium red wines from Shiraz and Cabernet Sauvignon and blends are born in the vineyards of Coonawarra; some wines rank amongst the best reds in the world. Many wineries located in other parts of Australia also source grapes from this premium area. Coonawarra cellar door sales outlets include Balnaves, Bowen Estate, Brands Laira, Haselgrove, Highbank, Hollick, Katnook Estate, Ladbroke Grove, Leconfield, Majella, Mildara, Parker Estate, Penfolds, Penley Estate, Redman, The Ridge, Rouge Homme, Rymill, Wetherall, Wynns and Zema Estate.

Balnaves Winery at Coonawarra

Wynns Coonawarra Estate Winery

Other areas in the South-East of South Australia

Viticulture is expanding rapidly in this south-east corner of the State, as major wine companies are developing vineyards in areas such as Koppamurra and Robe. Since these new areas have similar elevation, soils and climates to Coonawarra, there are great expectations as to the quality of wines that will emerge from these new vineyards. The zone which takes in Coonawarra, Padthaway and these new areas will be known as the Limestone Coast.

QUEENSLAND

The Queensland wine industry is mainly centred around Stanthorpe, west of Brisbane. Vineyards are planted on the slopes of the Great Dividing Range at altitudes of 700 to 1,000 metres above sea level, these conditions moderating the warm temperatures of the area. Typically the wines are well flavoured medium- to full-bodied styles, mainly made from Semillon, Chardonnay, Shiraz and Cabernet Sauvignon. Some Shiraz wines can show distinctive peppery, cool climate characters. Well established wineries such as Ballandean Estate, Robinsons Family, Kominos and Rumbalara have built a reputation for the quality of their table wines. As in most other wine producing states, the wine industry in Queensland is in a stage of expansion, and many new small wineries are being established. Along with vineyard expansion around Stanthorpe, new plantings are now being established at Mount Tamborine, Toowoomba, Oakey and the Burnett Valley. As well as the well known varieties, some plantings include Verdelho, Viognier and Sangiovese, suggesting an interesting future for Queensland wine. Some new wineries include Bald Mountain, Preston Peak, Rimfire and Mount Tamborine. Queensland's oldest winery, Romavilla Vineyard (the home of Basset's wines), is situated at Roma and makes some excellent fortified wines.

The sign to Ballandean Estate in the Granite Belt wine region near Stanthorpe

Preston Peak's new vineyard site near Toowoomba

TASMANIA

The climate of the Tasmanian vineyards is cool, ideally suited for the production of superb, tightly structured sparkling wine from Chardonnay and Pinot Noir and crisp, delicately flavoured table wines from Riesling, Gewürztraminer, Chardonnay and Pinot Noir, wines notable for their finesse and naturally balanced acidity rather than sheer power, typically wines that age well. Moorilla (near Hobart), Pipers Brook and Heemskerk wineries (just north-east of Launceston) pioneered the wine industry in this State, and now others have followed their lead and established small vineyards and wineries throughout the state. Now vineyards are scattered in the rolling hills around Pipers River and Pipers Brook north of Launceston, along the banks of the Tamar River to the west of Launceston, in the valleys and bays around Hobart and at Bicheno on the east coast.

Vineyards in this state are proving to be very suitable for the production of high quality sparkling wine. One of Australia's premium sparkling wines, Jansz, comes from the Heemskerk vineyard. Several mainland wine companies have also established vineyards or source fruit from Tasmania for their premium sparkling wine blends.

Generally, Cabernet Sauvignon and Merlot need to be planted in the warmer sites to ripen fully. These warmer mesoclimates, which allow full ripening of Pinot Noir, Cabernet Sauvignon and Merlot in most years, are to be found along the Tamar Valley and at Bicheno, where the Freycinet vineyard is sited.

On the banks of the Tamar River, just outside Launceston, visitors can enjoy dramatic views of the Tamar Valley while tasting wine at either the Strathlynn Wine Centre or Marion's Vineyard.

There are many smaller wineries and these include Delamere, Marion's, Rochecombe (in the north), Freycinet (on the east coast) and Bream Creek, Elsewhere, Domaine A/Stoney, Hood, Fishburn and O'Keefe, Meadowbank and Stefano Lubiana (in the south).

Vineyards at Heemskerk Winery

The entrance to Pipers Brook Winery

NORTHERN TERRITORY

In the centre of Australia near Alice Springs is Chateau Hornsby winery. Here you can try wines from varieties such as Shiraz and Chardonnay, as well as visiting their restaurant complex.

VICTORIA

Central Victoria

This zone takes in the vineyards and wineries around Bendigo and the Goulburn Valley, and to the east it extends into the foothills of the Alps. The districts near Bendigo are well known for their reds with powerful fruit flavours from Shiraz and Cabernet Sauvignon. Discover them at wineries such as Balgownie Estate, Jasper Hill, Passing Clouds, Tisdall and Waterwheel. In the Goulburn Valley, Chateau Tahbilk and Mitchelton wineries have made the area famous for wines made from Marsanne, Shiraz and other Rhône varieties, as well as other fine table wines made from Chardonnay and Riesling. In the vineyards of Chateau Tahbilk some of the vines are over one hundred years old. More recently viticulture has expanded into cooler climate regions, and vineyards have been developed in the foothills of the Alps, in areas known as the High Country. Near Mansfield you will find Delatite Winery which, amongst other table wine styles, produces delicate cool climate Riesling and Gewürztraminer wines.

Mitchelton Vineyards and Winery — located in the Goulburn Valley region near Nagambi in Victoria

Trentham Estate — on the banks of the Murray River near Mildura

North-west Victoria

The vineyards stretch from Mildura to Swan Hill, following the path of the Murray River. Just outside Mildura is Lindemans Karadoc, probably the largest single winery in the southern hemisphere. Other wineries include Allambie, Best's, Buller, Deakin Estate, Robinvale and Trentham Estate. Most varieties ripen in this warm to hot climate to provide grapes from which a range of wine styles is made, including well flavoured dry whites from Chardonnay, flavoursome reds from Shiraz, Cabernet Sauvignon and Merlot, and fortified wines. The Murphy family has grown grapes in the Mildura district since 1909 and has recently established Trentham Estate Winery and restaurant just south of Mildura on the banks of the Murray River.

Western Victoria

In the late 1800s, the lure of gold brought many people to this district and reminders of these gold rush days can be seen on some wine labels. Vineyards and wineries are located around the cities and towns of Ballarat, Ararat, Avoca and Great Western. A diversity of styles is made, from cool climate Shiraz wines to elegant, complex Chardonnays and a range of sparkling wine. Mount Langi Ghiran is well known for its deeply flavoured, peppery Shiraz. The wineries around Avoca, collectively known as the Pyrenees wineries, consistently produce impressive, richly flavoured reds from Shiraz and Cabernet Sauvignon and flavoursome dry whites from Chardonnay and Sauvignon Blanc. Pyrenees wineries include Blue Pyrenees, Dalwhinnie, Kara Kara, Mount Avoca, Mountain Creek, Redbank, Summerfield, Taltarni and Warrenmang.

Seppelt Great Western, Blue Pyrenees, Taltarni and Yellowglen (near Ballarat) craft some of Australia's finest sparkling wines. At each of these wineries you can experience the taste of a range of sparkling wine styles. At Seppelt Great Western and Blue Pyrenees you can tour the underground cellars and experience the atmosphere of sparkling winemaking. And for a touch of history visit Best's Great Western, established in 1866, where you can sample excellent wines covering a large array of styles, including a varietal Pinot Meunier.

The historic cellars of Best's Great Western

North-east Victoria

This zone covers four viticultural districts and includes the locations around Rutherglen and Glenrowan and the King and Oven Valleys. The best known are the vineyards and wineries around Rutherglen, famous for their Tokays, Muscats and Port-style wines but also producing good dry reds and whites from mainly Shiraz, Durif and Chardonnay. Families such as Buller, Campbells, Chambers, Killeen, Morris and Sutherland Smith have established their wineries over many years; in some cases the fifth generation is now carrying on the tradition. The character of their fortified wines reflects the many years that the wines have spent gently maturing in their cellars. Other fine fortified wines, as well as a range of table wines, can be found at Baileys of Glenrowan, which is the oldest winery in this district, having been established in 1870.

Morris Winery at Rutherglen

Boynton's of Bright vineyards with Mount Buffalo in the background

At Milawa, in the King Valley area, the Brown family has carried on the wine-making tradition since 1899. Brown Brothers is the largest winery in north-east Victoria and offers an opportunity to taste a large range of quality varietal wines. Recently more vineyards have been planted in the King Valley, including those of growers of Italian descent who have changed over from growing tobacco. These vineyards are providing many of the grapes for wines made from the Italian varieties that are now starting to appear on the Australian market. There are also small wineries producing excellent handcrafted regional wines, including Sorrenberg and Gioconda near Beechworth and Boynton's of Bright.

Gippsland

Wine grapes were planted here in the 1970s and a pioneering wine industry developed. Bass Phillip, a small winery near Leongatha, produces some of the best Pinot Noir wine in Australia, while further east the Nicholson River Winery near Bairnsdale has a great following for its complex, full-flavoured Chardonnay wines.

Visitors to Phillip Island can include a visit to the cellar door of Phillip Island Wines, one of the new wineries in the Gippsland area. Here, the vineyard is protected from wind, marauding penguins and hares by a spectacular two hectare net.

Oakridge's 'Reserve Block' vineyard, the source of the fruit for their Reserve range of wines

Port Phillip

The city of Melbourne is encircled by vineyards and wineries. To the east of Melbourne is the Yarra Valley, where Domaine Chandon has chosen to centre their sparkling wine production. It is also the home of many boutique wineries including Coldstream Hills, Yarra Valley De Bortoli, Diamond Valley, Long Gully, Mount Mary, Oakridge, Seville Estate, Shantell, St Hubert's, Tarrawarra, Yarra Burn, Yarra Ridge and Yarra Yering. There is a range of mesoclimates but generally the area is classified as cool. Some of Australia's best sparkling wine and table wines from Chardonnay, Pinot Noir and Cabernet Sauvignon and blends are skilfully crafted in the Yarra Valley. The Yarra Valley is now regarded as one of the regions consistently producing high quality Pinot Noir wines.

Stonier's vineyard — on the Mornington Peninsula overlooking Port Phillip Bay

The Hickinbotham family winery near Dromana has established a Wineworks Museum which includes an interactive training in wine tasting. This activity is aimed at all ages, as the tastings are prepared in non-alcoholic solutions.

A short drive south-east of Melbourne brings you to the picturesque Mornington Peninsula. The vineyards nestled in this strip of land produce excellent Chardonnay and Pinot Noir wines from wineries including Dromana Estate, Hickinbotham, Main Ridge, Stonier's and T'Gallant. Take the opportunity to try wines from Italian grape varieties at Dromana and T'Gallant. Across Port Phillip Bay, the vineyards and wineries located around Geelong, Bannockburn and the Bellarine Peninsula, including those of Bannockburn Vineyards and Scotchmans Hill, produce distinctive Pinot Noir and Chardonnay wines, while good examples of Gewürztraminer and Cabernet Sauvignon can be found at Idyll Vineyard and Winery just north of Geelong.

North of Melbourne, near the towns of Sunbury, Macedon and Kyneton, the wineries offer a great choice of table wines. Craiglee Winery near Sunbury makes a cool climate Shiraz which is consistently among the best in Australia. Crisp, delicate Rieslings and peppery Shiraz wines come from Knight's Granite Hills Winery near Lancefield. The reds from Virgin Hills Winery near Kyneton are often superb, while the wineries in the Macedon Ranges, including Cope-Williams (Romsey Vineyards) and Hanging Rock Winery, produce impressive sparkling wines as well as cool climate whites and reds.

A game in action at the Cricket Pitch at Cope-Williams Winery

WESTERN AUSTRALIA

South Western Australia

Wines that are putting Western Australia on the world wine map come from vineyards planted in this region. All the classic varieties perform well in the special mesoclimates that can be found across this vast expanse of bushland bordered by oceans. Skilfully crafted wines from Cabernet Sauvignon and blends, typified by those from Margaret River, have intensity of flavour and fine tannin structure. They are some of the best red wines in Australia, keenly sought after both nationally and in overseas markets. The wines from Margaret River have received many accolades, not only those from Cabernet Sauvignon but also for wines from Chardonnay, Semillon, Pinot Noir and Shiraz. However, any critique of the ability of the south-west corner of Australia to produce fine table wine must also highlight the areas around Capel Vale, Pemberton, Mount Barker, Denmark and Albany, where some excellent wines have been made.

The wines from the Geographe region are typified by strong mid palate flavours and fine grain tannins in the red varieties. Varieties that excel are Chardonnay, Merlot and Shiraz close to the coast and Cabernet Sauvignon, Sauvignon Blanc and Verdelho show great promise in the hills. Further south in the areas around Pemberton and Albany, the variety Riesling appears to be perfectly suited, some sites giving exceptional wines that display a harmony of delicate flavours, freshness and steely structure. Other sites are particularly suited to Chardonnay, Cabernet Sauvignon, Pinot Noir and Shiraz producing wines with intense flavours and fine structure. With continued expansion in this south-west corner of Australia we can expect even more exciting wines in the future.

Wineries in the area surrounding the town of Bunbury include Killerby and Capel Vale.

Some of the wineries of the Margaret River region are Ashbrook, Amberley, Cape Mentelle, Cullen, Devil's Lair, Evans and Tate, Happs, Leeuwin Estate, Moss Wood, Pierro, Sandalford, Sandstone, Vasse Felix, Voyager, Wrights and Chateau Xanadu.

Vineyards of the Pemberton wine region include — Donnelly River, Salitage, Chestnut Grove and Smithbrook.

Wineries of the Great Southern Region (the areas around Mt Barker, Denmark and Albany) include — Alkoomi, Chatsfield, Frankland, Goundrey, Jingalla, Patersons, Plantagenet and Wignalls.

Voyager Estate— one of the newer wineries in the Margaret River Region

Goundrey Estate — located in the Mount Barker region of the Great Southern Zone

Greater Perth

The wine industry of Western Australia began in the area known as the Swan Valley in the suburbs of Perth. The oldest winery in Western Australia, Olive Farm, was established in 1830 and is situated here, along with others including Evans and Tate, Sandalford and Houghton. One of Australia's favourite and largest selling wines, Houghton White Burgundy, has been made at the Houghton winery continuously for 60 vintages. The major varieties planted in the Swan Valley include Chenin Blanc, Verdelho and Shiraz. Typically the wines are soft, flavoursome, medium- to full-bodied styles. Several wineries also have vineyards in and/or source fruit from the more southern regions to produce attractive, well flavoured blended wines from, for example, Chenin Blanc, Sauvignon Blanc, Semillon, Chardonnay and Verdelho.

Roxburgh vineyard — the source of fruit for Rosemount's Roxburgh Chardonnay

At Hunter Cellars in the McGuigan Hunter Village, visitors can taste a range of wines from the Upper and Lower Hunter Valleys.

Rothbury Winery situated in the Lower Hunter Valley

The cellar door sales entrance of Craigmoor Winery in Mudgee

NEW SOUTH WALES
Hunter Valley

Although vines were part of the cargo when the first fleet arrived in Sydney in 1788, it was not until the 1820s, when the Hunter Valley plantings were established, that Australia's wine industry really began. George Wyndham (still a famous name in the wine industry) and James Busby were the early pioneers, and then the Tyrrell, Drayton, Lake, Evans and McGuigan families were heavily involved in building the wine industry in this area. Just north of Sydney, the Hunter Valley is easily accessible to visitors and offers a wide choice of quality wines as well as fine dining and accommodation, all intermingled in an Australian bush setting with a hazy blue backdrop of the Brokenback Ranges. The Lower Hunter near the town of Cessnock is home to many wineries such as Tyrrells, Rothbury, McWilliams Mount Pleasant, Lake's Folly, Draytons Family Wines, Brokenwood, Lindemans, Pepper Tree, Tullochs, Briar Ridge, Sutherland and Evans Family Winery.

Aged Hunter Semillon, which we feature on page 92, is the great wine of this region; so distinctively different to other Semillons of the world, it is regarded as a classic Australian wine style. Other wine styles include soft, generously flavoured reds from Shiraz and Cabernet Sauvignon and rich complex Chardonnays. The apparent hotness of the district is moderated by the high humidity and cooling breezes that wrap their way through the valley. This moderation relieves vine stress, allowing the vines to ripen their fruit fully.

In the Upper Hunter, near the towns of Denman and Muswellbrook, the scale of vineyard plantings is bigger, as it is here that several of the larger companies are established. Rosemount Estate and Arrowfield wineries, two larger enterprises, and several boutique wineries including Reynolds Yarraman, Sernella Estate and Cruickshank Callatoota are situated in this area. A range of dry white and red wine styles is produced. Chardonnay is the major grape variety. The Roxburgh vineyard, from which Rosemount's famous Roxburgh Chardonnay is made, is planted on a patch of limestone soil nestled into a rolling hillside near Denman.

Mudgee

Wine has been made in Mudgee for more than 150 years and some excellent white wines from Chardonnay and full-bodied reds, mainly from Cabernet Sauvignon, have been crafted here. Some of the wineries include Huntington Estate, Montrose, Thistle Hill, Botobolar, Miramar, Craigmoor, Pieter van Gent, Seldom Seen and Lawson Hill. Botobolar has been a leader in the development of organic viticulture, which we cover on page 87. Fruit from Mudgee has always been sourced by wineries outside the area, indicating the acceptance of this area for the quality of its fruit.

Canberra District

The small wineries along the shores of Lake George and those of the Yass Valley around Murrumbateman are part of the Canberra wine district. Some excellent Riesling wines have been produced from wineries such as Clonakilla and Doonkuna Estate. Chardonnay and Cabernet Sauvignon are the other major varieties, and plantings of Shiraz are increasing.

Riverina

The Riverina district, of which the city of Griffith is the centre, is one of the largest grapegrowing areas in Australia. Vines were first planted in the district in 1913 by J.J. McWilliam. After the First World War, the Australian Government sponsored soldier settlement schemes, resulting in rapid expansion of the farm holdings. Over the years, Italian families including De Bortoli, Rossetto and Miranda immigrated to the area and contributed to its wine culture. The major wineries in this area are McWilliams Hanwood, De Bortoli, Miranda, Cranswick Estate and Rossetto. Many wine styles are produced, from medium-bodied dry reds and whites to sweet whites through to sparkling and fortified. Varietal wines include Semillon, Chardonnay, Marsanne, Verdelho, Shiraz, Cabernet Sauvignon and Merlot. Typically these are good quality wines at reasonable prices, but it is the botrytis-affected sweet white wine styles made from Semillon (featured on page 111) for which the region is famous.

McWilliams-Hanwood cellar door sales outlet.

Other areas

The expansion of vineyard area throughout Australia is staggering. As well as increased plantings in traditional areas, vineyards are being established in new areas, including higher altitude sites in the highlands of central New South Wales. McWilliams chose Barwang, and some of their early wines have been exceptional cool climate styles, both red and white, while Stephen Doyle searched out sites on the slopes around Orange to establish his vineyards, which he called Bloodwood Estate. Rosemount and Reynolds (both from the Upper Hunter region) have also established interests in this area. These sites around Orange are showing promise in producing medium-bodied, finely structured, elegant red and white table wines.

The vineyards around Cowra have been established for some time now and larger vineyards dominate this area. Typically the Chardonnay wines are rich with peachy tones, Verdelho wines are tropical fruit-like and the reds also have plenty of flavour. Try the wines from Richmond Grove Cowra and Cowra Estate to see the characters of this region.

John Cassegrain and his family set up their vineyard and winery at Port Macquarie, and they pioneered in Australia a vineyard concept known as Clos Farming. This system of farming originated in France, where many small farms, adjoining yet separately owned, are linked together under one management scheme. They produce quality wines from the classic varieties and from the French hybrid grape variety Chambourcin.

Cranswick Estate, very successful in the export market with its imaginatively named 'Barramundi' range of wines, is now focussing on the domestic market with its Cranswick Estate wines.

Their new vineyard, located near the Cocoparra range on the outskirts of Griffith, uses drip irrigation controlled by computer technology. This approach to irrigation scheduling, aimed at improving grape quality, is typical of the modern viticultural approaches now being utilised in this area.

Cassegrain Winery — located close to Port Macquarie

The development of all these new areas and the evolution of regional characters add to the diversity of wine styles and can only enhance the interest and enjoyment of exploring Australian wine.

Cellaring wine for future enjoyment

The entrance to the cellar door sales of Plantagenet Wines: in a natural bush setting in the Great Southern region of Western Australia

CHOOSING WINE

Most people have a favourite place to purchase their wines, be it a liquor outlet, fine wine store or winery cellar door. Specialist wine stores have staff who are very wine knowledgeable and who can offer advice on many aspects of wine. They may also be able to help you choose the right wine for that special occasion. Some of these stores regularly conduct tastings, which offer a great opportunity to try the wine before buying.

Most wineries have cellar door sales areas where you can try their range of wines. You will find the staff well informed and in some places you may even get to meet the winemaker. An added bonus in visiting these outlets is that some wineries reserve special wines for purchase only at the cellar door. There are also many fine restaurants in our wine districts, providing an opportunity to match regional food and wine. Visiting the wineries is also a chance to experience the Australian environment, as many wineries are located in unique Australian bush settings.

Information on wines, winery and winemaker profiles, and other wine news can be obtained from wine magazines and newspaper columns. In 'Winestate Magazine', a bimonthly publication, you will find tasting notes and wine reviews by experts, information on wine regions, wine and food matches and other wine features. Other valuable sources are the annual wine guides from wine authors including James Halliday, Huon Hooke and Mark Shield, Robin Bradley and Jeremy Oliver. Mail order organisations such as the Australian Wine Society and Cellarmasters offer another way to purchase wine. Here you can choose from a range of pre-selected quality wines offering excellent value for money.

And for those wine lovers seeking that rare or special wine, there are the wine auctions such as those run by Langtons in Sydney and Melbourne and by Oddbins in Adelaide. Langtons produce a guide listing possible prices that you may expect to pay for some of Australia's most sought after wines. At an auction in 1996, a set of Grange (from the years 1951 to 1991) sold for about $80,000.

Peter Lehmann Wines cellar door sales

Margaret Lehmann of Peter Lehmann Wines in the Barossa Valley highlights the role of cellar door in these terms.

• The Cellar Door is a winery's showcase. It is here that a visitor discovers the wine styles and learns about the history, philosophy and aspirations of the winery.

• For us, it also means giving the winemakers an opportunity to use their skills to make 'limited edition' wines and to introduce new styles and varietals to the public.

Understanding Australian wine labels

Currently Australian wines can be labelled in the following ways.

• *Varietal identification* — the grape variety/varieties from which it was made, for example, Riesling, Chardonnay, Marsanne, Pinot Noir, Shiraz or Cabernet Sauvignon.

• *Descriptive labelling* — where additional words are used to further describe the style. For example, sweet white wines can additionally have the words 'spätlese', 'late picked' or 'botrytis' on the label to indicate the degree of sweetness/style. Port-like styles can be labelled vintage, tawny, liqueur or ruby.

• *Generic classification* — relates to a style and is often named after the vine-growing districts where the style originated. For example, Champagne indicates a sparkling wine style. Claret, Moselle, Sherry and Port are other generic names that you will be familiar with. However, confusion arises because wines labelled in this manner may not necessarily be made from similar varieties or by similar methods to those of the region of origin. Thus, they do not truly represent the characters of that style. Words such as Champagne, Chablis, Burgundy, Moselle and Chianti should only be used for wines produced in those regions of Europe. These names were adopted by our early wine producers, many of whom were of European descent. However, the use of these names has always been a contentious issue, which has been resolved by negotiations between the Australian Government and the European Community. The current agreement is detailed below. This agreement (part of The Bilateral Treaty for Trade in Wine between the European Economic Community (EEC) and Australia) provides for the phasing out of use by Australian winemakers of the following terms.

by 31 December 1993:	by 31 December 1997:
Beaujolais*	Chianti
Cava	Frontignan
Frascati	Hock
Sancerre	Madiera
Saint Emilion/St Emilion	Malaga
Vinho Verde/Vino Verde	
White Bordeaux	

*except where agreements with individual producers provide otherwise.

At a date to be agreed by the parties, having account of the commercial significance to both parties and the number of names used by Australia:

Burgundy	Chablis	Champagne
Claret	Graves	Marsala
Moselle	Port	Sauternes
Sherry	White Burgundy	

In return, the EEC has accepted the variation in grapegrowing and winemaking practices that are part of making wine in Australia. These concessions will further open up opportunities for Australian wine companies to export their wines to Europe, adding to our ever expanding export industry. Australian wines are now widely enjoyed in many parts of the world, including New Zealand, Europe, the USA, the United Kingdom and Asia.

Wine show medals

In wine shows, wines receive awards as shown below

Gold Medal
18.5 - 20.0 points

Silver Medal
17.0 - 18.4 points

Bronze Medal
15.5 - 16.9 points

Various capital city and district Agricultural Societies conduct wine shows where wine companies can enter wines to be judged by a panel of expert judges. Wines are awarded points out of 20. As well as medals, trophies may be awarded to the best wines in particular classes. These medals and trophies can then be displayed on the bottle. If a wine consistently wins silver and/or gold medals at a number of wine shows, it is highly likely that it is a very good wine. Good wines will consistently score bronze medals. However, the absence of any wine show awards on a bottle of wine does not necessarily indicate failure at wine shows, as not all Australian wine companies enter their wines in these shows.

What the words on the label mean

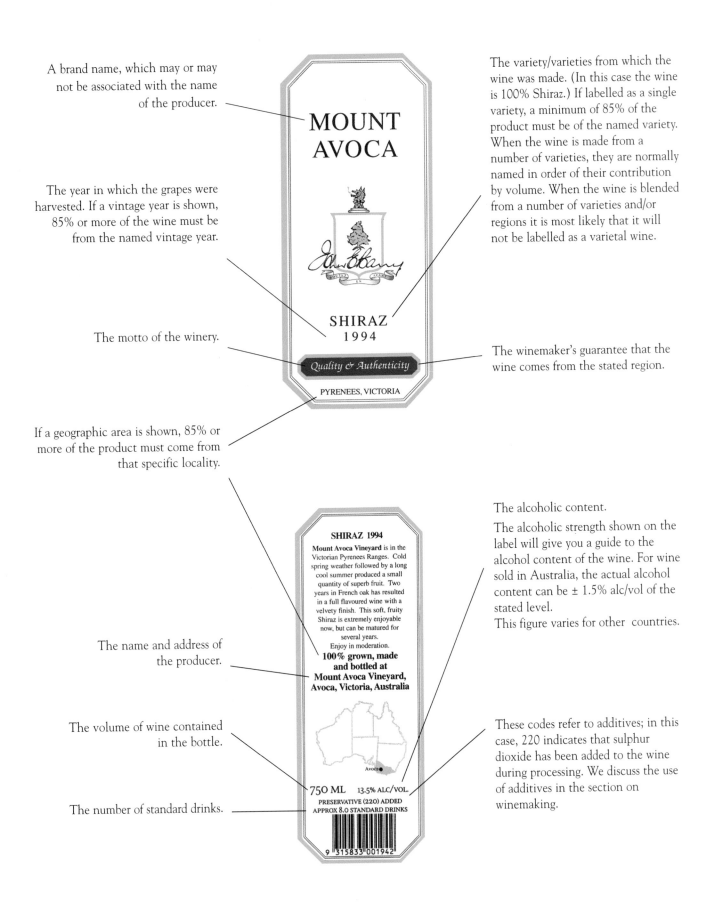

A brand name, which may or may not be associated with the name of the producer.

The year in which the grapes were harvested. If a vintage year is shown, 85% or more of the wine must be from the named vintage year.

The motto of the winery.

If a geographic area is shown, 85% or more of the product must come from that specific locality.

The name and address of the producer.

The volume of wine contained in the bottle.

The number of standard drinks.

The variety/varieties from which the wine was made. (In this case the wine is 100% Shiraz.) If labelled as a single variety, a minimum of 85% of the product must be of the named variety. When the wine is made from a number of varieties, they are normally named in order of their contribution by volume. When the wine is blended from a number of varieties and/or regions it is most likely that it will not be labelled as a varietal wine.

The winemaker's guarantee that the wine comes from the stated region.

The alcoholic content.
The alcoholic strength shown on the label will give you a guide to the alcohol content of the wine. For wine sold in Australia, the actual alcohol content can be ± 1.5% alc/vol of the stated level.
This figure varies for other countries.

These codes refer to additives; in this case, 220 indicates that sulphur dioxide has been added to the wine during processing. We discuss the use of additives in the section on winemaking.

MOUNT AVOCA

SHIRAZ
1994

Quality & Authenticity

PYRENEES, VICTORIA

SHIRAZ 1994

Mount Avoca Vineyard is in the Victorian Pyrenees Ranges. Cold spring weather followed by a long cool summer produced a small quantity of superb fruit. Two years in French oak has resulted in a full flavoured wine with a velvety finish. This soft, fruity Shiraz is extremely enjoyable now, but can be matured for several years.
Enjoy in moderation.
100% grown, made and bottled at Mount Avoca Vineyard, Avoca, Victoria, Australia

750 ML   13.5% ALC/VOL.
PRESERVATIVE (220) ADDED
APPROX 8.0 STANDARD DRINKS

Some hints to help you understand Australian wine labels

Grape varieties

Australian wine producers, unlike their European counterparts, grow a number of grape varieties in any particular area. Thus, you are likely to find Riesling, Chardonnay, Shiraz and Cabernet Sauvignon vines (and wines made from them) in most Australian wine regions. Each region will produce a different style of wine from each variety.

Grape growing and winemaking methods

Further, our winemakers are not obligated to produce wines according to regional traditions and/or regulations, as in some areas of Europe. Australian winemakers may make their wines by traditional methods, newer approaches, or perhaps a blend of both philosophies; it all depends on the style of wine they intend to produce.

Blending

Freedom to source grapes from a range of areas and to blend wines from different varieties and/or regions offers the opportunity for wine companies:
- to increase and enhance their range of wine styles, and
- to produce larger volumes of popular 'brand' names of consistent quality.

Regional wines

Sometimes wine producers will blend wines from different regions to obtain a particular style, while at other times they will make wines exclusively from grapes grown in one region. Some regions have introduced a more detailed system to indicate the origin of the wine, eg when a wine from the Mudgee Region carries the appellation mark on the bottle, it is a guarantee that the wine was made at the vineyard from grapes grown on the property. However, even though a region such as Mudgee may be well recognised for producing quality wines, these systems are only a guarantee of the origin of the wine and not a statement of any quality rating.

There are also hundreds of small wineries (often referred to as boutique) that form another significant part of the Australian wine industry. Most of these make their wines only from grapes grown in their own region and produce mainly premium varietal, regional wines, wines that not only express the characters of the region but often the personality of their maker.

The mark of the Society for the Appellation of the Wines of Mudgee

The Tasmanian Appellation of Origin System

The same winery but with different labels

Many wine producers, irrespective of where they are based, may own vineyards in or source grapes from many grapegrowing regions of Australia. The grapes may be used to produce a wine that is labelled as a variety coming from a particular region, or as a blend of varieties with a region either declared or not, or as a 'brand' name.

Wine producers (both large and small) may make a range of wines of varying styles, often under different labels. The two examples below illustrate this point.

The Rosemount Estate Winery is located near Denman in the Upper Hunter Valley with extensive vineyards in Australia's best regions. The Estates wines are made from vineyards chosen for their ability to produce unique varietal flavours such as Semillon and Chardonnay from the Upper Hunter, Shiraz from Mudgee, Chardonnay from Orange, Cabernet Sauvignon from Coonawarra, Shiraz and Cabernet Sauvignon from Langhorne Creek and McLaren Vale and Sauvignon Blanc from the Adelaide Hills.

Dromana Estate is a small, family owned vineyard on Victoria's Mornington Peninsula. As well as the Dromana Estate range of wines, which highlights the qualities of the Mornington Peninsular area, another label, known as Schinus, is also produced. Dromana Estate wines are produced from grapes grown in the Mornington Peninsula, while those under the Schinus Label may come as well from specially selected vineyards in areas as diverse as the Yarra and King Valleys in Victoria and Coonawarra and McLaren Vale in South Australia. The label on each bottle will indicate the source of the grapes.

Quality wines maturing in the cellar

CELLARING WINES

To most of us a cellar is our collection of wine in wine boxes in the cupboard or under the bed, while to others it is an underground cellar or a specially built temperature controlled room. Wherever you store your wines, it is recommended that they should be in a dark, well ventilated environment which is free of odours and vibrations. To ensure that your wine is maintained in its ideal condition, it should be held at a temperature of about 12-15°C with minimum temperature fluctuation and with a humidity of about 70-80%.

Why are these conditions important?

Temperature

High temperatures advance the development of the wine, while very low temperatures may accelerate the precipitation of tartrates and colouring matter. Conditions where the temperature fluctuates over a large range are most detrimental, as they cause random rapid ageing and/or precipitation. As the temperature increases and decreases, the volume of wine expands and contracts, putting pressure on the cork, potentially causing cork movement and contraction. This may lead to seepage between the cork and the inside of the neck of the bottle and, ultimately, leakage of wine from the bottle. Fluctuation in temperature can be monitored by a maximum-minimum thermometer placed in the storage area.

Humidity

If the atmosphere is too dry, corks can lose moisture and hence their elasticity, resulting in a poor seal. However, if conditions are too damp, there is a possibility of fungal growth occurring on top of the cork, and labels may become moist and damaged as well.

Good ventilation and freedom from odours

Well ventilated conditions prevent any odours from building up and possibly being absorbed by the cork and consequently into the wine.

Darkness and freedom from vibrations

Storing the wine in the dark prevents any damage from light. Ultraviolet light is damaging to wine, particularly sparkling and delicate white wines. Wherever possible, it is best to leave the wines in their original cartons, boxes or wrapping. Vibration, or any movement for that matter, can unsettle any deposit in the wine and also disturb the harmony of the ageing reactions.

Obviously, not everyone will be able to store their wines under these ideal conditions, but try to follow these guidelines as much as possible, to ensure that your wines age in optimal or near-optimal conditions.

Bottles of table wines and vintage ports should be stored lying down, while other fortified wines (tawny ports, muscats and tokays) are best stored upright. Depending on the size of your cellar, they can be stored either in boxes or racks. A number of companies produce wine racks suitable for storing various numbers of wine bottles. If using any of these systems, it is important to set them up in an environment which is as close to the ideal storage conditions as possible. Arrange the bottles so that those intended for more immediate consumption are more accessible, as this prevents unnecessary movement of bottles each time you select a wine.

It is best to align the bottles so that their corks are visible to enable checking for leakage. Regular inspection of your wines will not only remind you of future drinking pleasures, but will also help you notice any problems, such as leakage. If there are signs of leakage, check the ullage level. However a low ullage level does not always indicate a problem, as fill levels during bottling can vary slightly. But if the ullage level is below the shoulder of the bottle then the wine should be assessed and either recorked (if in good condition) or consumed as soon as possible.

the cork

head space — ullage level

When the bottle is upright the ullage level is the level of the wine in the bottle.

Penfolds is one of the few wine companies in the world that offer recorking clinics for bottles of their red wines.

What happens when wines age?

The period of time during which the wine is handled and stored in the winery is called the maturation stage, while ageing usually refers to the time in bottle. However, both processes are intimately linked, ageing being a progression of the maturation, albeit at a slower rate. The most obvious change is in the colour of the wine, but aromas and flavours and mouthfeel are also modified.

Ageing of wine distinguishes wine from almost every other drink and most food products. If these other products are aged, for example some cheeses, it is normally by the producer prior to sale, whereas with wine it is most often the customer who takes responsibility for its ageing.

Why age wine?

Simply, wines are aged to increase their complexity.

The chemical reactions that occur during ageing add new aromas, flavours and textures to the wine. The primary fruit compounds are gradually transformed into their developed forms, and as these reactions occur, the number of chemical compounds increases. The complexity of the wine grows as the aromas and flavours of youth intermingle with those that form with the progress of age. If the wine is aged for too long and all the reactions progress through to their final steps, there will be fewer chemical compounds in the wine and these are likely to all smell and taste very similar. The wine will have lost its complexity and will, in wine terms, be 'over the hill'.

Reactions other than those that lead to changes in the colour and flavour profile also take place; for example, some of the acids and alcohol present can react to form volatile compounds, but the impact of these changes on the character of the wine is generally regarded as minimal. These reactions involve only very small amounts of acid and the overall acid level of the wine actually does not change significantly as the wine ages. However, the acid may appear to soften as complexity increases.

The ageing of white wines

With age the colour of white wines intensifies. The straw and yellow colours associated with younger wines change to deeper yellow and even golden tones in older wines. With further time, however, the striking yellow and gold hues will progressively turn to brown as the wine succumbs to the final steps in its ageing process. These changes in colour are associated with alteration in the phenolic nature of the wine, but the actual reactions that are responsible for the deepening of the colour are poorly understood.

The aromas and flavours that develop in white wines as they age are similar to toast, fig, honey and caramel. Interestingly, these are smells and flavours that we associate with heating foods. They represent the slow transformation of the primary fruit characters to their more mature forms. Both temperature and oxygen play a role in these reactions. Although there can be small amounts of oxygen present in wines when they are bottled, it is thought that this is consumed early in the ageing process, perhaps within a few months of bottling. The ageing reactions following this are then essentially anaerobic and temperature becomes the major factor controlling the rate of ageing. Higher cellaring temperatures will advance the ageing processes, while cooler temperatures can slow them.

White wines develop more yellow/golden colours with time.

The aromas and flavours that develop with time can be similar to those associated with heating foods.

The ageing of wine, whether the wine be white or red, is not a simple process. It involves a multitude of chemical reactions, many of which are interrelated. Some wines begin their ageing process already with considerable intensity of flavour and complexity, for example many Chardonnays. With time these wines develop additional nutty, almond and honey characters, increasing their complexity and interest. They hold this complexity over a number of years before gradually becoming more one dimensional as caramelised and oxidised characters become more obvious.

On the other hand, many of our Rieslings and classic Hunter Valley Semillons destined for ageing begin their life as quite subdued wines. However with age in the bottle not only do they develop wonderful toasty, honeyed characters, but they also build in weight and texture. It is almost as if they become different wines, but it must be remembered that the potential for these changes lies in the character of the fruit. Riesling and Semillon wines that have the potential to age come from grapes that are delicately flavoured and have high acidity which, when carried over into the wine, contributes to its structure and ageing potential.

John Wilson of The Wilson Vineyard, in the Polish Hill River district near Clare in South Australia, describes the changes he has observed in his Riesling wines in these words.

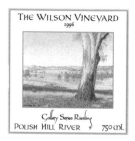

'Typically these wines emerge from vintage with citric flavours (predominantly limes) and a steely backbone. Very quickly they acquire flavours of tropical fruit (passion-fruit, pineapples, monstera fruit) and reach a peak at between one and two years old. The steeliness starts to fade early, and by two years the fresh tropical flavours are declining. There seems to be no change in the apparent level of citrus and lime flavours over time. With age a honeyed character emerges, although it appears that the intensity of this may be related to the sugar content of the wine, and possibly the level of ripeness at which the grapes were picked. Later still, there appear cedar-wood characters. Bear in mind that these wines have no wood contact at all.'

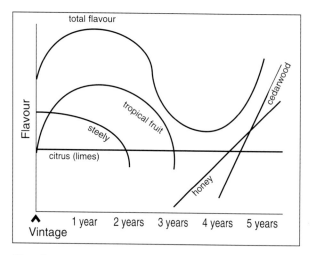

This is how John Wilson (winemaker of The Wilson Vineyard in the Polish Hill River region of South Australia) describes changes in his Rieslings with time.

The ageing of red wines

Anthocyanins (the coloured compounds in the skin) and other phenolics in the skin and seeds of the grape, after being extracted during fermentation, can combine with each other to form tannins in the wine. The tannins are initially small but with time combine to form larger tannins. The anthocyanins and the smaller tannins are red coloured, whereas the large tannins are brown. Thus, the colour of red wines changes with time from red, red/purple and sometimes almost black (in young wines with high concentrations of anthocyanins) to brick red, red brown and brown (in older wines). When the tannins get large they may precipitate; if this occurs after bottling, they form the red, red/brown crust often seen in bottles of older red wines.

The tannins interact with the saliva in the mouth, nullifying its lubricating actions, and thus the mouth feels dry. The interaction between tannins and saliva is stronger when the tannins are smaller. This is why some young wines which are high in tannins may be very astringent. The larger tannins which form as the wine ages do not react to the same extent with the saliva; the impact of the tannins in the mouth is less astringent and the wine is more pleasing to taste. There is now greater opportunity for the flavours of the wine, and particularly the more subtle flavours that come with age, to manifest themselves in the wine. Thus many medium- to full-bodied wines require time to mature and soften so that both their flavours and mouthfeel can be fully appreciated.

Intriguingly, red wines appear to age in a way similar to the annual changes observed in the vineyard. During the ripening period the grapes develop distinctive aromas and flavours which, when carried over into the wine, are the main aromas and flavours of the young wine. In the vineyard, after the grapes are harvested and the leaves have fallen, the shoots brown and harden and take on a more woody, earthy smell. These aromas are also apparent in wines as they age. When the vine is pruned, the shoots fall to the ground to join the mass of fallen leaves and other matter that accumulate on the vineyard floor. The process of decay continues, and smells reminiscent of earth, fungi, mushrooms and farmyards are associated with this environment. Interestingly some of the aromas and flavours of older red wines can be very similar to those of the vineyard floor, suggesting that the ageing of red wines could be perceived as simply a controlled progression of the changes that would naturally happen in the fruit if it were unharvested and with time returned to its environment.

Apart from these characters associated with the vineyard floor, other characters can also emerge during the life of a red wine. Older red wines can also take on impressions of coffee, cigars and tobacco, although one could argue that these are also closely linked to modifications in the nature of plant material. They are all part of the network of reactions that make red wines more complex with time. The aromas, flavours and mouthfeel of great old wines tasted in their prime are things to be savoured; this 'genesis of complexity' can create an overall character that can be absorbing and captivating. Regrettably these changes continue until the wine loses its intensity of aroma and flavour and lessens in complexity. By this time the wine will normally be quite brown and will start to taste more acidic. At this stage, when the wine has lost its flavour and the acidity is more dominant, it is said to be 'drying out'.

Red wines become more red/brown and brown with time.

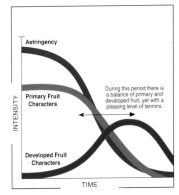

A representation of how the sensations of primary and developed fruit characters and astringency may change with time. Each wine will have different levels of intensity of these characters and a different pattern of change.

The vine loses its leaves

and they return to the vineyard floor.

Maturation and ageing, properly conducted, increase the complexity and quality of the wine. We believe that wines are most enjoyable when the characters of youth and age are harmoniously intermingled. Even old or very old wines can have tantalising reminders of their primary fruit characters.

How long will a wine improve in the bottle?

It is difficult to predict when a wine will be at its best. This depends somewhat on individual preference and whether you enjoy the vibrant flavours of youth or the developed characters and textures that come with time. Most white wines and light-bodied reds are best enjoyed as young wines, one to three years old, as their primary fruit characters are their most appealing feature. Other wines, particularly full-bodied, more complex whites and reds, are at their peak when the flavours of youth intermingle with those of age to evolve complexity and harmony and where the mouthfeel is softer and more pleasing. However, one must be cautious about how long to store different wines. Early drinking styles are usually consumed within 1-2 years after they are made. For white wines intended for cellaring, it is best to check the wines within a few years of their making and then to reassess them every year. For red wines intended for cellaring, however, it is recommended to check them about 5 years after their making and then to reassess them every couple of years or less, depending on the development of the wine.

Wines that have the propensity to age gracefully over many years (ten, twenty years or more) will typically, as young wines, have an intensity of aromas and flavours coupled with fresh acidity, and, in red wines, moderate to high amounts of tannins. They are wines that are well balanced and structured. They can be light-, medium- or full-bodied wines depending on the grape variety from which they were made. Generally they come from well-managed vines grown in cool to warm and warm sites, from lower yielding vines and from excellent vintages and reputable makers. Often a wine's track record from previous similar vintages is a good indication of its ageing potential.

Does the size of the bottle make a difference?
Yes. One of the reasons is that in smaller bottles, the proportion of air in the ullage space to the volume of wine is higher than in larger bottles, and hence it is likely that ageing will occur more readily in the smaller bottle and the wines will mature earlier. Some special wines are bottled in magnums (or larger) so that the wine will retain optimum flavour and freshness during long cellaring. On the other hand, some winemakers will bottle a portion of their red wine in half bottles to offer greater choice to consumers who appreciate a more mature wine, but with less cellaring time involved.

In deciding how long to cellar particular wines, be guided by your own assessment and advice from wine merchants, winemakers and wine reviews. Ideally it is best to purchase a case and regularly assess the wine over a number of years. Although this may initially be expensive, in the long run it is the cheapest way to build up a collection of good, mature wines. Hedonistic as it may be, developing a wine cellar can be a very rewarding experience.

The climates of Australian vineyards vary immensely, not only across states but also within relatively small distances, and thus it is difficult to generalise about the quality of the vintage in particular regions. However, generally through the 1980s the even years were considered to be the better vintages, while in the 1990s, 1990 and 1991 are regarded as being excellent vintages.

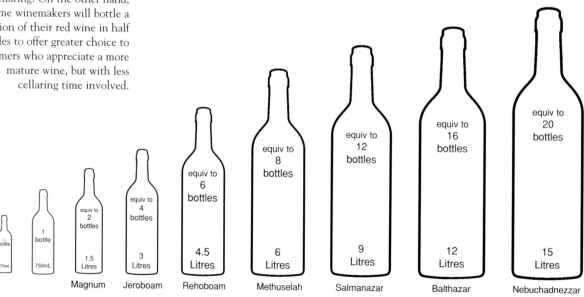

These names are associated with different size bottles. They mainly relate to sparkling wine bottles.

SERVING AND ENJOYING WINE

The way the wine is prepared and presented for serving can make a difference to the enjoyment of drinking it.

When the bottles are brought from the cellar prior to serving, allow them to reach the recommended drinking temperature; some may require refrigeration. Ideally red wines (particularly older wines) should be retrieved at least a day before they are required and stood upright to allow any deposits to settle on the bottom of the bottle before opening. This would also apply to white wines that may have thrown a deposit of tartrate crystals during storage. Inspect the top of the cork to check for any leakage and then observe the ullage level. If there is leakage or if the level of the wine is low, it is recommended that the wine be opened carefully and tasted prior to serving to any guests, as these signs indicate that the wine may not be in its best condition, and may possibly even be oxidised.

A range of equipment used to open wine bottles and to serve wine:
1. The midan wine pourer — used to make it easier to pour the wine without drops of wine forming at the end of pouring;
2. screwpull ®foil cutter;
3,4,5,6,7,8. various bottle openers;
9. a sparkling wine bottle closure used to retain the pressure after the cork is removed;
10. a decanter.

Some guidelines for opening a bottle of still wine

Cut the foil capsule under the lower lip of the bottle. Remove the top of the capsule and then wipe the top of the bottle with a clean, damp cloth to remove any sediment and/or pieces of capsule. A foil cutter (shown above right) can also be used to remove the top of the capsule.

Insert the tip of the corkscrew into the centre of the cork with the corkscrew at an angle, so that you do not push the cork in when inserting it. Straighten the corkscrew and twist it in a clockwise direction until it is inserted almost fully into the cork, with about one to two turns visible above the cork. Place the end of the lever on the lip of the bottle. Pull the handle of the corkscrew up with a gentle, even pressure. Change the pivotal contact point of the lever on the lip of the bottle during cork extraction so that the cork is removed vertically. As you are raising the handle it also helps to hold the bottom of the lever in place on the lip of the bottle with the fingers of the other hand. The last stage of removal should be completed by hand. Be careful with old, crumbly corks and proceed cautiously when inserting the corkscrew. If the cork breaks during extraction and crumbles, it is best to decant the wine through a funnel with a metal filter, to remove the pieces of cork prior to serving.

These pictures show a double sided cork screw (in this case a Screwpull ®). The even pressure exerted by the two arms ensures that the cork is removed vertically. Hold the base of the arms around the neck of the bottle while turning the screw. As the handle is turned the cork is extracted.

Pour the wine in a continuous action, and twist the bottle to prevent any drops of wine forming at the end of pouring.

Some guidelines for opening a bottle of sparkling wine

 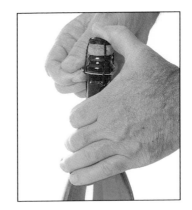

Find the pull to tear the capsule and remove the top of the capsule. Untwist the wire ring which holds the wire cage around the cork. Untwist the wire carefully and separate the strands of wire. While doing this, hold the thumb of your other hand on the cork to prevent it popping out of the bottle. Remove the wire cage, being careful that the cork does not pop out.

Hold the bottle firmly in one hand and hold the cork with the other hand. Ensure that the bottle is pointed away from yourself and others. Hold the cork firmly and slowly twist the bottle. Do not twist the cork. As the bottle is twisted the cork should start to ease out of the bottle. Apply downward pressure on the cork so that it does not come out suddenly. At the last stage of removal ease the cork out slowly, holding it between your fingers at all times. Do not let the cork pop out. Wipe the neck of the bottle with a clean, damp cloth.

If the cork is very tight and difficult to remove, it can be removed with an aid such as a Strachan Champagne cork extractor.

Hold the base of the bottle with your thumb in the punt and the fingers along the underside of the bottle. Pour a small amount of wine into the glass. Allow the foam to subside before pouring more wine into the glass until it is about half to two thirds full. Return the bottle to the ice bucket.

To decant or not?

Not all wines need decanting; normally most whites and lighter bodied reds can be poured directly from the bottle. However, during ageing red wines can throw a crust and decanting the wine prior to serving removes the sediment. Decant carefully, gradually and in one action, until you see any sediment just below the neck of the bottle; placing a candle or torch under the neck of the bottle can help you observe the sediment. The use of a funnel with an in-built metal filter also helps to remove any deposits. The other purpose of decanting is to aerate the wine slightly, allowing it 'to breathe', and to liberate any off-odours. In addition to red wines, some full-bodied, wooded Chardonnays may benefit from decanting and breathing.

On the question of 'how long to decant the wine prior to serving', there is much debate. Our view is that the wine should be decanted immediately prior to serving. The aromas and flavours of wines, particularly older wines, can be quite delicate, and excessive contact with air may not be beneficial. The decanting action will aerate most wines sufficiently and if they do require further time to breathe, it is best that this occurs in the decanter or glass where the changes can be more readily observed. Remember that you can swirl the wine in the glass to further aerate the wine and release its aromas. The exception to the above advice might be when, through experience, you know that a particular wine will require and can handle a longer breathing time.

If the wine is taken directly from the cellar and there is no time to allow it to stand before decanting, then the wine should be carried in the horizontal position from the cellar and then decanted from this position, preferably in a decanting cradle.

A decanting machine

What about double decanting?

Double decanting occurs when the wine is initially decanted into a decanter or jug, the bottle is rinsed to remove any deposits and allowed to drain, and then the decanted wine is returned to its original bottle. The practical benefits of this are that only one decanter is required for a number of bottles of wine, and the wine can be served in the original bottle, maintaining the association of the label and the wine in the glass. This is important as wine is one of the few food products that is presented at the table in its original packaging, and knowledge of the wine's identity can enhance the anticipation of drinking it.

These three photographs demonstrate various stages of decanting a red wine

Wine glasses — is there a difference?

Glasses for tasting wine should be clear, clean and ideally unadorned and should be thoroughly washed, rinsed and wiped with a lint-free cloth. If glasses have been stored in cardboard boxes they should be washed and dried before use to remove the smell of the packaging, ie the powdery, cardboard and dusty odours. Traditionally, there are different shapes of glasses. The different glass shapes enhance the perception of the aromas of each wine style. The delicate aromas of a Riesling or a sparkling wine are more readily perceived in a narrow glass with a small opening as the aromas are concentrated into a smaller volume and the aroma impact intensified. A glass with a large bowl, but still with a tapered top, is more suitable for red wines and some whites as the wine can be easily swirled to release the less volatile and more powerful, complex aromas.

Any advantages of the shape of the glass on the impact of the characters of the wine on the palate are somewhat debatable. It is now thought that the different taste buds are not localised on specific areas of the tongue, except for bitterness which is more pronounced at the back of the tongue and mouth. Thus, placement of the wine on different sections of the tongue may not particularly aid in discerning the different tastes, perhaps with the exception of bitterness. Further, once the wine enters the mouth and is moved around to fully appreciate its flavours and textures, then it could be argued, that any advantage of the placement of the wine in the mouth via a particular shaped glass is minimal. However, many wine lovers would argue that when drinking wine, as opposed to a rigorous conscious assessment of its qualities, that the shape of the glass does appear to add to the enjoyment of its characters in the mouth as well as on the nose.

While the role of the shape of the glass on the impact of the perception of the characters of the wine on the palate can be debated, the importance of the shape of the glass in appreciating the aromas of different wines and the added ambience that the use of a finely crafted glass brings to the overall pleasure of drinking wine cannot be challenged. Thus there will always be a need for fine glassware produced by companies such as the Riedel glassmaking family of Austria. This company has designed and produced a large range of glasses for the different wine styles made around the world and recently has developed a glass specifically for enjoying the characters of Australian Shiraz wine. Admittedly, Riedel glasses or other special glasses are not necessarily required every time you drink wine, but for those wine lovers who want to appreciate fully the subtleties of the characters of wine, using special glasses can add to the overall pleasure and experience.

The International Standards Organisation (ISO) glass, a suitable glass for tasting most wines

The Riedel Riesling glass and the Riedel Shiraz glass — classic glasses for two classic Australian wine styles

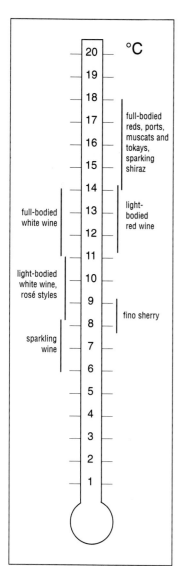

°C	
20	
19	
18	
17	full-bodied reds, ports, muscats and tokays, sparkling shiraz
16	
15	
14	
13	light-bodied red wine
12	
11	
10	
9	
8	fino sherry
7	
6	
5	
4	
3	
2	
1	

full-bodied white wine

light-bodied white wine, rosé styles

sparkling wine

The suggested temperature range to enjoy different wine styles
While there are no set rules, there is general agreement regarding the best temperature range at which to drink wines. The above diagram provides a guide to the appropriate temperature ranges.

Serving the wine

Normally a small portion of wine is poured into the glass and the wine smelt and tasted to check if there are any faults. If the wine is free of faults it can then be served. Preferably the glass should be only half filled (or less, depending on the size of the glass) so that the wine can be easily swirled to heighten the perception of its aromas.

The temperature of the wine — does it make a difference to its characters?

There are hundreds, perhaps thousands, of compounds which make up the aroma and flavour of a wine, and different groups are released from the surface of the wine at different temperatures. Aromatic, fragrant aromas are released at lower temperatures, while the more complex compounds evaporate at higher temperatures. The temperature of the wine also affects the perception of basic tastes and mouthfeel sensations. The lower the temperature, the less the perception of sweetness, and the wine can appear to be more acidic and refreshing. Also at lower temperatures the bitter and astringent sensations can be accentuated. At higher temperatures the hotness of alcohol can be more apparent.

The temperature effect — a summary

Higher temperatures:
• enhance the smell of stronger flavours,
• increase the perception of sweetness,
• lessen the impact of the tannins, and
• increase the warmth / hotness of alcohol.

Lower temperatures:
• lift the more aromatic aromas,
• decrease the perception of sugar,
• increase the perception of acid, and
• accentuate bitter and astringent tastes.

Within these general guidelines there are some other suggestions that need to be considered when serving different wines.

• Wines should not be served above 20°C as this can dull their apparent freshness and enhance the hotness of the alcohol.
• Wines with obvious oak characters can be served towards the upper limit of the recommended temperature range as this dulls the sensation of oak tannins.
• More subtle, older red wines may be best served towards the lower end of the recommended temperature range to preserve their delicate flavours.
• Fortified wines can be served slightly chilled as this lessens the effect of the spirit.
• With all wines, it is better to err towards the lower end of the suggested temperature range as normally the wine will warm up in the glass. If the wine needs to be warmed further, you can cup your hands around the glass to warm the wine.
• Wines can be chilled by placing the bottle in the refrigerator for a short time until it reaches the desired temperature.
• Sparkling wine is best served chilled but not ice cold. It can be chilled by placing the bottle in a bucket filled with ice and water and leaving it for about thirty minutes, or by storing it in the refrigerator for about four hours.
Do not place the bottle in the freezer compartment.

What is the best order in which to taste wine?

It is normally recommended to taste light-bodied before full-bodied, white before red, dry before sweet and young before old, but common sense should prevail and some light-bodied red wine or older reds may be more appropriately tasted before full-bodied whites. Further, on some occasions, it may be best to enjoy an older red wine before a younger one. It depends very much on the accompanying food.

Talking about wine

If you wish to share your opinion of the wine with others, it is best if you are familiar with some wine terms and how to talk about wines. We cover this in the chapter on 'The wine in the glass'.

Wine and food — a perfect combination

WINE WITH FOOD

Flavour, taste and texture in the glass, flavour, taste and texture on the plate; it comes as no surprise that the worlds of wine and food are so closely linked. Usually wine is selected to be served and enjoyed with food, and Australia, being a multicultural nation, provides a wide and exciting choice of cuisines, Mediterranean, Pacific, Japanese, Chinese, Thai, Indian and many others. Australians are certainly becoming more creative in exploring the taste of food and wine. Sauces, spices and textures that were alien to our grandparents are now readily available, as well as a much wider and more interesting choice of wine styles. The old accepted rules of white wine with fish or white meat and red wine with red meat do not necessarily apply now. There are no real rights or wrongs in pairing wine with food, only some guidelines based around personal taste and experience. These less prescriptive guidelines allow for the combination of wine and food to be adventurous, imaginative and enjoyable.

Some guidelines for matching food and wine
Aim for matches where the characters of the food and wine complement each other. Match the power of the food with the power of the wine, while taking into account the texture and the types of flavours present in each.

The power of a wine or a food is the combination of the impression of weight with the perception of the intensity of the flavours when taken into the mouth. The weight of a wine is largely determined by its alcohol, extract and sugar content, while the flavour intensity of a wine is linked to the variety and to where and how the grapes were grown. The weight of food relates partly to its fat and sugar content, while the flavour intensity is influenced not only by its inherent components but also by the way it is prepared and cooked.

Food can be cooked in a variety of ways: steamed, poached, sautéed, stir fried, pan fried, deep fried, roasted, baked, braised, stewed, grilled or charcoal grilled. The order in which these methods of cooking are listed here signifies a progression in flavour intensification. Generally a more full-bodied wine would be chosen to accompany food with increased flavour intensity, for example poached whiting fillet could be matched with a light- to medium-bodied Riesling or a Rosé, but when the whiting is grilled, a medium-bodied barrel fermented Chardonnay or Semillon or even a Pinot Noir may be a better choice.

The sauces and spices used in cooking can alter the perception of the intensity of flavour as well as the texture, and this fact needs to be taken into consideration when selecting the wine. For example, a fillet steak served with a creamy mushroom sauce may match either a medium-bodied red or a rich, complex Chardonnay, but served with a tomato based sauce it marries better with a medium- to full-bodied red; try a Grenache, Shiraz or blend.

As well as the power of the food and the wine, the types of flavours and the textures should also complement each other. Some foods which are light in texture, eg salads or calamari, are best matched with light- to medium-bodied wines, while other foods can have more weight and texture, eg a beef stew or kangaroo steak, and require a more full-bodied wine. Another guide is to coordinate the types of flavours, eg foods with lime flavours paired with the lime characters of a Riesling, or richly flavoured caramel based desserts married with the luscious flavours of a muscat or tokay.

Our tastes for food and wine and their many combinations vary from person to person. The essence of drinking wine is to accompany it with tasty foods, and the synergy is best enjoyed when shared with family and friends.

POWER = WEIGHT + FLAVOUR INTENSITY

Food Alchemy
Successful pairing of food and wine is a magical matching of their chemistry. We have already mentioned weight, flavour and texture, but there are some other factors to be considered.

Foods with an acid taste, such as salad with a vinaigrette dressing, are best aligned with refreshing, higher acid wines. Wines that accompany sweet foods should be as sweet or sweeter than the food, so that the wines are not dominated by the richness of the dish. Highly flavoured, young, tannic red wines are difficult to match. Their tannins are too dominant for fish; they require food with plenty of power, such as a char-grilled steak. Foods that contain fat or those cooked in oil are best paired with high acid white or red wines. The acid cuts through the fat. Salty foods appear to be better balanced by the taste of sweet wines.

Artichokes contain a compound that often makes the accompanying wine taste sweeter and metallic, and it is difficult to pair this vegetable with wine. However, the best match seems to be a light fruity wine with plenty of acid.

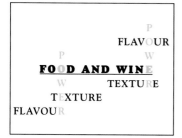

FLAVOUR

FOOD AND WINE

TEXTURE

TEXTURE

FLAVOUR

The three guidelines to matching food and wine: power, flavour and texture

The way we combine food and wine is a personal choice; perceptions of power, flavour and texture can vary greatly between individuals. Differences occur depending on the way the food is prepared, whether it is steamed or grilled, with or without spices, with or without sauces, and whether it is served with accompanying vegetables or salad. Some dishes are relatively simple, while others offer a cornucopia of flavours and textures. The challenge is to cater for these differences and to be creative in enhancing the enjoyment and appreciation of food.

We have designed a 'food power chart' to provide a guide to the power of some foods. Foods are grouped without taking into consideration cooking method or any combination with spices or sauces. It is a general representation and the positioning of some foods may vary slightly within the scale, particularly when it is appreciated that the taste of food, like wine, varies depending on where and how it was grown or farmed. However, from the lighter flavoured seafood at one end to the gamey red meats at the other, it provides a starting point in appreciating that foods vary in their tastes and that these are complemented by the characters of different wines.

FOOD POWER CHART

LIGHTER FOOD   **HEAVIER FOOD**

Seafood

oysters calamari mussels   coral trout crab crayfish tuna
  prawns whiting octopus john dory scallops   Morton Bay bugs
    yabby shark marron barramundi   Murray cod
                    Atlantic salmon

White meat

emu   quail
chicken   crocodile   pheasant
pork   pigeon   turkey
        rabbit/hare   duck   wild duck

Red meat

veal   beef
    lamb   kangaroo
        mutton   venison
            ox/buffalo

*The food may be prepared by different cooking methods, or with spices or sauces.
If so, its positioning may move across the chart, and the accompanying wine may need to
be one with more weight, flavour intensity and complexity.*

Light- to medium-bodied wines such as sparkling wine, Riesling, Gewürztraminer, Frontignac, Chenin Blanc, Colombard, Sauvignon Blanc, unwooded Chardonnay or Rosé are good matches for the foods towards the lighter end of the chart.

Medium-bodied wines including white and red sparkling wine, Sauvignon Blanc, barrel fermented Chardonnays and Semillons, Marsanne and reds, especially Pinot Noir, Sangiovese, Merlot and Grenache, complement more textured and sweeter seafood and most white and lighter red meats.

Medium- to full-bodied wines such as some Chardonnay, Pinot Noir, Shiraz and blends, Cabernet Sauvignon and blends and Sparkling Shiraz match the weight and stronger flavours of those foods towards the right of the chart. Generally a robust red is required to complement the foods at the far right end.

Variations around the food and wine theme —

Here we have taken the approach of focussing on the characters that are found in different foods, rather than selecting food specifically from different countries. These suggestions are only that, and you should feel free to experiment with different combinations.

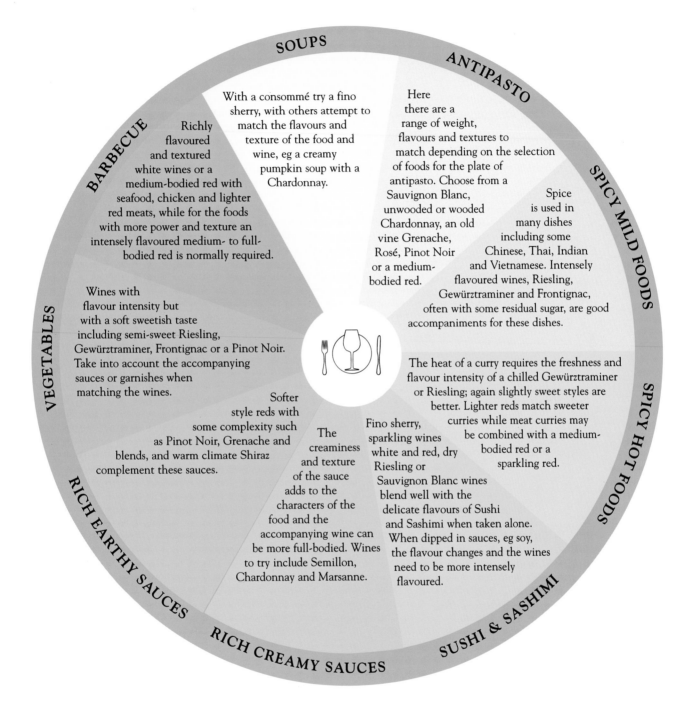

SOUPS

With a consommé try a fino sherry, with others attempt to match the flavours and texture of the food and wine, eg a creamy pumpkin soup with a Chardonnay.

ANTIPASTO

Here there are a range of weight, flavours and textures to match depending on the selection of foods for the plate of antipasto. Choose from a Sauvignon Blanc, unwooded or wooded Chardonnay, an old vine Grenache, Rosé, Pinot Noir or a medium-bodied red.

BARBECUE

Richly flavoured and textured white wines or a medium-bodied red with seafood, chicken and lighter red meats, while for the foods with more power and texture an intensely flavoured medium- to full-bodied red is normally required.

SPICY MILD FOODS

Spice is used in many dishes including some Chinese, Thai, Indian and Vietnamese. Intensely flavoured wines, Riesling, Gewürztraminer and Frontignac, often with some residual sugar, are good accompaniments for these dishes.

VEGETABLES

Wines with flavour intensity but with a soft sweetish taste including semi-sweet Riesling, Gewürztraminer, Frontignac or a Pinot Noir. Take into account the accompanying sauces or garnishes when matching the wines.

SPICY HOT FOODS

The heat of a curry requires the freshness and flavour intensity of a chilled Gewürztraminer or Riesling; again slightly sweet styles are better. Lighter reds match sweeter curries while meat curries may be combined with a medium-bodied red or a sparkling red.

RICH EARTHY SAUCES

Softer style reds with some complexity such as Pinot Noir, Grenache and blends, and warm climate Shiraz complement these sauces.

RICH CREAMY SAUCES

The creaminess and texture of the sauce adds to the characters of the food and the accompanying wine can be more full-bodied. Wines to try include Semillon, Chardonnay and Marsanne.

SUSHI & SASHIMI

Fino sherry, sparkling wines white and red, dry Riesling or Sauvignon Blanc wines blend well with the delicate flavours of Sushi and Sashimi when taken alone. When dipped in sauces, eg soy, the flavour changes and the wines need to be more intensely flavoured.

The age of wine and how it matches with food

Often it is difficult to complement the strong, robust flavours and mouthfeel of a young red, but with time the wine mellows and develops a softer feel and more complex and interesting flavours, characters that lend themselves to matching food more readily — an added incentive to cellar red wines.

Wine in cooking

Wine adds flavour to the food, and the wine used should have characters and quality similar to those of the food. Good food deserves good wine both in the dish and in the glass.

CHEESE AND WINE

There are hundreds of cheese types, and their tastes are as diverse as those of wines. For ease of matching them with wine we have divided them into three groups: soft, hard and blue.

Soft

The soft cheeses, Brie, Camembert, goat and sheep cheeses, are more lightly textured, and light- to medium-bodied wines are better partners, such as wines with high acidity like sparkling wine, Riesling and Sauvignon Blanc. The creamier, richer styles of cheese may require more complex wines including some Chardonnay wines, sweet whites and mature muscats.

Some suggestions

Jindi Brie, Adelaide Brie, Heritage Camembert and Timboon Farmhouse.

Hard

The stronger flavours and textures of these cheeses match medium- to full-bodied wines like barrel fermented Chardonnay and Semillon. Generally red wines, particularly young wines because of their high tannin content, do not combine well with cheese. If you wish to serve red wine with these cheeses, it is best to focus on low tannic wines like Rosé, Pinot Noir, Sangiovese, Tarrango and some of Australia's medium-bodied reds that are more fruity, rounded and soft. Old red wines, where the tannins have mellowed, may also be suitable.

Some suggestions

Mersey Valley Cheddar, Cradle Valley extra tasty and Mt Barker matured.

Blue

The powerful, complex and often pungent flavours of these cheeses require strongly flavoured, complex wines, including sweet whites such as botrytis Semillon and fortified wines such as port, muscat or tokay.

Some suggestions

Milawa Blue, King Island Admiralty Blue, Heritage True Blue and Gippsland Blue.

When serving a platter of cheeses it can be difficult to match one wine with all the different textures and tastes. We suggest that you serve one superb cheese accompanied by an excellent wine.

DESSERTS AND WINE
Ice creams and sorbets

Ice cream is difficult to serve with wine as the coldness on the palate dulls the characters of the wine. When the ice cream is flavoured *eg custard apple ice cream or orange and cardamom ice cream*, and thus more flavoured and textured, then a more complex, higher alcohol wine like a rich oloroso sherry or a muscat may complement it. Sorbets are designed to cleanse the palate and thus it is best to enjoy them alone.

Fruits

Aim to match the flavours of the fruit with the flavours of the wine. Try unwooded styles including dry or semi-sweet Riesling, Gewürztraminer or Frontignac and dry Sauvignon Blanc, Chardonnay and Verdelho.
Some refreshing combinations include — *fresh figs with ginger and lemon juice with a Chardonnay, or cinnamon pears with a Riesling or Gewürztraminer.*

Cakes, pastries and puddings

Combine their richness, texture and flavours with botrytis Rieslings and Semillons, sparkling Shiraz, tawny port, muscats and tokays.
Indulge in — *passionfruit soufflé or an orange and cumquat bavarois with a botrytis Riesling, steamed apricot pudding with a botrytis Semillon, or a muscat with a macadamia and coconut tart.*

AUSTRALIAN CUISINE

Australian cuisine is tasty and exciting, expressing a fusion of the influences of different cultures. Many dishes are based on the native produce that grows, lives or is farmed in our 'clean and green' lands and waters. Here we have chosen to feature the fascinating and unique dishes created by Andrew Fielke, of the Red Ochre Grill in Adelaide, from native ingredients that have formed part of Australia's landscape for thousands of years, and the wines of one of Australia's oldest family-owned wineries, Angove's.

MATCHING AUSTRALIAN FOOD AND WINE	
Australian food from the Red Ochre Grill	*Australian wine from Angove's*
Marron with pickled turnip and Kakadu plums	Classic Reserve Rhine Riesling
Yabby, wild lime and leek terrine	Classic Reserve Colombard
Rabbit, wallaby and pancetta roulade with pepperleaf and black fungus glaze	Sarina Farm Chardonnay
Char-grilled kangaroo fillet with wild mint polenta and quandong chilli sauce	Classic Reserve Shiraz

The Restaurant at Moorilla Estate Winery, near Hobart on the banks of the Derwent River

De Bortoli's Yarra Valley vineyard and restaurant complex in the Yarra Valley

Bridgewater Mill Restaurant nestled into the hillside at Bridgewater in the Adelaide Hills. The complex is also home to Petaluma's sparkling wine cellars.

The Milawa Epicurean Centre at the Brown Brothers Winery at Milawa

Roberts Restaurant situated in the Pepper Tree complex at Pokolbin in the heart of the Hunter Valley.

The Magill Estate Restaurant overlooking the historic Magill Estate Vineyard in the suburbs of Adelaide.

CLASSIC COMBINATIONS

Australia produces a diverse range of wine styles. Here we explore some of Australia's distinctive wine styles and offer suggestions on how to enjoy their characters with a range of food.

Sparkling Shiraz

Sparkling Shiraz has the strength of flavour and texture to match the weight of a range of medium to heavy foods. The earthy and chocolate tones of older wines enhance the richness and complexity of flavours of these stronger foods. Interestingly their attractive colour often complements the reddish and brown hues of the accompanying food.

Some recommendations for enjoying these wines — turkey with cranberry sauce, cold meats, spicy sausages, Peking duck, roast squab, rich patés, raw tuna, smoked salmon, steamed caramel pudding and sharp cheddar cheeses.

Aged Hunter Valley Semillon

These medium-weight wines begin their development quite subdued but with age build in strength and texture, displaying rich toasty, honeyed and fig-like tones.

Appreciate them with — yabby tails, prawns, mussels, spicy pork dishes, asparagus or asparagus quiche, pasta with creamy sun-dried tomato sauce and chicken with apricot sauce.

Riesling

The lifted freshness and flavours of Riesling wines complement most light- to medium-weight food. The cooler climate styles with their floral, fragrant tones and high acidity enhance the flavours of the array of seafood that abounds in the waters around Australia, while wines with intense aromas and flavours of lime and lemon characters and soft but crisp mouthfeel complement the spicy cuisine originating from Asian regions. The toasty and honeyed characters of aged Riesling marry with the stronger, more complex foods.

Enjoy our Riesling wines with — a platter of nuts and dried fruits, apples with spice, oysters, whiting, salmon, lime soufflé and Asian seafood or chicken dishes mildly flavoured with coriander, lemon grass, ginger and other spices.

Shiraz

Young or old, the strength and velvety tannins of Australian Shiraz marry with strongly flavoured and textured foods. Cool climate styles, with their pepper and berry characters, can accompany spicy, medium-weight dishes. The warm, richer, stronger and more complex flavours of Shiraz from warmer climates blend magically with more strongly flavoured dishes.

Match Shiraz with — stewed lamb shanks, roast duck, crusty peppered steak, kangaroo and game sausages.

Botrytis Semillon

The strong marmalade and apricot flavours and rich tastes of these wines combine superbly with luscious desserts, richer creamy cheeses and blue cheeses.

Enjoy them with — crème brûlée, zabaglione, almond orange cake, date torte, blueberry mango tartlets with strawberry sauce and King Island double brie cheese.

Muscat

This is probably the best style of wine to balance the richness of chocolate, although the luscious rich tastes of muscat also form a superb combination with Christmas puddings and other richly flavoured and textured desserts.

Savour the taste of muscat with — macadamia nut and mango ice cream, chocolate fudge cake, Christmas pudding and pecan pie.

The potential benefits
of moderate and regular
wine consumption and a
healthy diet and lifestyle
are inseparably linked.

WINE AND HEALTH

Drinking wine regularly, in moderation and with food can be beneficial to health, when coupled with a health-focussed approach to diet and lifestyle. On the other hand, abuse of alcohol can lead to serious health and social problems. Wine, like any other alcoholic beverage, requires a sensible approach to its consumption.

Is wine good for you? Are its effects different to those of beer and spirits? To help clarify issues of the debate on the benefits of drinking wine, Ms Creina Stockley, Information Manager, The Australian Wine Research Institute, has kindly offered to share some recent findings.

Often when the benefits of drinking wine are discussed, the story of the 'French Paradox' is raised.

What is this 'French Paradox'?
A high dietary intake of saturated fats or primarily animal fats is usually associated with a high rate of cardiovascular disease. However, the results of studies conducted over the last 30 years by Dr Serge Renaud, Director of the Nutrition and Cardiology Department of the French National Institute of Health Research, found that this was not always the case. He and his colleagues showed that the French, in spite of a diet high in saturated fats and a high level of risk factors such as high blood pressure and smoking, have one of the lowest rates of cardiovascular disease in the Western world. This study became known as the 'French Paradox'. Interestingly, wine is central to the French diet and lifestyle, and this has been suggested as a contributing factor in the reduced rate of cardiovascular disease in France.

Since 1965, more than 60 population studies have been published, with similar observations that regular moderate alcohol consumption, (one to two glasses, or 10 to 20 grams of ethyl alcohol, per day for both men and women) has a cardioprotective effect.

What are the protective effects of moderate alcohol consumption?
It may help first to understand the cholesterol story. The lipid or fat called cholesterol is produced by the liver from saturated fatty acids in our diet. It can also be absorbed into the blood stream via the gastrointestinal tract when we consume food containing animal fats. Cholesterol is carried in the blood stream by lipoproteins labelled HDL (high density) and LDL (low density). The LDL form, referred to as 'bad cholesterol', can be oxidatively modified in the blood and plaque can form on the arteries, which can lead to atherosclerosis (hardening and clogging of the arteries) and cardiovascular disease such as high blood pressure, heart attack or a stroke. The HDL form, referred to as 'good cholesterol', transports cholesterol from the arteries to the liver to be removed from the body and also inhibits some of the bad effects of LDL.

Medical studies have shown that a regular and moderate intake of alcohol:
• increases the blood concentration of HDL,
• prevents the oxidative modification of LDL, and
• reduces the formation of blood clots.

Because of these changes in the amounts and mechanisms of action of HDL and LDL, it is generally accepted that consuming alcohol in moderation is cardio-protective, reducing the risk of cardiovascular disease.

A number of studies have demonstrated a link between consumption of alcohol and life expectancy. As an example, it is reported that studies by Dr Arthur Klatsky, Chief of the Division of Cardiology at Kaiser Permanente Medical Center in Oakland, California, have shown that moderate drinkers live longer than abstainers or heavier drinkers, with the lowest risk of mortality found in those who consume one or two standard drinks per day.

Are the beneficial effects of wine different from those of other alcoholic drinks?

Wine, beer and spirits all have cardioprotective effects due to their alcohol content. Wine, however, contains other chemicals, including antioxidants, that also increase HDL and inhibit the oxidation of LDL and, in addition, prevent blood clotting. These antioxidants are phenolic compounds, which are present in the skin and seeds of grapes. They are extracted in varying amounts into the wine during the winemaking process. As the concentration of phenolics is high in the skin of black grapes and red wine is made with some skin contact, red wines have much higher concentrations of these antioxidants than white wines. It is, therefore, possible that red wine is significantly more cardioprotective than white wine which, in turn, is more cardioprotective than beer and spirits.

Why not eat grapes?

The pH value and temperature conditions of the stomach are not conducive to the extraction of these phenolic compounds from the seeds and skins of grapes. The cardioprotective effect of wine may also be partly explained by its usual consumption with meals, which slows its absorption into the blood stream, resulting in a relatively low concentration of alcohol being presented to the liver at any one time, and a correspondingly low concentration of unmetabolised alcohol circulating in the blood stream.

Wine and food - a good combination
The most beneficial way to enjoy wine is to drink it with a meal, and most Australian wine consumers are doing just that. A study commissioned by the Australian Wine Federation demonstrated that 88% of bottled wine and 81% of cask wine is consumed most often in conjunction with a meal.

Enjoying wine with food

Drink wine wisely

Women are more at risk from the harmful effects of alcohol than men. One of the reasons for this is the difference in the water content of the body for men and women. In men, about 65% of the body weight is made up of water, whereas in women it is about 50%. Women also have a larger fat content than men, 33% compared to 12%, into which the alcohol diffuses slowly because of the poor blood supply in fat. When alcohol is consumed it is distributed through the body fluids, so the alcohol is more diluted in men than it is in women, and this dilution occurs more rapidly. Because of this it is advisable that women should drink less than men. When considering appropriate amounts to drink we use the concept of a standard drink. This is the amount of wine that contains 10 grams of ethanol (alcohol) measured at 20°C. Because different wines contain different amounts of alcohol, the volume that is equivalent to a standard drink is also different.

The effects of alcohol can vary from person to person for many reasons, including gender, individual body weight and metabolism. A sensible approach to tasting and drinking wine must always be advised.

As a guide, the recommendation of The National Health and Medical Research Council is that a sensible and moderate alcohol consumption, with reference to wine, is four standard drinks a day for men and two for women.

Having a high blood alcohol concentration is associated with car and motor bike accidents. In Australia there is a maximum blood alcohol concentration above which it is not legal to drive. There is no accurate way of telling how much you can drink before you reach the legal blood alcohol concentration limit. It varies with each person depending on their weight, gender, age, if they have just eaten, what they have just eaten and what type of drink they have consumed. A guide to maintaining a blood concentration below the legal limit is that the body metabolises approximately one standard drink per hour, so if you have consumed one to two standard drinks in an hour for women and two to three standard drinks in an hour for men, it takes approximately two to three hours for your blood alcohol concentration to fall to zero. If you wish to keep track of how many drinks you have had, do not refill your glass until it is empty. Please note: the above information is only a guide. To be certain of your blood alcohol content, you should have a breath or blood test.

It is important to eat while drinking, as this slows the absorption of alcohol and lowers your maximum blood alcohol concentration. However, because of the slower absorption it also takes longer for your blood alcohol concentration to fall to zero, and this needs to be taken into account before you drive.

What is a standard drink?
Table wines
The alcohol content of dry white, semi-sweet white, sweet white, sparkling and dry red table wine is between 10 and 14% v/v (alcohol by volume), and a standard drink is in the order of 120 mL.

Fortified wines
For fortified wine, where the alcohol content is about 20% v/v, a standard drink is about 60 mL.

Brandy
For brandy, where the alcohol content is about 40% v/v, a standard drink is about 30 mL.

The formula for calculating the number of standard drinks in a bottle of wine is:
volume of wine in litres x alcohol content % v/v x 0.789 (specific gravity of ethanol)

In a 750 mL bottle of wine (with an alcohol content of approx. 12% v/v), there are approximately 7 standard drinks, while in a 750 mL bottle of fortified wine (with an alcohol content of approx. 19% v/v) there are approximately 11 standard drinks.

It is mandatory to show the number of standard drinks on any bottle of wine labelled on or after 22nd December 1995.

INDEX

References

Anon. (1994) The Rewards of Patience (3rd Edition), Penfolds Wines Pty Ltd, Nuriootpa, Australia.

Anon. (1995) Wine Regions of Victoria. Tourism Victoria.

Coombe, B.G. and Dry, P.R. (1988) Viticulture, Volume 1 Resources. Winetitles, Adelaide, Australia.

Gladstones, J. (1992) Viticulture and Environment. Winetitles, Adelaide, Australia.

Kolpan, S., Smith, B. and Weiss, M. (1996) Exploring Wine. Van Nostrand Reinhold, New York.

Peynaud, E. (1987) The taste of wine. The art and science of wine appreciation. Macdonald & Co (Publishers) Ltd, London and Sydney.

Rankine, B. (1990) Tasting and Enjoying Wine. A guide to wine evaluation for Australia and New Zealand. Winetitles, Adelaide, Australia.

Robinson, J. (1994) The Oxford Companion to Wine. Oxford University Press, Oxford and New York.

Simon, J. (1996) Wine with food. Mitchell Beazley, part of Reed Consumer Books Ltd, London.

Photographic acknowledgements

The following photographs by Prima Photographics were commissioned specifically for this book.
Photographs: authors iii, wine bottles 1,5; fruit 22; pumping over and plunging a red wine fermentation 54; oak barrels (2nd from top) 55; wine glasses - sparkling 61, sparkling red 76, white wine 79, sweet white 105, red wine 113, fortified 147, brandy 156; pouring a sparkling wine 62; cellaring wine 174, 180; heating food 181; vineyard floor 183; equipment 185; opening a bottle of still and sparkling wine 186, 187; decanting machine and decanting 188; Riedel glasses 189; wine and food 192; cheese and wine 196; dessert and wine 197. We thank Lucy Cheesman and Frank Priolo of Prima Photographics.

Photographs that refer to wineries, vineyards and/or bottles of wine, and where the associated wine company is mentioned in the photograph or in the caption, were provided by the respective wine companies, unless stated below.

Photographs were kindly provided by people/companies as shown below:

The photographs of the bunches of the different grape varieties, shown at the beginning of the section on each variety, were reproduced from the following publications held in the Rare Books Collection, State Library of South Australia — Pinot Noir, Shiraz, Semillon, Sauvignon Blanc, Riesling and Cabernet Sauvignon were from Ampélographie Vol. 2, Paris 1901; Chardonnay from Ampélographie Vol. 4, Paris 1903; Grenache from Ampélographie Vol. 6, Paris 1905 by Viala, P. & Vermorel, V. and Merlot from Ampélographie française. Paris 1857 by V. Rendu. We thank Ms Valmai Hankel for her assistance in obtaining these photographs.

A vineyard showing the effect of phylloxera 17 by Greg Buchanan of The Victorian Dept of Agriculture

Machine harvesting and rods 47 by Gordon Lonnon of Gregoire

Oak trees and barrel making 52, 53; oak barrels 95 by Geoff Schahinger of CA Schahinger

Botrytised juice oozing from the press 110 and large vats 146 by Southcorp Wines

Botrytised grapes 104 by Les Worland of De Bortoli Wines

Barrels at the 12 o'clock and the 2 o'clock position 55 and the barrel of flor sherry 148 by John Kleinig of Southcorp Wines

Profile of Coonawarra soil 41 by Katnook Estate

G.D.C. trellis, bottom right 35 by Peter Dry of The University of Adelaide

Cork trees & corks 58 by Bruce Priestley of J.B. Macmahon Pty Ltd.

Bottle of St Helga and food 83 by Simon Griffiths, St Kilda, Victoria and supplied by Gourmet Traveller

Bottle of Eileen Hardy and glasses 101 supplied by Read McCarthy Group, Ultimo, Sydney

Yalumba Heggies Vineyard 109 by Milton Wordley, supplied by Southlight Photo Library, Adelaide

Shottesbrooke Winery 164 by John Vivian Graphic Design, Adelaide

The vineyard and bottles 11; vineyard top right 35; Coriole sign 164; wine bottles 189; wine and food 202 were supplied by the South Australian Tourism Commission

Balnaves Winery 166 by Milton Wordley, Adelaide

Wine bottles 4; wine glasses 6,10, 181,183,189; grapes with and without skins 20; wine bottle 56; sparkling wine corks 70 by Stan Richards Photography, Adelaide

Angove's Wines and food 197 supplied by Angove's Wines. We thank Angove's Wines and Andrew Fielke of The Red Ochre Grill for giving us permission to use the wine and food matches from their Classic Combinations Booklet.

Chardonnay vine - before and after leaf removal 34 by Inca Lee

Shiraz bunches and Shiraz grapes 135 by Tony Proffitt

Filling barrels 11; veraison 20; bunches of grapes 32; vineyards top left, centre, bottom left 35; machine pruning and four different pruning methods 38; scarecrow 39; soils 40; hand harvesting 47; grapes in receival bin and crushing grapes 48; pH meter 49; presses 50; yeast settling and oak barrels 51; red ferment (top), treading ferment, Leconfield Winery 54; red wine colour 55; remuage 60; grapes 65; Chardonnay grapes 78; bunches of botrytis grapes 109; red ferment 112; Woolshed Winery 165; Heemskerk vineyard 167; vines 183 by Patrick Iland.